1930

1930 EUROPE IN THE SHADOW OF THE BEAST

ARTHUR HABERMAN

WILFRID LAURIER
UNIVERSITY PRESS

Inspiring Lives.

Wilfrid Laurier University Press acknowledges the support of the Canada Council for the Arts for our publishing program. We acknowledge the financial support of the Government of Canada through the Canada Book Fund for our publishing activities. This work was supported by the Research Support Fund.

Library and Archives Canada Cataloguing in Publication

Haberman, Arthur, [date], author
    1930 : Europe in the shadow of the beast / Arthur Haberman.

Includes bibliographical references and index.
Issued in print and electronic formats.
ISBN 978-1-77112-361-7 (softcover).—ISBN 978-1-77112-363-1 (EPUB).—
ISBN 978-1-77112-362-4 (PDF)

    1. Intellectuals—Europe—History—20th century. 2. Europe—Intellectual life—20th century. I. Title. II. Title: Nineteen thirty.

CB205.H33 2018   940.5'2   C2018-900842-3
                                                                 C2018-900843-1

Front cover image: Georges Braque, *The Blue Mandolin* (1930). Cover design and interior design by Angela Booth Malleau, designbooth.ca.

This book is printed on FSC® certified paper and is certified Ecologo. It contains post-consumer fibre, is processed chlorine free, and is manufactured using biogas energy.

Printed in Canada

To the memory of my teachers:

Joan Kelly Gadol (1928–1982) *and*
A. William Salomone (1915–1989)

And what rough beast, its hour come round at last,
Slouches towards Bethlehem to be born?

—Yeats, "The Second Coming"

CONTENTS

INTRODUCTION

THE YEAR 1930 was hardly a happy one for Europe and the West. The effects of the disaster of the Great War were still seen and felt. Economically, the Wall Street crash in October 1929 began a time when the viability of liberal capitalism was seriously questioned. In Italy there was a new authoritarianism claiming to be the wave of the future. Communism was a hope, a fear, and, mostly, an unknown.

A number of European writers and artists dealt with the time as a crisis of culture and civilization. Some were friends, others were hardly known to the rest. However, 1930 saw a coming together on the part of the major intellectuals of Europe about European values and stability, and the future of the continent. What makes 1930 such a watershed is that rarely have so many important minds worked independently on issues so closely related.

All argued that something was seriously amiss and asked that people become aware of the dilemma. Writers such as Thomas Mann, Virginia Woolf, José Ortega y Gasset, Sigmund Freud, and Bertolt Brecht acted as public intellectuals, asking hard questions about the survival of a Western tradition that went at least as far back as the Enlightenment and sometimes to the Renaissance and its classical revival.

The central issues were:

- **The viability of a secular Europe with Enlightenment values**
  Most wondered whether the direction of modernity had taken a dark turn with the event of the Great War and the rise of a strident and violent ethnic nationalism. Could the best of European culture survive a turn inward to destruction and fear?

- **Coming to terms with a new, darker view of human nature**
  Now, in place of a view of human nature as either Cartesian (*Cogito, ergo sum*), as one that claimed we are distinguished by our capacity to reason, or as one that says we create with our labour (*Homo faber*),

1

there is introduced the idea of humans as guided by instincts that pit Eros versus Thanatos—life versus death. We are beings with sexual desires and with an instinctual violence. "Homo homini lupus," said Freud: "Man is wolf to man." Hence, what now does it mean to have a moral, viable civilization?

- **The rise of the politics of irrationality**
  The old Liberal view was one that gave humans the right to decide their own path in life based upon self-interest and rational choices. However, now it will be asked if, because of our new view of human nature, we make political and social decisions based on irrational desires and unconscious choices. How, then, do we develop a body politic that makes us responsible for our choices? Is there a danger in mass society that was not foreseen?

- **Mass culture and its dangers**
  "The characteristic of the hour," wrote Ortega in 1930, "is that the commonplace mind, knowing itself to be commonplace, has the assurance to proclaim the rights of the commonplace and to impose them wherever it will."[1] Does the victory of liberal democracy mean that those who benefit from it will destroy the very society that raised them up?

- **Identity and the Other in the midst of Western civilization**
  There were three main Others in Europe in 1930—women, Blacks, and Jews. Woolf and Nardal asked about the first; Nardal and Langston Hughes were among many who began to redefine Black identity into something that would later in the decade be called Negritude; and many Jewish and non-Jewish figures dealt with the virulent and increasing anti-Semitism of the times.

- **Finding ways to represent the postwar world**
  The crisis was not seen simply as one of politics and society. It also became one of art and form. How do we now tell what is happening when the old world and its forms of representation are no longer adequate? How do we paint? How do we make music? How do we write? It was a period of artistic invention, one in which experimentation became the norm.

- **The epistemological dilemma**
  The problem of knowledge had not been so serious in the West since the Scientific Revolution. In many ways, it still exists. Nietzsche proclaimed in 1882 that "god is dead." He added, "and we are his murderers." What he meant is that we no longer have the certainty afforded by systems of belief that were more or less universal. In effect, we have lost our

Weltanschauung and substituted relativity at best, total anarchy at worst. This problem, for many, including Mann, Freud, and Ortega, threatened the very existence of civilization itself.

- **The new Fascism: is it a new norm or an aberration?**
  A number of intellectuals recognized something frightening in the rise of Fascism, three years before the coming to power of Nazism in Germany. Is what is happening in Italy something that will sweep the continent? Can it happen anywhere?

- **The dystopian trend of thought**
  Very few utopias were written in the West after 1914. Rather, in place of the reforming utopia as the good place, the dystopia, the cautionary tale of where we already might be and where we are going, gained legitimacy.

The year 1930 can be seen as the dawn of a period of darkness, the beginning of what Auden would in 1939 style "a low, dishonest decade,"[2] one of the most deeply reflective moments in the history of the West. Civilization stumbled into a war without precedent in 1914, managed to survive its conflagration, but did not immediately create something viable and valuable afterward. Intellectuals asked, Where are we heading? Who are we, and how do we build moral social and political structures? Can we continue to believe in the insights and healing quality of our culture? Big questions. After the optimism of the nineteenth century, Europe questioned itself and its own viability.

Major thinkers—Mann, Woolf, Ortega, Freud, Brecht, Nardal, and Huxley; a number of artists, including Picasso and Magritte; musicians like Weill—all sought in and around the year 1930 to grapple with these issues still central to our lives.

EUROPEANS, 1930

LET US IMAGINE a European couple in 1930. He was born in 1890, she in 1892. He is the son of a teacher and is now an engineer, working for the civil service of a city in their country. She is the daughter of shopkeepers, small grocers. She has a nursing certificate, and is now a housewife. They have two children, ten and eight.

Our couple married in 1915, just before he went to war for their country. They had a better war than some other couples, for they survived and had a future. He fought in the trenches and witnessed horrors that still give him occasional nightmares, though he will not talk about them. He was wounded in his left leg and has a permanent slight limp. She did some nursing on the home front during the war, lived mainly in a residence with other nurses, and is admired by family and friends for her compassion and decency.

The couple corresponded during the war, remained in love, and longed only for the conflict to be over, whatever may come. Afterward, they purchased a small house in a suburb of their city, settled into something called normality, had their children and led regular lives.

They are an intelligent pair. They read the newspaper, perhaps *The Times of London*, *Le Figaro*, *La Vanguardia*, the *Frankfurter Zeitiung*, or the *Corriera della Sera,* and try to keep abreast of current affairs. They like to read current serious novels aloud to each other, and in the last ten years might have read and discussed Thomas Mann's *The Magic Mountain*, Jaroslav Hašek's *The Good Soldier Schweik*, André Gide's *The Counterfeiters*, or Eric Maria Remarque's *All Quiet on the Western Front*. They have developed a taste for popular literature, especially mysteries; they love Poe and Conan Doyle, and recently found the contemporary Agatha Christie.

In 1928, they purchased a radio for their home and it has brought them some information and pleasure. They listen to the news, and also now have access to entertainment. They are especially fond of classical music and search for favourite symphonies in the evening so that the family can enjoy them together. On special occasions, they might attend a live musical performance or the theatre. They are fascinated by the new development of cinema and recently saw some films, perhaps *Battleship Potemkin* or Charlie Chaplin in *The Circus*. They especially liked Fritz Lang's *Metropolis*, which they saw three years ago and still discuss.

Our family takes a one-week holiday at the seaside each year, staying in a pension or a bed and breakfast that caters to others like themselves. There is a public park near their home, and the family uses it in good weather for picnics and Sunday outings.

They are very good citizens, decent, responsible, law-abiding, wonderful neighbours. Their children have manners, are respectful of others, and try hard in their public schools. The couple is ambitious for their children and see education as the road to social mobility. She spends some of her time as a volunteer in the local school.

If there was one word to describe how our couple felt about their lives and the future, it would be uneasy. They are uneasy about much in their lives: the economic future, the political stability of their country, the world their children will inherit, the durability of peace.

European culture has changed profoundly since the time our couple was born. Indeed, Europeans worried now about the viability of European culture itself. Paul Valéry stated in 1919, "the swaying of the ship has been so violent that the best-hung lamps have finally overturned."[1] The term doubt is usually associated with theology and reflections about the nature and existence of god or the gods. Now doubt has penetrated the spirit of Europe itself.

It had been assumed during the *fin de siècle* era that Europe was at the forefront of human development. Many behaved as if it would simply go on forever. The Great War ended this illusion and introduced a deep cultural malaise. In his 1922 essay "The European," one often cited by his generation, Valéry articulated the general mood:

> We hope vaguely, we dread precisely; our fears are infinitely more precise than our hopes; we confess that the charm of life is behind us, abundance is behind us, but doubt and disorder are in us and with us. There is no thinking man, however shrewd or learned he may be, who can hope to dominate this anxiety, to escape from this impression of darkness, to measure the probable duration of this period when the virtual relations of humanity are disturbed profoundly.

> We are a very unfortunate generation, whose lot has been to see the moment of our passage through life coincide with the arrival of great and terrifying events, the echo of which will resound through all our lives.[2]

Valéry noted that everything has been questioned and norms have been overturned—the economy is fraught with danger, states wonder what policies to follow, individuals question the meaning of their lives. He concluded, "*The Mind itself has not been exempt from all this damage.* The Mind is in fact cruelly stricken; it grieves in men of intellect, and looks sadly upon itself. It distrusts itself profoundly."[3]

European readers were faced with a plethora of novels documenting the horrors of the Great War and the senselessness of its violence and deaths. Many artists produced images that vied with those of the hell of Bosch, but were contemporary. Poets used terms like "The Wasteland" to evoke the present mood.

The reminder of a Europe wounded was everywhere. In France and Belgium especially, there were the ruins of war. However, there were also the returning soldiers, many of whom were wounded, some permanently disabled, and others with lost limbs. A common sight on the streets of Europe was young men using canes and crutches. The metaphor of sickness and a need to be healed was part of everyday life.

This unease was also reflected in the puzzlement about the war's resolution. Winning a war is useless if it is not followed by a durable peace. Our couple and their friends, with whom they sometimes discussed politics, did not know what to make of the international relations that arose out of the Versailles treaty.

For them, the settlement did not seem to hold. It violated several of the principles of balance of power politics in an era of national sovereignty. First, the treaty was made without the presence or consent of both Russia, engaged in its revolution after having left the war in March 1918, and Germany, defeated. It is axiomatic that a comprehensive treaty cannot create a peace that will last unless the major powers involved in the conflict agree to its provisions and are willing to act to uphold it. Of the five major powers, only three deliberated and wrote the documents: the United States, Britain, and France.

Moreover, by 1930 it was clear that the United States was following a policy of withdrawal from European affairs, regularly called isolationism. Though the idea of a strong League of Nations was put forth during the Great War and at the Paris peace negotiations by its president, Woodrow Wilson, the US Senate refused to endorse it in 1920; the country cooperated with the League on occasion but never belonged to it. Wilsonianism was never put into practice in the decade of the 1920s.

The treaty had economic consequences, predicted by the English economist John Maynard Keynes, that would unsettle both the European economy and relations among the major states. Germany was declared guilty of fomenting the Great War and was required—forced, really—to pay reparations, mainly to France, which had endured great destruction.

France was obsessed with Germany and its place in European affairs. This was the result of events following the German victory over the French in the Franco-Prussian War of 1870–1871, the creation of a united Germany, and the new status of Germany as the most important of the powers on the European continent. The insistence in France and elsewhere that Germany and Austria alone were responsible for the outbreak of the Great War added to this concern. France believed that a weak Germany was necessary for the stability of Europe.

Germany had difficulty raising enough funds to deal with the costs of reparations and requested a two-year moratorium in 1922, something the French vetoed. When no payments were forthcoming, the French took it upon themselves to send troops to occupy the German industrial area of the Ruhr. Eventually, an arrangement was made, but it was clear that the Versailles Treaty was tottering.

The economic side of the reparations issue resulted in severe inflation in Germany and the further alienation of the middle class from the treaty. In order to deal with occupation and reparations, the German government printed money. The mark, worth 62 marks to the US dollar in May 1921, dropped to 100,000 to the dollar in June 1923, and lower still to 4.2 trillion to the dollar in November 1923. Most German citizens had their savings wiped out.

All of this resulted in a quest for some measure of stability. Many agreements between countries were proposed. Two, designed to strengthen the powers of the League of Nations in international disputes—a 1923 Treaty of Mutual Assistance, and a 1924 proposal called the Geneva Protocol, which required compulsory arbitration in the event of international disputes— failed because, among others, Britain refused to sign. Now it seemed the United States had withdrawn, and Britain was behaving as "little Englanders." France was distraught. It seemed to be the only one of the five powers committed to the treaty.

There soon came to be some positive signs. A Treaty of Locarno was made in December 1925 that dealt with the borders between Germany, Belgium, and France, signed as well by Britain and Italy. Germany joined the

League of Nations in 1926. Some small progress was made on the limitation of armaments. And in 1928 the Pact of Paris (also known as the Kellogg-Briand Pact) was signed by fifteen states, and eventually agreed to by sixty-five. The latter was an agreement to outlaw war between the signatories.

Optimists took these agreements to mean that Europe was making progress toward a lasting peace. Pessimists wondered why it was necessary to do all this in light of a postwar comprehensive settlement emanating from 1919. They came to believe that the fact that Locarno and the other treaties were signed at all implied that Versailles was not quite binding, that Germany and others had to somehow be brought into an agreed, systematic peace.

As for the Pact of Paris, it gave great psychological satisfaction to the optimists, and the few years after 1925 were described by those hopefuls as the "spirit of Locarno" or the "Locarno honeymoon." The pessimists claimed it was easy to sign a pact outlawing war, but it was the diplomatic equivalent of agreeing on the virtues of parenthood, and made no real difference. For the pessimists, including our couple and some of their friends, there was need for a clear and certain order, and a fear of what some called a "revision" of the treaty.

The economic problems in Europe in the early 1920s troubled many and left serious psychic worries on the minds of some, including our couple trying to raise two children. Prior to 1914, Europeans accepted the fact that there were economic cycles, but they expected in the main to experience a steady prosperity. Things got better over time.

Not so after 1918. First, Europe had to accept that it was no longer the centre of the world economy. Europe was important, but the United States was now more important, as it became the largest producer of goods and services in the world and a creditor nation.

In the first half of the 1920s the European economy seemed to struggle. Unemployment rose considerably in Britain and Germany. The French agricultural sector was weak throughout the decade. In the two main liberal democracies there were monetary problems, as the French franc fell from being worth twenty cents to the US dollar before the war to two cents in mid-1926, and the British pound, worth nearly five US dollars at the end of the war, was below four dollars in the first few years of the 1920s. On top of all this there was German inflation, the effects of which were seared into the minds of all who experienced it.

In 1926 Britain experienced a General Strike of nine days, which caused some to worry about British democracy itself. France in 1926 had such an acute financial crisis and such a frozen parliamentary body that for the first time in the peacetime history of the Third Republic (begun in 1871), it granted its president the power to take measures by decree to end a cycle of nasty inflation and stop the decline of the franc. Democracies seemed to be stumbling.

As in the area of diplomacy, the end of the decade was better than its beginning. From the end of 1926 stability was achieved, and it lasted for three years. However, Europeans in 1930 came to worry about the consequences of what began happening in the United States on "Black Thursday," October 24, 1929, when the New York Stock Exchange crashed spectacularly. The United States was gripped by depression and high unemployment as the year 1930 wore on. World trade suffered as a result of the financial collapse. Demand dropped in both the United States and Europe, so production slowed as well. Indeed, entire industries collapsed as the economy contracted.

In January 1930 our couple might have hoped that the crisis in the United States would be short-lived. By the end of the year it became clear that this was a new phenomenon, a depression that would affect the whole of the developed world. They considered themselves fortunate to have the stability provided by a job in the civil service, seeing other engineers lose work as companies downsized or failed.

Europeans in 1930 were experiencing two new political developments that were both intriguing and a bit puzzling: the rise and seeming success of Communism in Russia and Fascism in Italy. Some among the family and friends of our couple were attracted by one or the other as democracies seemed mired in a form of government that did not ably respond to crises. They were certainly not ready to give up on liberal democracy, though some thought that perhaps aspects of the new might help the old to operate better. A few friends began to vote for communist parties or to talk about the need for fascist order and discipline.

Communism was apparently successful in the one place in Europe where no one in 1914 predicted it could happen—Russia, which in 1924 officially became the Union of Soviet Socialist Republics. Two revolutions happened in Russia in 1917. The first, in March, ended centuries of tsarist rule, and resulted in a wobbly provisional government led by moderate socialists. It set out to continue the war and reorganize Russia into a democratic state but failed to achieve either goal. The military situation continued to deteriorate, and the various factions in Russian politics put pressure on the government for reforms it could not carry out under the circumstances.

The second revolution, really a *coup d'état* in the midst of the larger revolution, was led by the Marxist Bolshevik Party, a determined group willing to take power when it could rather than wait for Russia to industrialize, modernize, and become a bourgeois society in the orthodox Marxist manner. No democrats, they used force to dissolve an elected assembly in early

1918—the last elected assembly of that period—because they were not the majority party.

A new experiment in governing began—that of the single-party state in control of the whole government apparatus. They pulled Russia out of the war, and for their first few years, those calling themselves "reds"—the colour of the left—had to fight a civil war against a variety of opponents, including the "whites," a group who wanted a restoration of the aristocracy, supported by contingents of troops from foreign countries including Britain, Japan, Canada, and the United States.

The rhetoric of the Bolsheviks and the goals they articulated were enormously important in the early years in getting support internally and abroad. They borrowed from Marx and talked about a classless society, working on behalf of justice for all, providing education and health services, giving opportunities to people whose ancestors had been peasants and serfs in an authoritarian system.

What was happening in reality was the introduction of a system that brooked no dissent, demanded ideological conformity, and turned Communist party ideology into a state religion. No deviation from the doctrine of the party was tolerated, as the distinctive feature of this kind of Communism was a party elite in charge of creating and organizing a proletarian revolution and a utopian Communist state. In true Orwellian manner, it came to be called democratic centralism.

By 1930 Stalin was the leader of the Soviet Union and the party had total power. The policies that his government followed interested many in Europe as a whole. Stalin argued for "socialism in one country," that is, to cement the Communist revolution in Russia before trying to achieve the world revolution predicted by Marx. In 1928, Russia's first five-year plan was inaugurated, hoping to transform the underdeveloped country rapidly into one powered by heavy industry. Workers were asked to meet quotas. And it seemed to be working—Russia began to industrialize very quickly.

In 1929, the Communist Party's government began the collectivization of Russian agriculture. In December 1929 Stalin spoke about their goals. The party, he said, "have developed an offensive along the whole front against capitalist elements in the countryside." We will strike at the independent farmers, he proclaimed, "to break their resistance, to eliminate them as a class, and to *replace* their output by the output of the collective farms and state farms."[4]

We now know the cost in human terms of these efforts, including forced-labour camps, prisons in Siberia for dissenters, the purges of those who wanted some discourse or who queried the policy, show trials, and soon starvation in parts of the countryside and the Ukraine. This was not known in 1930, though a few years later some visitors to the Soviet Union would bring back tales of the horrors they witnessed there.

In the 1920s Communism won support in many countries. Germany had a strong Communist party, as did France and Italy. There was a Comintern, short for Communist International, begun by Lenin in 1919, which attempted to unite the various national groups behind a common policy whose stated aim was support of the "proletarian revolution" in Russia and "to fight by all available means, including armed struggle, for the overthrow of the international bourgeoisie." The organization "considers the dictatorship of the proletariat the only way to liberate mankind from the horrors of capitalism."[5]

The movement, and a movement it was, had some appeal. In 1930, the rhetoric overtook reality for many on the left in the rest of Europe, including some intellectuals. People like Arthur Koestler were sympathetic to Communism, and he joined the party in 1931. Distinguished writers like André Gide became fellow-travellers for a time, supporting Communist causes in their home countries. Some viewed it as the way to deal with the inequalities and difficulties of capitalism and liberal democracy. The "Russian experiment" was a subject of discussion among our couple and their community.

The new Fascism in Italy also intrigued many in 1930. Constitutional government failed in Italy as the Fascist party, led by Mussolini, took power in 1922 and used the next few years to dissolve Italian democracy in the name of providing order and opposing Communism. Beginning in 1925, a series of laws was enacted that soon put the Fascists in control of much of Italian life. A single-party state evolved from the right, made not by revolution but by a *coup d'état* of the very state it governed. In late 1925 Mussolini became "Head of Government" and was given authority to take executive actions without being responsible to parliament. By the end of 1928 the Fascist party took full control of the state; in practice the party and the government merged.

The Fascists claimed it was not about power, but that they were introducing a new form of government to protect the Italian people, reorganize, drive forward the economy, and oppose the radical left. Arising out of a spirit of fierce nationalism, Fascism emphasized the nation and solidarity above all else. "Political doctrines pass," said Mussolini, "nations remain." If the nineteenth century was the century of liberalism, socialism, and democracy, then, he said, "we are free to believe that [the twentieth century] is the century of authority, a century tending to the 'right' ... the 'collective' century, and therefore the century of the State."[6]

Fascism in Italy attempted to establish what was called the "Corporate State." This involved creating a series of institutions, called corporations or syndicates, to organize and regulate the economy. Each labour group, industrial group, or profession had its corporation, and each individual could take part in the civic and economic life of Italy only as a member of a corporation. Corporations would then bargain collectively under the authority of a central body to arrange contracts and settle disputes, with the government having the final authority in any settlement. "Lockouts and strikes are abolished," stated one of the laws that established these institutions.

Hence, Fascism was a "collective" doctrine. All belong to the state that represents the interests of the nation. Individuals were expected to subordinate their interests to the nation. Democracy, liberalism, capitalism, Marxism, and socialism were passé. Above all, it was a form of modern nationalism.

In 1930, Italian Fascism claimed success. Roads were being built and, whether it was true or not (it is certainly not true today), the famous slogan was that now the trains ran on time. There was order, there seemed to be stability, and Italians were given the illusion that they would once again be a great power modelled after ancient Rome.

Moreover, the Fascist state not only retained the monarchy as a symbol of continuity, it also made peace with the Roman Catholic Church, which had been an enemy of the modern Italian state since its reunification in 1870. Pope Pius XI and Mussolini signed The Lateran Agreements in 1929, in which the Italian state recognized "the full ownership and the exclusive and absolute dominion ... of the Holy See over the Vatican."[7] In addition, all differences between Italy and the Vatican, such as authority over the appointment of bishops, educational policy, and marriage laws were settled. In turn, the Church recognized the existence of the Italian state. For Italians and Europeans, this was a victory for Fascism—it put the papal stamp of approval on the regime and the new ideology.

Fascism claimed to be acting on behalf of the masses, but it changed little socially or economically for most Italians. The "corporate" organization favoured large industrialists, landowners, and landlords, many of whom strongly supported the new regime. A large part of the appeal of Fascism in Italy and elsewhere in Europe was that it was thought to be a new, viable alternative to the threat of Communism.

In the late 1920s Fascism also had appeal elsewhere in Europe. Poland established a military dictatorship in 1926 and Yugoslavia ended parliamentary democracy in 1929. Hungary had right-wing parties. Austria had its authoritarian right-wing politicians, and in Germany the Nazi party was gaining support. Fascist groups existed in France from the mid-1920s. Fascism would continue its growth after 1930 in many other countries, including Spain, Belgium, the Netherlands, Greece, and Romania.

Even in the established democracies, Fascism was seen as totally different from Communism. Some wealthy people in Britain and France viewed it with favour, seeing it as a way of retaining the traditional order and opposing the scourge of Bolshevism. They not only liked its nationalist rhetoric, they also saw it as protecting the traditional social and economic structure. You could do business with the Fascists, especially after the Church gave them respectability.

Our European couple did not quite know what to make of the two new ideologies and their reification in Russia and Italy. They liked some of the goals of both, especially their espousal of helping people to gain stability, equality, and prosperity. They continued to support moderation and democratic processes, but saw a need to make the democracies fairer and more efficient. They were troubled by the end of constitutional limits on the state, and discussed how an appropriate balance between liberty, authority, order, and prosperity could be achieved. They were loyal to their country, though they did not see themselves as superior to or in competition against others.

Some family and friends of our couple agreed with the Communists and Fascists that democracy might be failing. Some decided to support the communist party in their country, hoping to transform capitalism into something that would provide for all. Others moved to the right, arguing that fascism was the real wave of the future, and that the moderate politicians in power were unable to deal with the needs of the population in a time of economic and political crisis.

Both new ideologies attracted people who were not committed to a version of the status quo. Both also attracted many disaffected who chose a belief system that provided certainty, a community, and a sense of self-worth.

Our couple, well-read, informed, and concerned, looked to European intellectuals for some guidance on how to deal with their unease in 1930. They had read Thomas Mann, had attended the performance of a work by Brecht and Weill, had heard about the Spanish philosopher and journalist José Ortega y Gasset, knew about the ideas of Albert Einstein and Sigmund Freud, had reflected on a novel and some essays by Virginia Woolf, and went to the art museums in their city, where they tried to puzzle through the paintings of Picasso and Matisse.

They decided to read what would be written and see what would be painted at this time by those who they respected as the major public intellectuals of Europe.

They were not disappointed in 1930. It was a year in which outstanding minds, often not in contact with one another, had serious concerns about Europe and its future. The unease of our couple was mirrored by the intellectuals they admired, as they all grappled with what Europe had become and where it was heading.

1 THOMAS MANN
The Uncanny and Its Power

ON AUGUST 31, 1926, the German novelist and public intellectual Thomas Mann took a two-week holiday with his wife and their two youngest children, Michael and Elisabeth, in the Italian bathing resort of Forte dei Marmi. The town, located in the north of Tuscany, had been the home of Aldous Huxley for a time, and was well known to the cognoscenti of Florence and Milan as a pleasant place for a family vacation.

Mann had close ties to Italy. He was, after all, the author of the novella *Death in Venice* (1912), a work instantly regarded as a masterpiece upon publication. As well, he had vacationed in Italy often, and had written parts of another novella, *Tonio Kröger* (1903), and his great novel *The Magic Mountain* (1924) in that country.

Still, he wrote to his friend Ida Boy-Ed on September 8: "We send you our warm greetings from this beautiful place where we are spending some weeks with our children.... We are enjoying sea, mountains, and sunshine. Nevertheless, this time I believe we are not completely satisfied in the south. Next summer we will return to the Baltic Sea full of remorse."[1]

Mann was so disturbed by what happened on his holiday that three years later he turned the experiences into a new novella, originally titled *A Tragic Travel Experience*, published in late 1929 as *Mario and the Magician*. The novella is an important political tale, in which Mann deals with the rise of Fascism in Italy and Europe and its consequences.

Mann was not always interested in political matters. Until the start of the First World War he described himself as a non-political person, claiming that the artist dealt with other matters, those of the soul and heart. After the Great War, in which he articulated some patriotic and aristocratic feelings, he surprised many by supporting the Weimar Republic and the development of democracy in Germany.

Mann's own political development—he would later become an exile from Germany—came slowly. Yet by 1929 he could not ignore one of the new facets of life on the European continent. Life itself was becoming far more politicized than ever before, especially with the popularity of the new fascist and authoritarian parties, combined with the sentiment of nationalism, something like a secular religion replacing the old theology.

Now, Mann implicitly argued in his work, culture and politics were intertwined as never before. The threat to ideas and civilization came from the new modern state.

Mann claimed that his story accurately reflects the family's experiences in 1926. "Only the lethal outcome is invented," he stated.[2]

Mann opened the tale with an insight into what John Stuart Mill would have called the tyranny of the majority in society. The first words of the narrator signal an important consideration: "The atmosphere of Torre di Venere remains unpleasant in the memory," he says. Why atmosphere? Mann is suggesting that human relations take place in society, sometimes separate from the political sphere, though reflecting its values. And society can reveal its prejudices, its beliefs, in subtle and unusual ways that can make the outsider feel most uncomfortable.

The fictional family goes to Torre for their holiday in the middle of August. The narrator finds that the place is too busy to find proper peace. As well, it is very Italian, making the German family feel like outsiders. Better, he reflects, to go in May or September when the hotels and beaches are more cosmopolitan. Our narrator, something of a prig himself, feels "temporarily déclassé."

They take rooms at the Grand Hotel, not some small pension. Two incidents at the beginning of their stay make the family most uncomfortable. On their first night they go to dinner and are shown to their table inside the restaurant. However, they wanted to eat al fresco, on the veranda, where they could be close to the water and the red lamps created a holiday mood. Very politely they were told that the outside area was reserved. For whom? "*Ai nostri clienti*" ("our clients"). "Were we not their clients?" asks the narrator. Still, they obey quietly and take their meals in the dull interior room.

The second incident relates to a cough their children had, having recently recovered from the whooping cough. A principessa staying in nearby rooms took offence at having to be near this possible infection and complained. Our narrator explained that the illness was nearly over, and there was no possible "danger of infection to anybody." Told to have a consultation with the hotel doctor, the family agreed. He, too, indicated that no possible transference of the disease existed. Still, the management insisted that they move to the dépendance, rooms in an outbuilding.

Mann's choice of illness as a metaphor is something he and others in the West would use to discuss politics and society, from Jonathan Swift wanting to "heal" the world to Albert Camus's *The Plague*. The disease signifies they are different, not part of the important community, and therefore it is carried by the German family whether they like it or not. It foreshadows what is to come in the tale, for they are told often, sometimes directly, sometime subtly, that they do not belong and that they count for much less than those who are part of the Italian nation.

The illness metaphor goes further. It asks us to think about the illness of a society or civilization, one that is adopting values that are opposite to those ideals articulated in the Enlightenment. For Mann, Europe, the West, was defined by its cosmopolitan character and values that were universal. Here he is only beginning to suggest that modern nationalism can justify doing harm to the Other, and runs counter to inherited values.

At this point, the narrator and his family do take action. They move, though they stay in Torre. Nearby was the Casa Eleonora, a homier place looked after in the summer by a couple who had a larger hotel in Florence, the city of culture and art.

The smaller hotel was presided over by Signora Angiolieri and her husband. Signora Angiolieri was indeed angelic in her manner and her relations with others. Her hotel was named in honour of the great and legendary actress Eleonora Duse (d. 1924), with whom she had had a close relationship as a companion and aide. She worshipped Duse, and the cult of personality was evident throughout the hotel, which was decorated with numerous photographs and mementoes. Here Mann is noting that in modernity, the middle class often live through their association with others and that personalities are more fragile than we might think them to be.

The narrator remarks on another facet of the holiday that is typical of Mann. He notes the heat, the languor, the ever-present sun. In many of his works, going back to *Buddenbrooks* (1901) and *Tonio Kröger*, Mann discusses his belief in the differences between northern and southern European personalities. The south is sensual, somewhat erratic, and subdued by the southern sun. The north, his German origin, is more disciplined, orderly, sober, and deeper in reflection.

The distinction is one Mann would have known was made by Nietzsche, whom he studied carefully and respected, though he seriously differed with the philosopher on many matters. The south is Dionysian, the north Apollonian. In this story, in the south, the Dionysian element comes to the fore with the appearance of the magician Cipolla. Yet Mann would express in other writings the fear, correctly, that this side of human nature could dominate in Germany as well. Mann was deeply concerned that the irrational

Dionysian temperament, given legitimacy by some thinkers, would destroy culture and civilization.

Two other incidents added to the strangeness of the holiday experience. The narrator notes that even the beach and the play of children took on a political tone. There was no innocence, only a heightened sense of the new national honour. Hence, "patriotic children" now played with their own and insulted others. Adults accepted this, and there were conversations about the greatness of the new Italy. When his children questioned this lack of openness, troubled by being designated as outsiders, their parents explained to them that the Italians were experiencing something like an illness.

The second incident involved the daughter, whose bathing suit becomes filled with sand one afternoon at the beach. She is told by her parents to take it off and wash it in the sea. The eight-year-old child obeyed, and found herself the object of nasty hoots and whistles. An adult told the family that they had committed an indecent act, one that was "an insulting breach of his country's hospitality." The dignity of Italy was invoked. The family was forced to appear at the municipal offices and pay a fine.

At this moment the narrator poses a question he will return to later in the tale. He asks why they did not leave. His claim is that they thought it better to face adversity squarely and overcome it rather than to succumb to such bullying.

But now the tale turns fantastic. The narrator invokes the term "uncanny" to describe what is happening. He is in a place where there is a rupture with ordinary behaviour and experience; he has, unwittingly, left the normal world.

Posters appear advertising the coming of the magician to Torre. The children are excited by the prospect of a conjurer, a magic show, and the family purchases tickets for the performance, which is attended by the whole of the town. The family has seats, while the youth of Torre stand at the rear, many of them known to the family, including their waiter Mario and several young fishermen.

Mann immediately gives the magician something of a personality. First, there is his name and assumed title. He is Cipolla, and claims to be a Cavaliere, a kind of "knight." Cipolla means "onion" in Italian. Some commentators suggest that the name refers to a person with no centre. However, there is more to it. An onion has many layers, is far more complex than it appears, and one has to peel away a lot before finding the centre. He is a complex character, for whom appearance and reality must be distinguished.

The Cavaliere title has an intertextual reference. Mann was a great admirer of Goethe, and he not only knew Goethe's *Faust* well, he would later write his own *Dr. Faustus* (1947), using the Faust myth to deal with Germany's bargain with racism, fascism, and gratuitous violence. In Goethe's *Faust*, Mephistopheles, as the devil is known, first appears to Faust in his study. He introduces himself: "I am the spirit that negates…. [E]verything that you term sin, destruction, evil represent—that is my proper element." A bit later in the same scene he instructs Faust,

> Have but contempt for reason and for science,
> Man's nobles force spurn with defiance,
> Subscribe to magic and illusion,
> The Lord of Lies aids your confusion,
> And pact or no, I hold you tight.[3]

Many of Cipolla's images and behaviours allude to him as a devil. And he will, like Mephistopheles, promise an experience that is Dionysian.

Mann's north–south dichotomy also is used to start the performance. In the south, time is measured differently. "Everybody came late, but not too late. Cipolla made us wait for him." Mussolini was known to purposely appear late for his speaking engagements (performances might be a better term), a way of demonstrating his superiority and increasing the anticipation of the audience. To further the comparison, Cipolla regularly refers to the "Fatherland" and the importance of Italy. He even tells the audience he has performed for the brother of Mussolini, the Duce.

Yet more comes with the appearance of Cipolla. He is dressed oddly, wearing a pelerine, a short cloak decorated with velvet and satin to cover some of his body. And it was clear that he had a deformity, which turned out to be a hump on his hip and/or buttock. Physically, he seemed to evoke pity, yet he displayed a confidence and power totally distinct from his frame. This was accentuated by the riding whip he revealed under his garment.

Cipolla's style immediately changed the nature of the theatre. Whereas there is usually a clear distinction between the performer and the audience, he did everything he could—and succeeded—to efface the gap. Here, the audience was not passive, they were actors in their own seduction by the magician.

It began with some bantering between the youths at the rear and Cipolla. A young man (*giovanotto*) starts a conversation, and the audience is amused and appreciates his boldness and facility with language. Cipolla praises him, this youth who wears his hair, notes the narrator, in the style now used by those supporting the new national resurgence. He tells him also that "I've had my eye on you for some time. People like you are just in my line. I can use them."

To prove it, he suggests that the youth stick out his tongue to the audience. Never, replies the *giovanotto*, that shows bad manners. Cipolla suggests to the youth that he would only be acting on behalf of something else, a puzzling idea at the moment. Then the riding whip comes out, and Cipolla makes it whistle. And surprisingly, the young man turns and sticks out his tongue as far as possible.

Cipolla, for the first time, makes a claim. "That was me." The youth was obeying some power higher than his own volition. The magician goes on to explain that while he has a physical problem, "it is with my mental and spiritual powers that I conquer life." We have the first assertion that something arational is happening.

The children find the demonstration delightful, though the narrator and his wife see something puzzling, perhaps even sinister. Throughout the evening, Cipolla drinks cognac from a bottle on the stage and smokes cigarettes, fortifying himself. The performance continues, now with some traditional numerical tricks. But Cipolla takes care to include the audience and, as the narrator remarks, to erase the distinction between performer and witnesses. In the midst of this there occurs an altercation between Cipolla and the populace.

Two young men who Cipolla asked to write down some numbers claim, perhaps jokingly, perhaps seriously, that they cannot write. Cipolla responds with a nationalist diatribe—in the great Italy there is no place for this, he states, and he insults the "ignorance" of Torre.

A youth from the audience responds: stop your insults. These two fellows are our friends and good people.

Cipolla calmly takes the challenge and again the narrator invokes the uncanny. Cipolla comes near the young man, stares at him with "the strangest eyes" and tells him that he knows the youth does not feel well. You have a colic, you are in pain, you need to double over, he says. Do it. And the youth does so, clearly in great agony. Then out comes the whip and the episode is over. Cipolla drinks more cognac, shudders, and continues with his clever numerical games.

Some commentators attribute Cipolla's power to the suggestion that he is a hypnotist, a statement later made by the narrator. But this does not adequately explain what is happening. Cipolla comments regularly on the difficulty of his efforts. When a spectator claims that he will assert his own will in the face of Cipolla's powers in a trick involving the selection of cards, the magician remarks that resistance will not work. "Freedom exists, and also the will exists; but freedom of the will does not exist, for a will that aims at its own freedom aims at the unknown. You are free to draw or not to draw.

But if you draw you will draw the right cards—the more certainly, the more wilfully obstinate your behaviour."

Here, we enter the world of Nietzsche's will to power and the overman. Cipolla is representing the relationship between the leader and the led as it is playing itself out at the time. If you enter the reality of the leader, you will so relate to his will that you will be led. You can choose to remain apart from that world—at a very great social cost in the atmosphere of the era—but if you do enter, you will be guided by the will of another. You give up your freedom, whether you think so or not.

Cipolla emphasizes his powers by playing games that have him entering the space of the audience and moving about. He continues his commentary, elaborating on his comment about freedom and will. He even asks for the sympathy of the audience. He is the leader now, and he asserts that the people and leader are as one. He is willing the audience to obey, and the audience, in its self-surrender, must do so. However, claims Cipolla, this requires great effort on the part of himself. The audience must understand his hard task. The will to power requires massive work on the part of those who can do it.

In a last demonstration before the intermission, Cipolla puts on a display of clairvoyance, yet another break with the rational world. He is attracted to Signora Angiolieri in the audience, and slowly, with some effort, he tells the audience that this woman was closely associated with the great artist Eleonora Duse, "whose fame has long been bound up with the Fatherland's."

The audience is enraptured, applauding as if they were engaged in a patriotic act. Then the intermission. The narrator remarks, "our lord and master withdrew."

Our narrator pauses to reflect again: why did they not leave at that moment? After all, it was very late for the children, and that offered a simple way of dealing with the feelings of dislocation and the sense of finding oneself uncomfortable. He claims to hardly understand it, but then gives the reader some possibilities. Clearly, while the magician was entertaining, his performance elicited complex feelings, even contradictory ones. The narrator and his wife were entertained and disturbed at the same time, as was the whole of the audience. He admits to a "fascination" that went beyond the evening's experience and related to the whole of his stay in Torre.

The reason is clear. Our narrator and some of the audience are thrilled and repelled at the same time. They are experiencing the feelings of terror associated with the sublime, and the fear that goes with it. Yet they are also stunned by the uncanny nature of the performance. At once they are participants in the event and conscious observers of it. The line between consciousness and experience is also effaced.

When does terror turn into horror? When does the fascination with the grotesque turn into disgust? The border between the two, for a coherent observer, remains clear. As an outsider, the narrator is not quite certain; for the people of Torre, the new nationalists, their abandonment of the will simply ends the distinction. They become willing participants in a public event that defines the nature of the new relationship between the leader and the led.

Mann examines the end of reason in social and political relations. He, one must make clear, is the author, not the narrator. Mann is witnessing something about crowd behaviour that had earlier been examined by Gustave Le Bon and others, the abandonment of personality and individual responsibility on the part of the person who joins the crowd.

Mann is also telling the reader that there is an erotic element in the behaviour of the people in Torre—who represent what Mann is observing in Italian fascism—in relationship to the Cavaliere.

We now have the new view of human nature, one recorded unhappily by Mann, being played out in the social and political realm. What is the attraction? It is the ability to redirect Eros and Thanatos to the public realm. Now the state and the Fascist leader offer more than simple policies. They appeal to feelings deep in our unconscious and try to give them an outlet in which power is in the hands of a deified leader and an elite.

Eros and power had been tied together before, including in Shakespeare's *Othello* and Machiavelli's *The Prince* during the Renaissance. However, in modernity the belief of the liberal West was that we are defined by our capacity to reason. The image of human nature in an age when more people existed as a result of advances in health and demography, and when they engaged in making political choices, offered the hope that with universal education people would make sensible decisions based on rational thought. We behave as *homo economicus* in this utilitarian formulation.[4]

Mann, who earlier dealt with this issue in great depth in his *The Magic Mountain*, was witnessing something that contradicted this view and forced him to offer an alternative hinted at, but not elaborated upon, in the writings of Freud, a friend.

Humanity, Mann now saw, is far more irrational and complicated than liberal democratic assumptions. Now, Eros is part of the politics of modernity, and part of the essence of the mass society emanating out of the French and Industrial Revolutions.

Mann was not alone in wrestling with this matter. His contemporary, Robert Musil (1880–1942), was at the time writing his trilogy *The Man Without Qualities*, which he began in 1921 and continued to work on until his death in 1942. Musil published some of the work in his lifetime, but he never attained the notoriety given to Mann. It was only in the 1950s, the era of existentialism in Europe, that Musil's work was recognized as insightful and groundbreaking.

Musil reflected on the loneliness and emptiness of an era of rationality, his work set near the end of the Austrian Empire:

> Perhaps not all of these people believe in that stuff about the Devil to whom one can sell one's soul; but all those who have to know something about the soul, because they draw a good income out of it as clergy, historians or artists, bear witness to the fact that it has been ruined by mathematics and that in mathematics is the source of a wicked intellect that, while making man the lord of the earth, also makes him the slave of the machine. The inner drought, the monstrous mixture of acuity in matters of detail and indifference as regards the whole, man's immense loneliness in a desert of detail, his restlessness, malice, incomparable callousness, his greed for money, his coldness and violence, which are characteristic of our time, are, according to such surveys, simply and solely the result of the losses that logical and accurate thinking has inflicted upon the soul! And so it was that even at that time ... there were people who were prophesying the collapse of European civilisation on the grounds that there was no longer any faith, any love, any simplicity or any goodness left in mankind; and it is significant that these people were all bad at mathematics at school.[5]

One of Musil's most famous lines comes from an essay, "Helpless Europe" (1922): "We do not have too much intellect and too little soul, but too little intellect in matters of the soul."[6]

Mann and Musil anticipated the outpouring that followed the Second World War in this matter, including the highly influential works of Erich Fromm, *Escape from Freedom* (1941) and Eric Hoffer, *The True Believer* (1951).

This new phenomenon was witnessed by the American journalist William Shirer when he attended the Nuremburg gathering of the Nazi party in 1934, the famous event captured and interpreted by the young Leni Riefenstahl in her propaganda film *Triumph of the Will*, itself a brilliant work of art in a demonic cause.

Shirer recorded, in his *Berlin Diary*:

Nuremberg, September 4
About ten o'clock tonight I got caught in a mob of ten thousand hysterics who jammed the moat in front of Hitler's hotel, shouting: "We want our Fuhrer." I was a little shocked at the faces, especially those of the women, when Hitler finally appeared on the balcony for a moment.

They reminded me of the crazed expressions I saw once in the back country of Louisiana on the faces of some Holy Rollers who were about to hit the trail. They looked up at him as if he were a Messiah, their faces transformed into something positively inhuman. If he had remained in sight for more than a few moments, I think many of the women would have swooned from excitement.

Nuremberg, September 5

I'm beginning to comprehend, I think, some of the reasons for Hitler's astounding success. Borrowing a chapter from the Roman church, he is restoring pageantry and colour and mysticism to the drab lives of twentieth-century Germans and officers of the army and navy.

In such an atmosphere no wonder, then, that every word dropped by Hitler seemed like an inspired Word from on high. Man's—or at least the German's—critical faculty is swept away at such moments, and every lie pronounced is accepted as high truth itself.

Nuremberg, September 7

"We are strong and will get stronger," Hitler shouted at them through the microphone, his words echoing across the hushed field from the loud-speakers. And there, in the flood-lit night, jammed together like sardines, in one mass formation, the little men of Germany who have made Nazism possible achieved the highest state of being the Germanic man knows: the shedding of their individual souls and minds—with the personal responsibilities and doubts and problems—until under the mystic lights and at the sound of the magic words of the Austrian they were merged completely in the Germanic herd.[7]

As we shall see, Cipolla is not only dealing with power, he also directs desire. As he later says to the audience after one of his most diabolical acts, "there are powers stronger than reason or virtue."

The performance resumes. Cipolla keeps going, getting people to obey him in the most mysterious and difficult circumstances. An elderly woman is convinced she is on a journey to India, and gives a narrative of her voyage. A man who seems healthy and strong is told he cannot lift his arm, and the magician uses his whip to command him. Later, he will make some of the people in the audience dance in a scene that conjures up images of a bacchanalia. The narrator remarks that clearly much of the audience had lost their ability to act freely, that he was witnessing "a drunken abdication of the critical spirit."

Indeed, now the narrator sees that some of the participants were quite delighted to rid themselves of choice, to give it over to someone who he says is a Circe: the daughter of the Sun, a sorceress who, in *The Odyssey*, turns people into pigs. He suggests that "between not willing a certain thing and not willing at all—in other words, yielding to another person's will—there may lie too small a space for the idea of freedom to squeeze into."

Two moments stand out. The first involved Signora Angiolieri, in whom the magician had earlier discerned a desire to lose herself in another. Cipolla now had her follow him wherever he wished. He asked her husband to call her, to try to break the spell by using their long history and marital ties. But it was in vain. One display of the whip caused the signora to turn to Cipolla. He moves backward and she follows, "moonstruck, deaf, enslaved," seemingly in the throes of the power of the magician. She would have followed him any- where. Then, to end it, Cipolla breaks the spell and returns her, "unharmed," he says, to her husband. Mann uses another paradoxical duality to describe the scene: it is "at once comic and horrible." What clearer display could there be of the profound, disturbing, and menacing relationship between the leader and the led than that given after the intermission by the conjurer?

Finally, the reader arrives at the episode between Mario and Cipolla. After fortifying himself with a cigarette, Cipolla singles out Mario and sig- nals him to come onto the stage. Mario hesitates—who would not, for fear of being humiliated?—but then, as the narrator remarks, "obedience was his calling in life," and the twenty-year-old assents.

To make the analogy with Fascism clear, Mann has Cipolla praise Mario's name as appropriate to "the Fatherland" and then he gives the Fascist salute. He toys with the youth, enquiring about his background before asking whether Mario believes in him and his powers. Mario shrugs indefinitely.

Then, Cipolla circles into the mind of the youth. He suggests Mario is sad, and that the sadness is related to a relationship with a girl. Someone in the audience shouts the name: Silvestra.

Cipolla talks to Mario but is really addressing the audience. You think, he says, that someone with my physical deformity could not know about love. However, you are wrong. I understand how Mario suffers, and I will show you.

Cipolla then makes gestures of love and, in Mario's eyes, the hunchback transforms himself into his sweetheart. "Mario, my beloved! Tell me, who am I?" The drama turns the whole of the place silent. People are aware that they are in the presence of frightening and strange powers. Mario answers, "Silvestra."

"Kiss me," says the deformed Cipolla. And Mario does. Again, Mann has the narrator use an emotional oxymoron, as he describes the moment as "grotesque and thrilling" at the same time. Clearly, the audience sympa- thizes with Mario, as they had with Signora Angiolieri. Still, they are also mesmerized by Cipolla's powers.

The spell is broken with one snap of Cipolla's whip. Mario, now aware of what has occurred, beats his temples with his fists before leaving the stage.

Now comes the unexpected "lethal conclusion" that Mann invented. Amid the applause for Cipolla, Mario returns with a gun and shoots the magician twice. Not even Cipolla can manage this. The conjurer falls and dies.

Briefly the public chaos is acknowledged, and the narrator and his wife usher the children to the exit. The innocent children ask if this was the end of the show, for they see the event of the shooting as part of the theatrical performance.

However, the narrator (and in this case, Mann) states that this was indeed the end of something beyond terror, a horror. It is, he states, a "liberation."

Mann's politics had evolved to the point where in late 1929 he was certainly a democrat, and he had already articulated his contempt and fear of Fascism. Was he suggesting that the only way to deal with the fatal charisma of the Fascist leader was to assassinate him?

It is not clear, though it is certain that Mann realized Fascism represented a new threat to the values of Europe and its civilization. After all, there came to be several plots against Hitler after the Nazis took power, and the historical consensus has praised those attempts. We are in new moral territory in this tale—does democracy need to see certain threats as so dangerous as to confront them with anti-democratic acts? What is the line between free speech and moral degradation in a civilized society?

The answers to the above questions were not as clear then as they might be now, with our experience of the many decades from 1930. To ask the question was itself a suggestion from Mann that he was entering new ethical territory at the time he decided to write the novella and insert his own ending.

Mann's concerns and his relationship to these issues did not begin or end in 1930. He came late to a consideration of politics and life. His initial thinking led him to the belief that politics were not part of the realm of art. He was, as he put it in an essay of 1918, a non-political man. He confessed in exile in 1938, in the essay "The Coming Victory of Democracy,"

> I must regretfully own that in my younger years I shared that dangerous German habit of thought which regards life and intellect, art and politics as totally separate worlds. In those days we were all of us inclined to view political and social matters as non-essentials that might as well be entrusted to politicians. And we were foolish enough to rely on the ability of these specialists to protect our highest interests.[8]

The young Mann simply ignored the political, thinking that only culture matters. Here, he emulated Nietzsche, whom he studied carefully and with whom he silently debated regularly, not realizing that what was desperately missing from Nietzsche's reflections were questions regarding the moral nature of the political and social worlds in relationship to human nature and well-being. And he had precedent in his beloved Goethe, who worried that poets would be overwhelmed by politics.

What might have saved Mann from going down the path of Nietzsche into elitism and the praise of the will to power was a position he very early adopted against the Nietzschean posture in the semi-autobiographical story *Tonio Kröger* (1903), which deals with Tonio growing up as an artist and coming to terms with himself. At the end of the tale, Tonio writes a letter to the artist Lisabeta, with whom he had earlier developed an intimate friendship, and could discuss his desires and doubts. Lisabeta had called him a *bourgeois manqué* in an earlier exchange. Tonio now refers to himself as "a bourgeois who strayed off into art, a bohemian who feels nostalgic yearnings for respectability, an artist with a bad conscience." He writes,

> I admire those proud, cold beings who adventure upon the paths of great and demonic beauty and despise "mankind"; but I do not envy them. For if anything is capable of making a poet of a literary man, it is my *bourgeois* love of the human, the living and usual. It is the source of all warmth, goodness, and humour.[9]

At the start of the Great War, Mann was a patriot, supporting Germany and articulating sentiments about his country that were common on both sides of the conflict. They were, to put it kindly, conventional and somewhat simplistic. They reflect the fact that this wonderful mind simply had not thought very much about politics and diplomacy, nor did he consider it necessary to do so. As he again put it in 1938, "not long after the war, however, I recognized the threat to liberty which was beginning to take form in Germany."[10]

The change came in the 1920s. Mann supported the Weimar Republic and social democracy, abandoning both his conservative position and aristocratic stance. He attacked German Fascism as early as 1922 as opposed to humanism and, anticipating the critique in *Mario*, as "romantic barbarism."

By 1930 Mann had moved from the position of an artist on the margins of society to the role of public intellectual. This was helped by the international recognition he achieved when awarded the Nobel Prize in Literature in late 1929. In "An Appeal to Reason" (1930), he used strong language. German Fascism was "a wave of anomalous barbarism, of primitive popular vulgarity." The Nazi party is a movement of "fanatical cult-barbarism, more dangerous and estranging than the isolation and the political romanticism which led us into the war."[11]

His position had consequences. Mann was in Switzerland when, on January 30, 1933, the Nazis took power. He was advised by his children that it would be wise not to return. He would not set foot again in Germany until 1949.

Mann, now alongside his brother, the novelist Heinrich Mann—with whom he had quarrels about art and politics earlier in life—continued his attack on the Nazis and his support for social democracy. On December 2, 1936, under an announcement by the German government headed "Traitors of the People and Enemies of the Reich," Mann was stripped of his German citizenship. Fortunately, he had been granted Czech citizenship a few weeks earlier, so he was not to be stateless.

His position would anticipate that of De Gaulle's in France in 1940. "I have already on several occasions declared in advance that I am more deeply rooted in German life and heritage than the fleeting figures who rule Germany at the moment." More casually, he wrote to a friend about his loss of citizenship in this manner: "It is like receiving the Nobel Prize."[12]

An opportunity to formulate a clear public position soon arrived. On December 19, 1936, he received a letter from the Dean of the Philosophical Faculty at the University of Bonn: "as a consequence of your loss of citizenship the Philosophical Faculty finds itself obliged to strike your name off its roll of honorary doctors."[13]

Mann's reply became a famous document, reported and quoted in nearly every newspaper in Europe and North America, immediately published in book form in England, the United States and Switzerland.

A German author accustomed to this responsibility of the Word—a German whose patriotism, perhaps naively, expresses itself in a belief in the infinite moral significance of whatever happens in Germany—should he be silent, wholly silent, in the face of the inexpiable evil that is done daily in my country to bodies, souls, and minds, to right and truth, to men and mankind? And should he be silent in the face of the frightful danger to the whole continent presented by this soul-destroying regime, which exists in abysmal ignorance of the hour that has struck today in the world? It was not possible for me to be silent....

To what a pass, in less than four years, have they brought Germany! Ruined, sucked dry body and soul by armaments with which they threaten the whole world, holding up the whole world and hindering it in its real task of peace, loved by nobody, regarded with fear and cold aversion by all, it stands on the brink of economic disaster, while its "enemies" stretch out their hands in alarm to snatch back from the abyss so important a member of the future family of nations, to help it, if only it will come to its senses and try to understand the real needs of the world at this hour, instead of dreaming dreams about mythical "sacred necessities." The meaning and purpose of the National Socialist state is this alone and can be only this: to put the German people in readiness for the "coming war" by ruthless repression, elimination, extirpation of every stirring of opposition; to make of them an instrument of war, infinitely compliant, without a single critical thought, driven by a blind and fanatical ignorance.[14]

Mann defends his right to use the German tongue and to be deeply concerned with its current path and the future. He ends with, "God help our darkened and desecrated country and teach it to make its peace with the world and with itself!" As we know, it would get worse before ending in conflagration.

Mann's deep concerns in late 1929 and 1930 were relatively new in giving prominence to issues of irrationality, fanaticism, instinct, and the willingness to obey, but there are several precedents in the literature of the West, notably in that of modern Russia.

Dostoyevsky, whose works were well known to Mann, addressed these matters in several of his novels. In *The Brothers Karamazov*, there is the justly famous parable of the Grand Inquisitor, told by Ivan. In it Christ returns to earth, appearing in Seville during the time of the Inquisition. He performs several miracles and goes among the populace. The Grand Inquisitor confronts him, asking why he returned to earth when he is no longer relevant or necessary. You promised freedom, you resisted Satan, says the Inquisitor, but humans cannot handle freedom and do not want it. They want order, structure, to be told how to achieve salvation, and it is the Church and its priests who carry this burden. He tells Christ to leave, for there is nothing he can give that is useful any longer. Christ responds by kissing the Inquisitor and wandering away.

In his *Notes from Underground*, Dostoyevsky has his narrator mock the nineteenth-century European belief in reason, science, and optimism. "Man is so partial to systems and abstract deduction that in order to justify his logic he is prepared to distort the truth intentionally."[15] Look at what is happening in the nineteenth century in the West: "everywhere blood flows in torrents," in Napoleon's world, in North America, now on the continent of Europe. Underground Man argues that humans are guided by consciousness and will, both of which are far superior to science and "systems." Indeed, he claims that humans regularly act against their own rational best interests.

Dostoyevsky's successor in these considerations is Yevgeny Zamiatin, whose novel *We*, written in 1920–1921 (though not published in Russia until 1988) in the midst of the Russian Revolution and Civil War, is arguably the finest dystopia of the twentieth century. *We*, which served as the model for *1984* by George Orwell, presents the reader with a futuristic state built on "reason" and order. Freedom does not exist, for "the only means to rid man of crime is to rid him of freedom." As the novel progresses, the head of the state, the Benefactor, argues that human beings do not want freedom, that it causes suffering and confusion. He tells the first-person narrator of his justification for tyranny and repression:

> I ask this question: What is it that people beg for, dream about, torment themselves for, from the time they leave swaddling clothes? They want someone to tell them, once and for all, what happiness is—and then to bind them to that happiness with a chain. What is it we're doing right now, if not that? The ancient dream of paradise…. Remember: In paradise they've lost all knowledge of desires, pity, love—they are the blessed, with their imaginations surgically removed (the only reason why they are blessed)—angels, the slaves of God.[16]

The questions raised by Mann would be seen as central to considerations of social and political thought after the Second World War. Books such as Erich Fromm's *Escape from Freedom* (1941) and Eric Hoffer's *The True Believer* (1951) came to lend not only their contents but also their titles to the discourse about human nature, social movements, and the traditional assumption that humans wanted to be free.

It was Hannah Arendt, another German exile, who said that the fundamental question central to the aftermath of the First World War was that of death, and the fundamental problem related to the experience of the 1930s and the Second World War was about the nature of evil. It should be added that the whole of the twentieth century bequeathed to its heirs the issue raised so clearly by Thomas Mann—that of human nature and the relationship between freedom and authority.

2 VIRGINIA WOOLF
Transcending

VIRGINIA WOOLF WAS BY 1930 as famous in England as was Thomas Mann in Germany. Her novels, especially *Mrs. Dalloway* (1925), *To the Lighthouse* (1927), and *Orlando* (1928), were highly regarded by both mainstream and avant-garde critics. Her essays and opinions were important statements in public debate.

As well, Woolf and her husband were the founders and proprietors of Hogarth Press, a major publisher. She was a leading figure in the Bloomsbury group, a set of friends and intellectuals that included such luminaries as John Maynard Keynes, E.M. Forster, Lytton Strachey, Clive Bell, and Duncan Grant, and that set the tone of British intellectual life in its time.

Woolf had a fine pedigree in the rarefied and somewhat incestuous world of British letters. Her father was Leslie Stephen, author, critic, and editor of the *Cornhill Magazine* and the *Dictionary of National Biography*, himself the son of a Regius professor of modern history at Cambridge. Her mother, born Julia Prinsep Jackson, was painted in her youth by Burne-Jones and G.F. Watts, and was courted by Holman-Hunt, all Pre-Raphaelite painters. Her godfather was James Russell Lowell, the American critic and poet who was the US ambassador to Britain from 1880 to 1885.

Woolf was a person whose life and work were both experimental. She was bisexual and had several open affairs with women. She courted androgyny in her life and in her works, notably *Orlando*. She had deep, painful episodes of depression, suffered from visions, and was mentally unstable for a good part of her adult life, looked after by her husband and others. She was a woman who asked about women's place in the world, and a novelist whose works changed the way novels were regarded and written.

On July 2, 1928, Royal Assent was given to the Representation of the People (Equal Franchise) Act in Great Britain. Now all women over the age of twenty-one had the vote. This was a great victory for the suffragette movement after several decades of protest in the streets and in the press. To some, it ended a period when women were treated unequally in the civil state.

Woolf gave two lectures at Cambridge University in October of that year on women and fiction, indicating that she believed the battle for women had still just begun. The lectures were put into book form and published in 1929 as an essay, *A Room of One's Own*. The most famous phrase of the essay, one that has become a part of the canon of Western culture, appears in the first paragraph: "a woman must have money and a room of her own if she is to write fiction."

One of the main things Woolf was doing in the essay was announcing that women could not gain freedom simply by political means. Rather, money, which provided economic freedom, must be part of the equation. Simply, money gave one the power to shape one's own self apart from the social patriarchy that continued to dominate British society. There could be no freedom without equality of opportunity, and women therefore, like men, needed means and property.

As well, one needs a room of one's own—apart from the kitchen. One needs space and air. Men have studies; women need to carve out some place that belongs to them alone.

A simple idea, perhaps, but a profound insight. One cannot shape oneself independently of the surrounding social and economic circumstances. Political equality would mean little without a change in opportunity. Indeed, in order to be able to shape oneself, an oppressed group must work to change the conditions of existence.

Woolf's insight was not original, but her articulation of it began what has been called second-wave feminism. She certainly knew the history of her gender, and admired many women in the past, including Aphra Benn and Mary Wollstonecraft. It is not certain whether she knew the work of Charlotte Perkins Gilman, especially her harrowing short story "The Yellow Wallpaper" and groundbreaking *Women and Economics* (1898). But Woolf clearly understood that the ability to create required more than a pen and paper.

Woolf's essay is also unusual in its style. She consciously made "use of all the liberties and licenses of a novelist" in her presentation and argument. She states that while she will use the first person singular, the "'I' is only a convenient term for somebody who has no real being." She will, on occasion, invent characters and present events that may not have happened. Woolf is trying—and I argue that she succeeds—to invent an essay style appropriate to the condition of women rather than adopting the "normal" patriarchal form. This is something Woolf will deal with her whole life. How do women articulate their sense of reality? It is as necessary to invent form as well as to employ new content.

The "I" imagines herself sitting on the side of a river in Oxbridge in a natural setting lush with growth and the colours of autumn. She contemplates the timelessness and beauty of the place and the college, and recognizes the insignificance of herself and a larger, fuller world. And then she walks on the grass.

There appears a man in the distance, gesturing anxiously. He is the Beadle, an employee of the college, dressed formally, responsible for security and the rules. He informs her that she is not permitted to walk on the grass, that this privilege is reserved for Fellows and Scholars. Her place is the gravel path.

There are many beadles in the class-conscious world of Oxbridge and Britain. They are employed to make certain the rules are followed. Who makes the rules? The patriarchy. So someone like Virginia Woolf, invited to lecture, having published several well-received novels and many essays, regarded as a luminary in the firmament of British letters, still cannot walk on the grass because of her gender.

This recalls John Stuart Mill's lament in his *The Subjection of Women* (1871). Men use the patriarchy, he notes, as a way of elevating themselves. Indeed, the most foolish and ignorant male child will grow into adulthood thinking himself superior to one half of humanity by virtue of his gender.

The matter is underlined as the "I" wanders to the library. She opens the door and there appears "a guardian angel barring the way with a flutter of black gown instead of white wings," who informs her that ladies cannot be permitted to enter the library unless accompanied by a Fellow of the College or a letter of introduction. Of course, Woolf remarks, it is not about the library or its contents, it is about power and status.

Woolf then goes to lunch at the college. She notes such matters as what people eat seem unimportant to the novelist describing a lunch, but that this time she finds it significant. The lunch is abundant and sumptuous—sole, partridges, sauces, salads, a dessert that is "a confection which rose all sugar from the waves," white and red wine. All had leisure and abundance as the luncheon took its time and lasted for hours.

The essayist then seems to go on a tangent, but it is a meaningful one. She reflects (for to Woolf inner reflection is often more real than outer perception) on some poetry of Tennyson and Christina Rossetti, thinking that their pastoral and joyful lines were what would be appropriate to the luncheon. However, she suggests that those thoughts fit the experience of the same luncheon before 1914, before the war, but no longer.

The suggestion is that the luncheon has not changed, but the world in which it is happening has fundamentally transformed. The poetry no longer reflects our experience or illuminates it. We have new poetry—perhaps we also need new luncheons.

There are other nuances here in Woolf's analysis. The West, having thought itself superior to the rest of humankind before 1914, was guilty of many injustices. After all, it, like most societies, oppressed females; it countenanced and supported racial slavery for centuries; it colonized those whom it believed to be inferior and forced them to adopt its languages, religion, and mythology. The Great War, for many, punctured the ideology of superiority—the so-called most civilized people of earth committed unprecedented carnage on themselves. Is it not now necessary to think in new ways?

This point is punctuated with her dinner, in one of the few women's colleges. "Dinner was ready. Here was the soup. It was plain gravy soup. There was nothing to stir the fancy in that." The beef, greens, and potatoes form "a homely trinity." Then prunes and custard for dessert, no wavelike confection. Finally, biscuits, cheese, and water.

If Mann used the table at a restaurant as a social statement, Woolf now enters the world of the politics and economics of food. Why the contrast of meals? Because the women's college has no money. The traditional colleges have endowments and resources, whereas the women striving for education have the bare necessities. "Not a penny could be spared for 'amenities'; for partridges and wine, beadles and turf, books and cigars, libraries and leisure. To raise bare walls out of bare earth was the utmost they could do."

Hence, the few women's colleges could just supply its students with bare rooms of their own. The other necessity, money, was not forthcoming. Just as poetry had to change, so too did the social and economic balance. Her society, she remarks, is "inscrutable."

Woolf's character decides to go to the British Museum to do some research on matters of gender. What she finds is not helpful. Nearly all the books written about women are by men, and nearly all of those by learned professors have titles like *The Mental, Moral, and Physical Inferiority of the Female Sex*. She reflects that the so-called scholarship might not really be about the inferiority of females but the need for males to believe in their own superiority. Scholarship is guided by psychology, not data.

Then a segue back to the fictional self of the narrator. She reveals that an aunt (who died from a fall from her horse in India) left her a legacy of five hundred pounds a year. She muses that she now has the vote and money, but of the two, the money "seems infinitely more important." The money meant she no longer had to work at the mean jobs left to women of intelligence. Moreover, "I do not need to hate any man; he cannot hurt me. I do not need to flatter any man; he has nothing to give me." She is free—free to shape herself according to her own sense of her best interests, something liberal thought had as its goal for humanity since the Enlightenment.

Woolf's reflections on what it means to be free are not entirely new, though the context of gender gives them a novel direction in 1929. It was Marx and Engels who gave substance to the distinction between what they called the animal life and the human life. For them, the dilemma of capitalism is that it left the vast majority—men and women—in a position where they spent all their time and energy fulfilling their "animal" needs: food, clothing, and shelter. Hence, they had no opportunity to develop their human needs—self-definition, a relationship to art and beauty.

What the Industrial Revolution did was to create abundance. What it did not do (many would argue this is still the case) was to create a fair system of distribution. After all, if there was abundance, could we not all be free from our "animal" needs? Woolf adopts the Marx–Engels argument. If one has enough money to live decently, it frees one to shape oneself. It frees all of us from being subject to the limitations placed by social and political convention.

So, for Woolf and for Marx the vote seems to give you equality. But it is money that will set you free and make your relationships with fellow human beings far more honest.

Woolf speculates that perhaps a century hence, women will take part in all social, political, and commercial activities. "Anything may happen when womanhood has ceased to be a protected occupation."

This is another insight of great importance. Men's development has a model—men know what will happen to them, or at least what is supposed to happen. But if women are free, then any future is possible. Women's story is open-ended. They will make history, rather than repeat it.

Woolf returns to her central subject—why so few women have written literature compared to men. To understand why, she invents the character of Judith Shakespeare, one of several of her fictional women who are now part of the literary canon.

Judith Shakespeare is supposed to be the splendidly intelligent and creative sister of William, a sibling as gifted as was he. He goes to school, he marries young, he goes to London and to the theatre. Judith does not go to school, is told not to be interested in books, and is betrothed at sixteen to a local lad.

She protests to the marriage, but her father beats her, begs her, and perhaps even tries to bribe her with jewels and clothes not to shame the family.

Judith loves words, has the same gifts as her brother, and she occasionally secretly writes.

She runs away—to London and to the theatre. She wants to act, but no woman is thought to be able to be an actress. She is mocked and derided. Finally, an actor-manager, who Woolf calls Nick Greene (the surname is the same as that of a critic who in 1592 wrote that William Shakespeare thought too well of himself) takes her in and she becomes pregnant. How, asks Woolf, do we understand this phenomenon in the late sixteenth century: a great poet's mind and heart in the body of a woman?

Judith kills herself. She cannot live with the contradictions she finds herself always encountering. And, of course, it is we who are also the losers in this tale.

Woolf does not note that Judith has fictional sisters in kind, many of whom are closer in time to 1929. They are Anna Karenina, Emma Bovary, Hedda Gabler, Edna Pontellier, and others, women who try to break out of the mould in which they are placed and find they cannot do so because the social and economic circumstances of their lives do not permit them to be free.

Even fictional women who seem successful provide an enigma of not knowing how the story ends. The narrator of "The Yellow Wallpaper" breaks out of the confinement her doctor-husband placed her in, and Nora of Henrik Ibsen's *A Doll's House* slams the door, leaving her stupefied husband and children as the final curtain comes down. But the real question is not what happened to these two women, it is what will happen to them after they set themselves free. What is the end of their story? We do not know, in part at least because their actions are so unprecedented, we have no models to work from. Again, the endings are open.

Woolf reviews poetry and other writings of women, and notes that there is talent displayed, though it was not valued. Many women wrote for their own selves, solitary people who had no audience and who would garner no criticism or accolades. She finds that what we now call life-writing is a source for understanding how well some women could write and how insightful they could be. Letters by women, she demonstrates, are a powerful source of understanding.

She then asks yet another important question. Does being a woman make one a writer different from their male counterparts? Surely, one's social circumstances shape one's mind, and even some of the finest women writers, say Emily Brontë and George Eliot, stumble at times. Perhaps this is due to the fact that they have no tradition to work from—they cannot see themselves as continuing or transcending a customary practice. Perhaps it is, at least in its beginnings, the idea that women have to do what men do and do it so much better in order to be heard. After all, many women adopted men's names in order to get a reading and some consideration.

Woolf notes that there still are men who make statements like Sir Egerton Bridges in 1928: "female novelists should only aspire to excellence by courageously acknowledging the limitations of their sex." Bridges is a beadle, and Woolf insists that he may be able to control the lawn and library, but he cannot control her mind.

That women have something to offer far different from the sensibility of men was earlier acknowledged by Charles Dickens in one of the most famous critical reviews in the English language. Dickens read George Eliot's first published work, *Scenes of Clerical Life*. He admired it greatly and wrote to Eliot in January 1858:

> My Dear Sir,
>
> I have been so strongly affected by the two first tales in the book you have had the kindness to send me through Messrs. Blackwood [Eliot's publisher], that I hope you will excuse my writing to you to express my admiration of their extraordinary merit. The exquisite truth and delicacy, both of the humour and the pathos of those stories, I have never seen the like of; and they have impressed me in a manner that I should find it very difficult to describe to you, if I had the impertinence to try.
>
> In addressing these few words of thankfulness, to the creator of the sad fortunes of Mr. Amos Barton, and the sad love-story of Mr. Gilfil, I am (I presume) bound to adopt the name that it pleases that excellent writer to assume. I can suggest no better one; but I should have been strongly disposed, if I had been left to my own devices, to address the said writer as a woman. I have observed what seem to me to be such womanly touches, in those moving fictions, that the assurance on the title-page is insufficient to satisfy me, even now. If they originated with no woman, I believe that no man ever before had the art of making himself, mentally, so like a woman, since the world began.
>
> You will not suppose that I have any vulgar wish to fathom your secret. I mention the point as one of great interest to me—not of mere curiosity. If it should ever suit your convenience and inclination, to shew me the face of the man or woman who has written so charmingly, it will be a very memorable occasion to me. If otherwise, I shall always hold that impalpable personage in loving attachment and respect, and shall yield myself up to all future utterances from the same source, with a perfect confidence in their making me wiser and better.[1]

Dickens had the imagination to do what few male critics, if any (outside the philosopher John Stuart Mill), could manage in his time. He recognized that there was a whole realm of sensibility that would be opened with women as equals in the literary community. The canon still had much to do. Woolf's own novels and stories are among the works that deepened it.

Woolf then takes up yet another important issue, and invents another woman—Mary Carmichael, who is the fictional author of her fictional first novel, *Life's Adventure*. Her style is odd, says Woolf. She moved up and down, too many facts, seemingly afraid of the judgment of the reader, going somewhere but hesitating. And then Woolf says she realized what was happening. She read, "Chloe liked Olivia."

Mary Carmichael was going into uncharted territory, "for if Chloe likes Olivia and Mary Carmichael knows how to express it, she will light a torch in that vast chamber where nobody has been." We will have an honest, illuminating story of a lesbian relationship.

This was no small matter at the time. Woolf names Sir Chartres Biron in her discussion. He was the judge at the famous obscenity trial of Radclyffe Hall's novel *The Well of Loneliness* in November 1928. Hall's novel, with a foreword by Havelock Ellis, is about a female protagonist who sees herself as male, and who has a lesbian relationship. Some of the British press deemed the novel obscene, an obscenity trial was held, and all copies of the book were ordered destroyed by the eminent Sir Chartres.

Leonard and Virginia Woolf, E.M. Forster, and others publicly supported Hall's right to write freely, though some believed the book had little literary merit. No matter, said Biron, it depicted "moral and physical degradation" and "vice."[2]

Woolf's own *Orlando* (1928) involved lesbianism and androgyny, as did several other works by women at the time. But the matter was discussed in metaphorical code, and Woolf's book certainly had what critics call literary merit. Still, Woolf remarks, if women are free to write, then they will need deeply to explore territory heretofore closed.

The fear of lesbianism as part of public discussion on the part of the male patriarchy and their beadles was yet another example of the double standard. The establishment "public" (meaning independent, private) schools in England—Eton, Harrow, Winchester, and others—were notoriously places where young men grew to maturity while engaged in homosexual and sadistic acts. The British male establishment included a high number of individuals who were homosexual. The battle of Waterloo and others may have been won on the playing fields of Eton, but that is not all that was happening on that lush grass.

Mary Carmichael, Woolf claimed, had a large task. "The novels lie," claimed Woolf, because we have little understanding of such matters as to what was happening in the kitchen, how children were raised, how women thought and felt. Obscure lives remain to be recorded. Indeed, Woolf states, Mary Carmichael could also tell stories about men. In this Woolf, perhaps unknowingly, helped to direct other intellectual matters, apart from literature. Historians have finally taken up the lives of women and the poor. Archeologists and anthropologists have changed their emphasis from power to society. The humanities now deals far better with all of humanity.

At some point, Woolf states, the Mary Carmichaels will have a place different from women writers of 1929 and before. She will no longer have to start with anger against men, and men will no longer be "the opposing faction." She will lose the fear and rage, and be free to be herself. She will write as a woman, "but as a woman who has forgotten that she is a woman." Mary Carmichael is not Judith Shakespeare in her talent or her circumstances. She will write good, not great, literature and, at some point, she will be a poet. What she does not have to do is to kill herself; she can be free.

Woolf then asks that writers in the West transcend issues of gender. She cites Coleridge in saying "a great mind is androgynous." A writer must communicate the whole of human experience, and to do so she must be open and undivided. At some point, the grievances must be set aside "for anything written with that conscious bias is doomed to death." There will be writers who are male and writers who are female, but great writers—she refers to Shakespeare—will be neither female nor male.

Circumstances still matter, and Woolf joins Mann in referring to the oppression of Fascism. What is happening in Italy, she asserts, is masculine; Fascism is a patriarchal style and ideology as practised from Rome. She mocks the hope among Fascist supporters that a great literature, especially new poets, will appear to give voice to its desires. Nothing will come of it, she argues, for poetry needs "a mother as well as a father."

Later, in her essay *Three Guineas* (1938), Woolf will elaborate on her critique of Fascism and, like Mann, come to the conclusion that the writer must engage in politics in a world where men calling themselves Führer or Duce become tyrannical leaders of states. Behind this Man (Woolf's capital "M") "lie ruined houses and dead bodies—men, women, children."[3] Hence, she comes back to her premise of *A Room of One's Own*: the personal, social, and political are intertwined.

Woolf returns to Judith Shakespeare. She is certain that the time is coming when she can flourish. Life may be a struggle but, she says to her audience, if we continue to work "the dead poet who was Shakespeare's sister will put on the body which she has so often laid down."

For Woolf the world of 1929 is unjust, yet she is hopeful that women will not only be free but that at some time in the future we will all be judged equally. For Woolf, feminism turns out to be a branch of humanism, recalling Terence's dictum: "Nothing human is alien to me."

Woolf remained a novelist first and in 1929, 1930, and early 1931, she was engaged in writing her most experimental work of fiction, *The Waves*, which attempted to transcend the traditional novel.

The intellectual issue Woolf decided to address was one central to literature and epistemology in general after the First World War and with the introduction of Einsteinian physics and Einstein's and others' reflections on the problem of knowledge.

Toward the end of *The Waves* Woolf's main character, Bernard, reflects, "life is not susceptible perhaps to the treatment we give it when we try to tell it." How, now, do we relate what is real? What can the writer of fiction do to illuminate the nature of reality in a world where nothing appears to be firm? Are words and stories inadequate? Woolf asks whether the novel needs to take a new form in order to deal with the world as it is in 1930 and how we understand it.

The Waves is presented as a novel, but Woolf herself acknowledged that she was experimenting. In her diary she described it as "a new kind of play ... prose yet poetry; a novel and a play.... I am writing *The Waves* to a rhythm not to a plot."[4] In August 1930 she noted that "*The Waves* is, I think, resolving itself into a series of dramatic soliloquies. The thing is to keep them running homogeneously in & out, in the rhythm of the waves."[5]

The traditional novel—and we should remember that the novel itself is a relatively new form, invented in the early seventeenth century—was a social document with a narrator, characters, plot, and clear ending. Indeed, Thomas Mann's *Buddenbrooks* is an excellent representative of that form, whose masters include George Eliot, Dickens, and Balzac. There were also novels written in the first person, a narrator telling his or her story, usually advancing through the world.

However, in the early twentieth century, some novelists would pick up the issue of the importance of inner reality and write different works. In effect, they implicitly suggested that the novel needed to change in form because our notions of reality and personality were now different. The major figures using this approach were Marcel Proust, whose *Remembrance of Things Past* is often cited as a precursor to Woolf's work, James Joyce, and, though hardly well known in 1930, Franz Kafka.

Woolf's novels before *The Waves* treated reality as multi-faceted—socially and psychologically, most especially *Mrs. Dalloway* and *Orlando*.

But *The Waves* goes further than ever before. "Prose yet poetry" as Woolf stated, is correct. Much of the book can be treated as prose poetry, especially the nine italicized descriptions of nature that precede each section, in addition to some of the many soliloquies. It also has the quality of "a novel and a play," as Woolf adopts some dramatic forms from the theatre.

Further, Woolf talks about the book having a rhythm, and she means a rhythm that is not only poetic, but musical. In her diaries we learn that Woolf listened to Beethoven, especially the last quartets, while writing *The Waves*. These works by Beethoven are widely regarded as not only brilliant in themselves, but also a major development of the dominant musical discourse of the composer's time, the allegro sonata form. Beethoven was writing new music in an old guise, just as Woolf was writing new literature—with elements borrowed from psychology, poetry, music, and drama—while still calling it a novel.

"It occurred to me last night," wrote Woolf in her diary on December 22, 1930,

> while listening to a Beethoven quartet that I would merge all the interjected passage in Bernard's final speech, & end with the words O solitude…. This is also to show that the theme effort, effort dominates: not the waves: & personality: & defiance: but I am not sure of the effect artistically; because the proportions may need the intervention of the waves finally so as to make a conclusion.[6]

The Waves employs the narrative voices of six characters: Bernard, Rhoda, Neville, Susan, Louis, and Jinny, friends who have known one another since childhood. Directly at the beginning, the reader is faced with a dilemma. Woolf has each character, now a small child, quickly describe a single perception, all different. Critics have argued whether the six friends are each a separate character, or whether they blend together to form one whole. Both occur in the novel.

By abandoning the "appalling narrative business of the realist,"[7] as Woolf described her intentions in November 1928, she has her characters sometimes narrate their own lives, sometimes "melt into each other," as Bernard says early in the novel. Sometimes they simultaneously do both.

Woolf believed that we have multiple selves, not a single identity. Bernard notes, "I am not one and simple, but complex and many." Moreover, there are "several different men who alternately act their parts as Bernard."

Woolf adopts the idea that human nature is very complex, that we are sometimes defined by our consciousness of things, events, people, and ourselves, and that there are layers of personality. How do we get to this? Through language, though she is clear that language refers to our consciousness but is not to be confused with consciousness itself. "Nothing should be named," says Neville, who will be a writer, "lest by doing so we change it. Let it exist, this bank, this beauty, and I, for one instant, steeped in pleasure."

Woolf's relationship to Freudian thought has been the subject of much critical reflection. She claimed not to have read Freud until later in her life.

But in 1924, Hogarth Press became the publisher of Freud's works in English, and Leonard Woolf, Lytton Strachey, and others in her circle discoursed regularly about Freud's ideas.

Woolf dealt with some of the main issues raised by Freud in writing *The Waves*, asking what these concepts meant to the novel. First, there is the idea that the unconscious is a layer of our personality, perhaps the main layer. All of her characters attempt to deal with their inner lives, their perceptions.

As well, Woolf accepts and emphasizes that story is important to our identity. We have a past and that past matters. "I make stories," says Bernard. In addition, nothing is stable, all is flux, all is change. We are, but we are in a world where Becoming trumps Being.

As for the concept of an external objective reality, we "pretend that life is a solid substance, shaped like a globe, which we turn about in our fingers. Let us pretend we can make out a plain and logical story." We pretend, knowing we are pretending, for life is hardly plain or logical. Woolf asks, "but what is the thing that lies beneath the semblance of the thing?"

Woolf's novel is thus both fiction and metafiction. It is a work of art that is very self-conscious of itself as artifice. It reflects on itself as it unfolds, just as we reflect on ourselves as our lives unfold. Indeed, the six characters regularly take refuge in friendship, commitment, and connection, but they also meditate on both solitude and being alone.

The novel also has a different relationship to the reader than more conventional, realist works. What we as readers know, we know through the words and perceptions of the six characters. There is no omniscient narrator, nor is there information that the reader might have that is sometimes not known by some characters. We, as readers, must be active participants in getting meaning from the work. This fits a new Western understanding in which there is no formal, objective reality; rather, the subject—in this case the reader—is engaged in constructing reality from perceptions, reflections, memory, and so on.

There is a seventh character in the work, another friend, Percival, who is known to the reader only through the perceptions of the other six. He is a character of Platonic perfection, loved by all, seen as a model, a paragon of human potential. Percival dies in the middle of the book, absurdly. "He is dead, said Neville. He fell. His horse tripped. He was thrown. The sails of the world have swung round and caught me on the head. All is over. The lights of the world have gone out. There stands the tree which I cannot pass."

Through the death of Percival, Woolf also deals with important themes of the interwar years and all of modernity. Neville and Bernard perceive that though Percival has died, a shattering moment for them, ordinary life is going on about them. Woolf thus anticipates one of the great poems of the decade, W.H. Auden's *Musée des Beaux Arts* (1939), in which Auden reflects on both suffering and its loneliness.

After 1914, loss and suffering were no strangers to many people and families in Europe. Moreover, the loss of young people was a part of the experience of everyone, as Europe sent its youth to war and then dug cemeteries for many of them. Percival represents possibilities that have been lost irrevocably.

Still, there is order in the world Woolf creates in *The Waves*. The book is organized using three intertwined rhythms. First, there is the cycle of nature, represented by the continuous falling of the waves onto the shore. This cycle is circular, not progressive. It represents the largeness of the world and continuity.

The second is the cycle of the sun, the day. Each of the nine cursive sections introducing the chapters begins with a statement about the sun. The first recalls Genesis: "The sun had not yet risen. The sea was indistinguishable from the sky." In the middle of the work: "The sun had risen to its full height". At the end: "Now the sun had sunk. Sky and sea were indistinguishable." Woolf uses extraordinary colour imagery throughout the nine introductions, again indicating that perception is important. In the fifth introduction, two pages long, there are over thirty colour references.

The third is the cycle of our own lives, paralleling that of the rise and fall of the sun. We are born, we live, we will die. These two last cycles are developmental, linear, unlike the first. A larger metaphysical question is implicit: what is the meaning of our poor lives in the face of the wholeness and continuity of the waves?

If *The Waves* is a novel written in nine movements, a work with something of a musical form, the last movement is a kind of coda, summing up, as one narrator, Bernard, states in its opening. "Now to sum up," he says as an old man. "Now to explain to you the meaning of my life."

But the summing up and the explanation of meaning are messy, because life is not as coherent as we often present it.

> [L]ike children we tell each other stories, and to decorate them we make up these ridiculous, flamboyant, beautiful phrases. How tired I am of stories, how tired I am of phrases that come down beautifully with all their feet on the ground! Also, how I distrust neat designs of life that are drawn upon half-sheets of notepaper.

Bernard argues for an active life. "To let oneself be carried on passively is unthinkable." Woolf is here telling us that in the twentieth century lives are constructed, not given. As well, she is carrying on with the argument from *A Room of One's Own*, where she insists that all of us should be in a position to shape our lives. Passivity is tacit acceptance of the patriarchy and the existing structure of authority.

Some commentators suggest that here Woolf is being an existentialist, a term not yet invented in 1930. Certainly, she prefigures the stance that meaning is created by individual choices. Indeed, there is a kind of intertextuality in Bernard's reflections, for in his musings on "eternal flux," the reality of Becoming, he makes reference to Hamlet and Dostoyevsky's main figure in *The Possessed*, Stavrogin, two characters often cited by later existentialist philosophers. Woolf is part of a group of thinkers who set the stage for the more formal introduction of existentialism after the Second World War.

Bernard continuously contrasts the apparent orderliness of our outer lives—"this military progress"; "Tuesday follows Monday, then comes Wednesday"—to what is actually happening. Below this outward order there are our dreams, memories, images, half-understood perceptions, and experiences. There is "concord and discord." Bernard suggests it is more a symphony than an organized story.

He muses again on the death of Percival and he reveals, almost in passing, that one of the six friends, Rhoda, a person unable to find a place in the world, committed suicide. At the end it is death that clouds his mind.

But, although death is inevitable, it is to be resisted. Fight, he insists. "It is the effort and the struggle, it is the perpetual warfare, it is the shattering and piecing together—this is the daily battle, defeat or victory, the absorbing pursuit."

The waves continue, the cycle goes on, and we will disappear. Still, he is determined. Death is seen as "the enemy." And Bernard will continue the struggle against the inevitable. At the end of the book he states, "Against you I will fling myself, unvanquished and unyielding, O Death." Woolf adds one more sentence in italics, referring back to the nine cursive sections: "*The waves broke on the shore.*"

Woolf's two works cover a great deal of territory—everything from social and political analysis, moral considerations, the nature of reality, and the way to build a meaningful life, to the possibilities and limits of literature.

She belongs not only to literature but to modern philosophy. One of several things that happens to what we call philosophy, including aesthetics, ethics, and epistemology in the twentieth century, is that it adopts new modes of discourse to articulate its concerns and positions. Neither Kierkegaard nor Nietzsche develops his philosophy as Hume, Montesquieu, Kant, Hegel, or Marx did. Dostoyevsky and Mann explore philosophy under the guise of literature. Clearly, new modes of discourse seem to be needed to deal with the modern world.

Woolf sees this, and she experiments with both the essay form and the literary tradition. She not only thinks in a new way, she talks to us in a new manner in order to articulate clearly her concerns. Simply, you cannot deal with modernity in the inherited forms. Since it is Woolf, it is appropriate to adopt a musical analogy. The "classical" musical language needs to be reshaped—for in modernity there is a great deal of dissonance and discord, and things in life often do not get resolved.

Woolf thus not only opens the door for existentialism, she prefigures what we will later call postmodernity. She was important in her time. She is even more important after her time.

3 ORTEGA Y GASSET
Rethinking the West

JOSÉ ORTEGA Y GASSET (1883–1955) was one of two twentieth-century Spanish philosophers—the other is Miguel de Unamuno (1864–1936)—who became prominent European thinkers during their lifetime, and whose work influenced the discourse throughout the West.

Ortega was something of an intellectual wunderkind, taking his university examinations at a young age, going to Germany to study philosophy, and assuming the chair of Professor of Metaphysics at the University of Madrid in 1910 at the age of twenty-seven.

Still, he was not an ivory tower professor. He saw it as part of his responsibility to serve as a public intellectual. In 1923 he founded and edited the *Revista de Occidente*, the most important intellectual journal in Spain in the 1920s, and he regularly commented on Spain's tangled political life from his appointment through the 1920s and 1930s. In 1929 he resigned his university chair in protest against the Spanish dictatorship's attacks on the universities.

Ortega saw his role as twofold. The first was to help bring Spain back into the intellectual discourse of Europe as a whole. To this he brought a wide-ranging intellect, and his writings include commentaries on art and music, liberalism and socialism, the literary tradition of Spain, and the philosophy of history, in addition to metaphysics.

He believed his second role was to bring to Spain the philosophical tradition developed in Europe, especially Germany, from the eighteenth century. He was especially enamoured of the work of Immanuel Kant (1724–1804), a giant of a figure whose metaphysics, *Critique of Pure Reason*, and moral philosophy has occupied a central place in European thought right down to this moment.

Ortega's most important and influential work, *The Revolt of the Masses*, first appeared as a series of articles from October 1929 to February 1930 in the Madrid newspaper *El Sol*, which he had helped to found in 1917 and which had great influence on Spain's politics and ideology through the 1920s. The book appeared later in 1930, and it became immediately important through the West. Indeed, it is one of those works that shifted the political and social discourse.

Given its origins as a set of pieces written for a journal, the book is also an exercise in rhetoric, an attempt to use words and arguments to persuade his readers, members of the educated public, to think in new ways. And Ortega is sometimes repetitive, in order to more powerfully build his case.

The first paragraph has become famous. In part, it reads:

> There is one fact which, whether for good or ill, is of utmost importance in the public life of Europe at the present moment. This fact is the accession of the masses to complete social power. As the masses, by definition, neither should nor can direct their own personal existence, and still less rule society in general, this fact means that actually Europe is suffering from the greatest crisis that can afflict peoples, nations, and civilization…. It is called the rebellion of the masses.

Ortega argues that something new is occurring on the European scene, "entirely new in the history of our civilization." There is now something called the masses as a group, not simply a bunch of individuals. This group now claims the right to the benefits of Western civilization. Democracy has won, and the average person now has what only minorities obtained in the past.

What, then, is the problem? For Ortega, we are witnessing a "hyper-democracy in which the mass acts directly, outside the law, imposing its aspirations and its desires by means of material pressure."

He does not refer to Tocqueville, though it is a phenomenon Tocqueville predicted in his insightful analysis of American culture, *Democracy in America* (1835, 1840). The new masses, raised by the liberalism and Industrial Revolution of the nineteenth century, will insist on conformity and an instant gratification of their desires. As Ortega emphasizes, using italics, *"the characteristic of the hour is that the commonplace mind, knowing itself to be commonplace, has the assurance to proclaim the rights of the commonplace and to impose them wherever it will."* All that is unique, eccentric, excellent, unusual is, he believes, risking the danger of being crushed under the brutal will of the masses, represented by what he and others have come to call "mass man."

Ortega was a thinker, like many in the twentieth century, whose frame of reference was not only the present, but the past. *Yo soy yo y mis circumstancias* ("I am myself and my circumstances") he wrote earlier in his first major book, the *Meditations on Quixote* of 1914. Reality was not only in the mind of the individual, but also in the social, political, and historical circumstances in which one found oneself.

Ortega's thinking on this matter echoes Marx's justly lauded second paragraph of his *Eighteenth Brumaire of Louis Napoleon Bonaparte* (1852): "Men make their own history, but they do not make it just as they please: they do not make it under circumstances chosen by themselves, but under circumstances directly found, given and transmitted by the past."[1]

Both Marx and Ortega—along with Woolf in *A Room of One's Own* and Freud in *Civilization and Its Discontents*—are historicists. We cannot understand who or where we are without taking into account the full world around us and how it came to be. The present—how we live, and act, and know who we are—is great with the past.

And for Ortega, this new phenomenon of the growth and power of the masses is rooted in the nineteenth century. There is first the demographic fact. From roughly 1800 the population of Europe has grown exponentially, from 180 million in 1800 to 430 million in 1914. Europe, and the world at large, no longer is more or less stagnant. Ortega refers to this as a "dizzying rapidity of ... increase," though he would be staggered to learn that we added one billion people to the planet in the years between 1999 and 2011, bring the total to 7 billion.

To this demographic phenomenon, Ortega adds the growth of liberal democracy (from the French Revolution forward) and what he calls technicism—a combination of modern science and industrial development (from the Industrial Revolution forward).

Hence, much good has come from the nineteenth century. However, the West has also seen in modernity the coming of the masses and the presence of violence and authoritarianism in public life.

What Ortega perceives is that the new masses have no regard for the past or the struggles that came to produce them. Rather, they live in a kind of eternal present, taking for granted abundance and ease. The psychology of mass man believes that he can both universalize and obtain his present desires. However, he also has no appreciation for the past that gave him this material ease, and he possesses a certitude that his own will is correct and should be triumphant. The children of the nineteenth century, Ortega is claiming, are destroying the very basis of their freedom and success. Here, it is not the French and Industrial Revolutions that shall devour their children; it is the children who are destroying the benefits and civilization that came from the revolutions.

He states his thesis,

> the very perfection with which the XIXth Century gave an organi-
> zation to certain orders of existence has caused the masses benefited
> thereby to consider it, not as an organised, but as a natural system. Thus
> is explained and defined the absurd state of mind revealed by these
> masses; they are only concerned with their own well-being, and at the
> same time they remain alien to the cause of that well-being.

Ortega elaborates throughout the work on the qualities of this new type
of person. He contends that mass man has no respect for civilization, the
forces that created it, and the demands on the individual who participates
in it. Rather, he assumes that his desires will be automatically taken care of
as if the world were naturally like this.

Mass man is styled as "a primitive who has slipped through the wings on
to the age-old stage of civilization." The year 1930 is witnessing "the vertical
invasion of the barbarians." Mass man has no sense of the past or any appreciation for the complexities of society—it is as if he has been parachuted
into the present.

Ortega fears that this new type will now make decisions on many of the
important matters in Europe—who will govern, who will benefit, and who
will be left out. He suggests that we are entering a "self-satisfied age" when
the primitive will rule. He gives the psychology of mass man three characteristics: the sense that life is easy and simple, and requires no limitations
or reflection; a belief in his own excellence as a given, which means he will
not listen to or respect any discourse, and which gives him the sense he and
others like him are the only beings that matter; and a taste for "direct action,"
for imposing his own views on others by whatever means.

Who, precisely, is "mass man"? Ortega does not tell us explicitly, though
by discussing his characteristics he clearly makes the type something modern. There had been mobs that influenced politics in the past, from those
in the Roman Empire, to peasants in Germany in the Reformation, to the
chaos of the Thirty Years War.

Now, however, Ortega's mass man seems to come out of the suffrage
movements in the nineteenth century and the dilemmas faced by liberal
democratic thinkers such as Tocqueville and Mill.

The secular Liberals were on the side of universal human rights and the
equality of all citizens. Some talked only about males, though Mill insisted
that all rights and the vote should be extended to females.

Tocqueville and Mill had two matters that led them to reflect on the wis-
dom of their position. First, there was what Tocqueville styled "the tyranny

of the majority," the fear that in a full-fledged democracy the majority would impose its views and standards on the whole of the community.

Mill, in his *On Liberty*, among the most important documents of modern Liberalism, took this notion further and discussed the tyranny of the majority as both political and social.

> The "people" who exercise the power are not always the same people with those over whom it is exercised; and the "self-government" spoken of is not the government of each by himself, but of each by all the rest. The will of the people, moreover, practically means the will of the most numerous or the most active *part* of the people; the majority, or those who succeed in making themselves accepted as the majority; the people, consequently, *may* desire to oppress a part of their number; and precautions are as much needed against this as against any other abuse of power.... [I]n political speculations "the tyranny of the majority" is now generally included among the evils against which society requires to be on its guard.
>
> Like other tyrannies, the tyranny of the majority was at first, and is still vulgarly, held in dread, chiefly as operating through the acts of the public authorities. But reflecting persons perceived that when society is itself the tyrant—society collectively, over the separate individuals who compose it—its means of tyrannizing are not restricted to the acts which it may do by the hands of its political functionaries. Society can and does execute its own mandates: and if it issues wrong mandates instead of right, or any mandates at all in things with which it ought not to meddle, it practises a social tyranny more formidable than many kinds of political oppression.... Protection, therefore, against the tyranny of the magistrate is not enough: there needs to be protection also against the tyranny of the prevailing opinion and feeling; against the tendency of society to impose, by other means than civil penalties, its own ideas and practices as rules of conduct on those who dissent from them; to fetter the development, and, if possible, prevent the formation of any individuality not in harmony with its ways, and compel all characters to fashion themselves upon the model of its own. There is a limit to the legitimate interference of collective opinion with individual independence: and to find that limit, and maintain it against encroachment, is as indispensable to a good condition of human affairs, as protection against political despotism.[2]

Ortega's mass man is someone who will accept, even forward, both political and social tyranny.

In addition, Mill speculated that universal suffrage would elevate uninformed and unconsidered opinion to the fore and thought for a time that suffrage should be either limited or proportioned, based on the level of one's education. Both men loved democracy and feared it at the same time.

Ortega's mass man is modern because he appears out of the consequences and aftermath of both the French and American Revolutions. Universal manhood suffrage, after all, was recent for Ortega, having arrived in Spain in 1869, Portugal in 1878, France in 1875, Germany in 1871, and the United Kingdom in 1918. In these states, women in 1930 had the vote only in Germany (1919) and the United Kingdom (1928).

Mass man is also modern because the type appears out of the Industrial Revolution, the factory system, and the new urban environment. Indeed, one can speculate that he is also a product of the violence, carnage, and disillusionment coming out of the First World War. The new authoritarianism can partly be explained, claims Ortega, by this new type, which, he could not know, would reappear every so often in the later twentieth century and the early twenty-first century.

Ortega relates this new type of person to two movements in his own time: Syndicalism and Fascism. Both appeal to an individual who does not require reasons to have opinions and to believe that they can impose their opinions on others. The so-called ideas of these movements are "nothing more than appetites in words."

How do these movements impose their will? By action, using violence. The mass is encouraged to intervene in public affairs by the legitimization of its violence in the name of the rightness of its tastes. Force, claims Ortega, is coming to be part of public life of Europe. He argues this is barbaric and will radically transform Europe's public life and governance.

Bolshevism fares no better in Ortega's mind—the solution is not to be found in the Soviet Union. It, like Fascism, is a kind of regression, a movement of mass men led by mediocrities with no real sense of history. For Ortega, the Russian Revolution is just another revolution, not at all special, "a monotonous repetition of the eternal revolution," a commonplace event. Indeed, Ortega in 1930 has figured out what it took many Western intellectuals several more decades to determine—the Russian Revolution is important only as part of Russian history, it is not a Communist revolution at all. Russia is no more Marxist, as he puts it, than "the Germans of the Holy Roman Empire were Romans."

Civilization demands limitations, process, justice, reason, restrictions, and respect for the dignity of others. For Ortega, this new violence as a political style is "the Magna Charta of barbarism." He fears, and he turns out to be correct, that the so-called most civilized culture on the planet is overturning its values. Like Mann, he worries that Europe and the West are entering a time when force and the irrational will be elevated to power, even celebrated.

Ortega, like virtually everyone in 1930, did not foresee the extraordinary brutality of the next fifteen years, when many Europeans would adopt racist policies, accept the right to beat up one's neighbour because they existed, experience the cruelty of the Spanish Civil War, and have a world war in which millions were maimed or killed, and others "eliminated" in death camps. Europe's claims to be civilized were exposed as excessive in the period of colonization and the years from 1914 to 1945. It should be remembered that when Gandhi was asked what he thought of Western civilization, he replied that he believed it would be a good idea.

Ortega has mass man behaving from instinct and desire. Though he does not have a deep discussion of human nature in this work, he is at one with Mann and Freud in suggesting that we are not as benign as the Enlightenment thought us to be. We can be violent and brutal, and we look for outlets for our will. It has been said that the true fascist personality is a male who beats up people not because he dislikes them but because he takes pleasure in beating up people. There were ideologies—Fascism, Nazism, Bolshevism—that were being developed and practised in 1930 that gave legitimacy to this brutality. Ortega openly refers to Bolshevism and Fascism as retrograde and a new kind of primitivism.

There is another type in contrast to mass man, who is satisfied and acknowledges no standard outside of his own feelings and will. This is, says Ortega, the noble man, someone who makes great demands upon himself, who aspires to excellence, and who continually searches for the highest standard. He is, though Ortega does not directly refer to it, living according to Kant's categorical imperative—we universalize our behaviour as a way of moving it from will to morality.

This noble figure accepts the obligations of living in a community and wishes to transcend the present in the service of bettering himself and society. He struggles, he makes efforts, he is not as certain as he would like to be, and he is always in process, in opposition to the inert mass man.

Ortega, here and in other works, most especially his earlier *The Dehumanization of Art* (1925), claims that this nobility is not something most people can achieve, but it is to be valued nonetheless.

In introducing the type of the noble man, Ortega has been accused of being an elitist, of abandoning the very liberal democratic principles he claims to value. This is a misreading of his work, though Ortega could have been clearer by introducing some people who he believed were noble.

Ortega's noble man is not from an inherited class. Nor is he exempt from the limitations placed upon him by society and politics. He is, simply, someone who lives in a style that is critical and transformative, and who might make a special contribution as a result of his quest for excellence. It is an acknowledgement that while we are all equal in our civic lives, some of us will be outstanding and make more of a difference than others. Mann and Woolf qualify as nobles for Ortega, as do his beloved Kant and Goethe.

Part of the reason for the misunderstanding of the noble concept is the shadow of Nietzsche on Europe's intellectual life at the time. His Overman (sometimes translated as Superman in English at that time) is claimed by Nietzsche to have noble qualities. This, then, gives him the right to the will to power—to create his own values and decide on a destiny so transcendent that it can justify ignoring and/or harming those who are deemed inferior.

Ortega's noble man has no fraternity with either Nietzsche's idea or that of the libertarian Ayn Rand, who later in the 1940s would argue for the right of the superior individual to ignore the common good if he thought it appropriate. Rather, Ortega wants to acknowledge excellence and to give credit to a life of striving.

Ortega suggests that mass man will be repelled by the noble person to the point where he will choose one of his own to lead. He will want in power someone with whom he can relate psychologically and who will cater to his material and mental needs. Ortega strongly supports democracy but fears what the masses will do with their power, indeed whether they will destroy liberal democracy first at the ballot box and then in the street.

At the beginning and the end of the work Ortega discusses a fundamental question implicit in his full analysis. "Europe has been left without a moral code," he claims. We in 1930 are living at a time when humans believe they can do and create anything, but have no idea what to do or create. Modernity has abundance, but it is lost.

This phenomenon, commented upon by so many from roughly 1900, reified by the Great War, is sometimes referred to as the loss of the *weltanschauung*, the end of a clear and coherent world view. What is unusual about this change in world views in the early twentieth century, which after all occur regularly in Western culture, is that no new set of accepted beliefs or standards came to replace it. When the Italian Renaissance came to be, it altered and transformed a medieval world and introduced new ideas about knowledge and the human personality. When the Enlightenment developed a secular and rational point of view, it replaced other main ideas. New paradigms soon replace old ones, as Kuhn theorized. Not so for 1930.

Ortega and other public intellectuals of 1930 would agree with Yeats's lament in his *The Second Coming* (1919)

> Things fall apart; the centre cannot hold;
> Mere anarchy is loosed upon the world,
> The blood-dimmed tide is loosed, and everywhere

The ceremony of innocence is drowned;
The best lack all conviction, while the worst
Are full of passionate intensity.

....

The darkness drops again but now I know
That twenty centuries of stony sleep
Were vexed to nightmare by a rocking cradle,
And what rough beast, its hour come round at last,
Slouches towards Bethlehem to be born?[3]

The dilemma in the early twentieth century, perhaps in the early twenty-first century as well, is that an intellectual revolution occurred from roughly 1880–1920 that transformed everything—Newtonian physics was seen as inadequate; artists experimented with colour and form; human nature was seen as far more complex than anything the Enlightenment posited and far more irrational than we would like it to be; composers began writing twelve-tone and dissonant music; the Darwinian model became the basis of biological research; Euclidian geometry was supplanted by new mathematical constructs—but substituted no new, coherent world view. Rather, some, including Nietzsche, Picasso, and Proust, were excited about the openness it offered, the abundant possibilities.

However, Ortega states that his time is not witnessing the struggle of a new civilization with one that came previously. There is no dialectic. Mass man does not have a new morality, he argues, he "is simply without morality, which is always, in essence, a sentiment of submission to something." No new ethos, claims Ortega, is coming into being from a dominant group that recognizes no authority outside of its own will.

In this Ortega was in error. His mass man had something of a moral code, though it is one that repels Ortega. His type that supports authority and Fascism adopted a world view that included an abhorrent vision of social Darwinism. Mussolini took pains to have his belief system regarded as a coherent philosophy in many writings attributed to him, most prominently in his 1932 article on Fascism, written with the help of Giovanni Gentile, in the *Italian Encyclopaedia* and in *Fascism: Doctrine and Institutions*, published in 1935.

Moreover, Ortega wrote at a time when colonial rule was common. The British regarded their rule in India as beneficent, as did the French in Algeria. The British, French, and Spanish colonized the Americas, sometimes perpetuating genocides, using as justification their own Biblical and social Darwinian views. Liberal democracies in the colonial period behaved as badly as did authoritarian states in their treatment of indigenous people and colonials, viewing their policies and actions as moral, even God-given. The French introduced the term *mission civilatrice* as a rationale for justifying their condescending and harmful activities that violated basic human rights.

For Ortega, however, there is desperate need for a "new European code." We are capable of creating great things, but we know not what to create. He viewed the critical European of his day as an intellectual paradox: he has power beyond anything in the past and he is totally insecure in his soul.

Of all the major 1930 figures, Ortega is the one who deals most profoundly with the contemporary question of the viability of liberal democracy.

Liberal democracy was not doing well in 1930. It was viewed by many as not responsive enough to the needs of the times and something of a failure in practice. Many saw one of two new ideologies, Bolshevism or Fascism, as the wave of the future. The main democracies were struggling: France's Third Republic was staggering; Britain's parliamentary democracy had witnessed a General Strike and class battles throughout the 1920s; the Weimar Republic was stumbling in Germany with many on the left and right ready to end it; and the United States was leading the world into the Great Depression. As we know, the latter had no vital or even coherent response to its troubles until it revised its system from 1933. Spain itself had been under a dictatorship since 1923.

Still, Ortega was not alone in valuing the liberal tradition and its aspirations. In *The Revolt of the Masses* he defined Liberalism as "that principle of political rights, according to which the public authority, in spite of being all-powerful, limits itself and attempts, even at its own expense, to leave room in the State over which it rules for those to live who neither think nor feel as it does, that is to say and do as the stronger, the majority." Ortega called Liberalism a noble belief, the willingness to care for the minorities, the "determination to share existence with the enemy; more than that, with an enemy which is weak."

The Liberal tradition was developed in the West from the eighteenth century, with the introduction of the idea of universal human rights (though this part of its belief was never put into practice until the late twentieth century, with the extension of both humanity and rights to all. In many places it still remains an aspiration, not a fact). In the nineteenth century, John Stuart Mill helped to develop and refine Liberal thought in his works *On Liberty* (1859) and *Considerations on Representative Government* (1861).

A major piece of what Liberalism became was identified by Ortega as the defence of minority rights, an attack on what Tocqueville and Mill called "the tyranny of the majority." Hence, for Ortega, mass man is by his nature illiberal and anti-democratic, for he will impose his will on all around him, sometimes justifying that imposition by claiming this is the will of the majority.

The Liberal tradition as it developed asked that, insofar as it was possible, all humans should be able to shape the course of their own lives, to decide their own destiny. Thus, the state was limited—it could not interfere with those matters that Mill called self-regarding acts, those acts that are part of our tastes and inclinations and that affect only ourselves.

As it developed, the liberal democratic tradition also assumed a contract between government and the governed. Constitutional rule meant that the state accepted it could not interfere with rights and that it had an obligation to the law and due process.

The position of Liberalism on religion clearly differentiated it from aristocratic and conservative positions on the right, and the two new authoritarian systems, Bolshevism and Fascism. For Liberals, religion is a private matter, a self-regarding position. Therefore, they were opposed to the institution of a state religion to the point of advocating a clear separation of church and state. As well, they opposed any legislation that imposed a religious belief on the entire population, for example Sabbatarian laws. Nonetheless, they defended the right of people to form organized religious groups as part of the belief in the right of association, and to peacefully practise their faiths.

A piece of liberal democracy overlapped what came to be called social democracy (not democratic socialism) in the late nineteenth century. Liberals began to accept what Woolf discussed in her considerations about women—the need for some entity to make certain that individuals lived in a social and political community where they could be free to shape their destinies. Thus, though they worried about state power, Liberals realized that it could be legitimate for the state to have pension schemes, to be responsible for public health, to foster universal education, to build the infrastructure of a healthy economy, and even to regulate trade and commerce.

Ortega viewed this Liberal tradition as a civilized development, one that should be nurtured and valued. Bolshevism and Fascism appealed to what he called the barbaric side of human nature and would be both authoritarian and cruel.

A major piece of the Liberal tradition—in addition to the idea that minority rights trumps majority will, the notion that the state has some role in assuring that individuals can develop their own lives, and the importance of what has come to be called natural rights—is that of the importance of the depoliticization of as much of our lives as possible.

This latter belief became one of the tests of whether a system was indeed Liberal. Are we free to choose what we read? To form friendships with those whom we choose? To utter in public beliefs that do not conform to the majority, or to the position of those who govern us? Even to be wrong on occasion?

What was happening in the early twentieth century is that new doctrines were being articulated and put into practice that politicized much of what had heretofore been thought as private. Ortega and other Liberals saw this as a development that would destroy what is most valued in the inherited tradition of the West.

There were not all that many defenders of Liberalism in the years after the Wall Street crash of October 1929. On the right, the Fascists published essays and delivered speeches that mocked the Liberal tradition as outmoded, praising their new corporate state. Some on the right even talked about Liberalism as a doctrine of the weak, instead appealing to national and racist sentiments. On the left, the Bolsheviks with their five-year plan saw themselves as the wave of the future.

Many intellectuals agreed that the death of Liberalism and liberal democracy was near. What was happening (perhaps really what was said to be happening) in the Soviet Union attracted many intellectuals, from André Gide and André Malraux in France and Bertolt Brecht in Germany, to Antonio Gramsci in Italy, along with many others. Strangely, this would not be the last time that European intellectuals would forgive arbitrary government on the left while condemning it on the right. If religion was "the opium of the masses," Marxism (though it should be called Stalinism or Bolshevism, for as Ortega remarked it had little to do with Marx) was, as Raymond Aron later stated, the "the opium of the intellectuals."

In 1940 George Orwell wrote, "between 1935 and 1939 the Communist Party had an almost irresistible fascination for any [British] writer under forty."[4] In 1932 a number of United States intellectuals wrote a joint public letter urging voters to vote for the American Communist candidate for president, William Z. Foster, in the November elections in which Franklin Roosevelt and Herbert Hoover were the candidates of the two major parties. They wrote, "it is capitalism [with which Liberalism was associated] which is destructive of all culture and Communism which desires to save civilization and its cultural heritage from the abyss to which the world crisis is driving it." Those who signed the letter included the prominent authors John Dos Passos, Theodore Dreiser, Sherwood Anderson, and Upton Sinclair, the critics Edmund Wilson and Malcolm Cowley, and the philosopher Sydney Hook.[5]

Of course, Ortega and any Liberal would simply say that they have a right to be wrong and that it is important to have as wide a public discourse as possible. As we know, in the Soviet Union many intellectuals were sent to gulags or killed for much lesser offences.

Still, Liberalism had (still has) an ambivalent, even paradoxical relationship with the modern state. One of the later chapters in *The Revolt of the Masses* was entitled "The Greatest Danger, the State."

Ortega argues that the modern state is a product of the middle-class taking social power and then translating that into public power. Moreover, the state in his time is far different from what it had been in the seventeenth and eighteenth centuries. It is now more ubiquitous, in a role that touches everything.

On one level, thus, the state is a product of the growth of civilization and contributes to it. However, with the rise of the masses to power, Ortega fears that "mass man will tend to demand that the State intervene immediately and undertake a solution directly with its immense and unassailable resources." All that is new and spontaneous will either be absorbed by the state or crushed by it. The state becomes an end in itself.

He fears the bureaucratization of life, as do many liberal democrats, going back to both Mill and Max Weber. Moreover, he states, society will become more militarized than ever before. The warfare state will come into being. "The people are converted into fuel to feed the mere machine which is the state." Ortega predicted this six years before Charlie Chaplin's film *Modern Times*.

This dystopian worry would perhaps be seen as extreme if we did not know the history of the rest of the twentieth century. Ortega cites Mussolini's transformation of Italy as his example: someone who takes a state developed by liberal democracy—and he knows his Italian history—and turns it into what he calls Statism. The state now is the place where the violence and direct action demanded by the masses resides. Ortega is Cassandra-like in his analysis and prophecy, as one contemplates the next fifteen years of European history: the Bloodlands in Eastern Europe, the mass exterminations, the Spanish Civil War, the Second World War, the racist impulses.

The argument for liberal democracy thus becomes for Ortega a plea for civility and decency, not only a position about politics but about morality. Liberals and Democrats will continually argue for the primacy of human rights, the rule of law embodied in constitutions, the contractual relation between people and their state, an independent judiciary, and the importance of universal education. The state should never be a thing-in-itself, it should instead serve a higher purpose.

There is a solution, one that goes against the grain of the time in 1930, but is also prophetic. Ortega as a liberal democrat is a cosmopolitan thinker. In his work he challenges the ideology and ontology of nationalism. The concept of a nation united by tradition, history, and language is not something that is eternal, he argues. Rather, giving examples, "the community of blood and language in France or in Spain has been the effect, not the cause, of the unification into a State."

Ortega never used the more modern concept of Benedict Anderson, that the nation is an "invented community." But he came close to where Anderson landed in 1983 in his important contribution to the discussion about the nature of nationalism and the nation-state.

The modern ideal of nationalism is a creation for Ortega. He is well aware that in the European states where it has arisen there are and were localities that had their own language and traditions, and that the centralization of the modern state works to efface them. In Spain, in other works at the time, he clearly recognizes the importance of local tradition in Catalonia, the Basque country, and elsewhere. Indeed, there are moments when he sees a federalization of authority as a better way of organizing Spanish and European politics.

In *The Revolt of the Masses*, however, Ortega takes the cosmopolitan direction. In terms of culture, frontiers are artificial and limiting. In terms of where to go, it is more important to think about the future—he cites Renan, who argued "the existence of a nation is a daily plebiscite"—than to create an imagined community. Nothing about nationalism should cause it to be understood as something of an ontological entity.

Ortega thus argues that nationalism is a moment in history, something to be transcended. With what? Europe, he argued, should "perfect itself in a gigantic continental state." Nationalism, or the many nationalisms are, he claims, "blind alleys."

In this matter, Ortega is part of a line of thinkers who contemplate a united Europe as a cultural and political force, far better than the map as it existed from the Congress of Vienna to his time. He cites Renan, but there is also, among others, Henri de Saint-Simon in the early nineteenth century, and many later peace theorists and socialists.

Of course, Ortega is again prophetic. He did not argue that the only way to keep Europe from perpetual war was to integrate the economies and then the politics of the many states. But his intuition was correct—there are European values, and the only way to practise them is to foster being a European. Ortega's position as a European earned him a high compliment from Albert Camus, who said, "Ortega y Gasset, after Nietzsche, is perhaps the greatest 'European' writer, and yet it would be difficult to be more Spanish."[6]

Ortega published two books in 1930. The second, *Mission of the University*, under 100 pages, was the result of a lecture he gave on higher education late in that year at the request of Federacion Universitaria Escolar of Madrid. He was, after all, an esteemed professor in addition to being an essayist, philosopher, and political man.

Prior to the lecture, Ortega had written an important discussion of education in his time in *The Revolt of the Masses*.

The modern world, claimed Ortega, is producing a new type of scientist in its adoption of the idea of education as specialized study. Now, the so-called educated person "knows the small corner in which he is an active investigator." This new specialist knows only his "tiny corner of the universe; he is radically ignorant of all the rest."

Heretofore, humans could be divided into those who were learned and those who were not. Now there appears a new type, who Ortega calls "a learned ignoramus." The new specialist has knowledge but is entirely devoid of culture. He, too, is part of the new power of the masses and a barbarian. Hence, he says, we have in 1930 more scientists than ever before, and fewer people who are cultured—by which he means someone who has a breadth of knowledge about the history, literature, and philosophy of the West, and who critically brings that knowledge to bear on his intellectual and personal life.

In a way, Ortega is referring to the earlier nineteenth century division of knowledge into two categories, natural philosophy and moral philosophy. The latter includes all those areas that reflect on our social, political, and ethical lives, including economics. Though he does not refer to it, he is dealing with the issue raised by Mary Shelley in one of the first works to contemplate this idea, her 1818 novel, *Frankenstein*. Dr. Frankenstein is a scientist who deals only with natural philosophy. He creates life and is then unable morally to deal with the consequences of his creation. He is a great scientist and a failed human being. In the decades following the Second World War, the creation of weapons of mass destruction will continually raise this issue for all of humanity.

In *Mission of the University*,[7] Ortega elaborates on the place and role of higher education in society. First, he asserts that the university has a mission of social justice. In 1930, it is mainly the wealthy who are able to attend. Thus, efforts must be made to make higher education accessible to the working class as well.

Specialization is again attacked, even more angrily than in his earlier work. We see in the twentieth century, he declares, how brutal, stupid, and violent is the person educated in one small area of knowledge and ignorant of all else. The teaching in the university has three parts:

I   The transmission of culture
II   The teaching of the professions
III   Scientific research and the training of new scientists

However, professionalization and specialization without the first are destructive to the purposes of the institution.

Throughout the lecture, Ortega makes the point that the university should ask what is it that the ordinary person should obtain in higher education. He is very clear that he believes teaching is of prime importance. Scientific research can be done, but it can also be done outside the university.

Ortega asserts that the role of the institution is to make the ordinary person someone who is cultured. Hence, he states that there are five branches of knowledge that must be taught to all:

1. the physical scheme of the world (Physics)
2. the fundamental themes of organic life (Biology)
3. the historical process of the human species (History)
4. the structure and functioning of social life (Sociology)
5. the plan of the universe (Philosophy)

It is also necessary "to make the ordinary man a good professional," but only on top of the teaching of culture. His examples of professionals are doctors, judges, and teachers.

If this seems familiar, especially to North Americans, it is because it has become institutionalized in many universities in the United States and Canada, though the trend is moving back to specialization. It is usually called General Education and it became the introduction to university for millions of North American students since its introduction into the curricula in the 1950s. Ortega has a claim to being one of its fathers.

Further, Ortega asked that the university be active in public life, implying that it has an important role to play in a liberal democratic society. He gives the university of 1930 a noble task, to help rescue Europe from the new barbarism he sees on the rise. The university "must intervene, *as* the university, in current affairs, treating the great themes of the day from its own point of view: cultural, professional, scientific." He argues for what he has been: an intellectual engaged in the active life of the community. The university must stand "for serenity in the midst of frenzy, for seriousness in the grasp of intellect in the face of frivolity and unashamed stupidity."

Sadly, as in the case of Thomas Mann, many universities in Europe would not live up to this standard as the decade moved on.

Events in Spain in 1930 and thereafter affected Ortega's life deeply. Between January 1930 and April 1931, Spain's politics absorbed all. The dictatorship of Primo de Rivera ended with his resignation in January 1930, followed by a new government that was still monarchical and authoritarian. Ortega publicly attacked it, and brought together a group of intellectuals who supported a Republic, challenging a solution that might lead to Bolshevism or Fascism. In April 1931, to the surprise of many, including the Republicans themselves, the Second Spanish Republic was declared.

Ortega continued his activity, was elected to parliament in 1931, and was one of the founders of the Group at the Service of the Republic, a loose collection of intellectuals and others of liberal persuasion. His name was mentioned as a possible president of the Republic. However, events overtook him and most liberal intellectuals to the point where he, Unamuno, and others were no longer active in politics after 1933. He was ill in June 1936 when the Spanish Civil War began. He managed to leave Madrid with his family in August and went to France, where he lived in an exile that lasted until 1945.

He remained a European figure, lectured on that continent and in South America, but could no longer affect events in Spain. It was not a happy ending for a man who, as many have commented, demonstrated to Spain and Europe that it was once again possible to think profoundly in Spanish.

Ortega was not a systematiser, as is the case with most moral philosophers after Nietzsche. Modern philosophy is rightly suspicious of those who think they have included all knowledge and solved metaphysical and moral problems in one system. Indeed, systems are seen as limiting, even authoritarian, in their insistence that they can answer all questions. The systematisers around 1930 were those on the right and left who would arbitrarily destroy anyone who might get in their way.

Ortega remained true to his culture and his liberal democratic beliefs at a time when many saw them as outmoded, seduced by nation, race, closed beliefs, and power. He was right often, though perhaps right at the wrong time. He remains worth reading almost a century later as Europe and West have developed. The issues he raised have not gone away in our world.

4 BRECHT AND WEILL
Rethinking Theatre, Remaking Opera

ON MARCH 9, 1930, the new opera *The Rise and Fall of the City of Mahagonny*, written by Bertolt Brecht and Kurt Weill—creators of the extraordinarily successful *Threepenny Opera* two years earlier—had its premiere in Leipzig.

During the day, Nazis in brown shirts demonstrated in front of the opera house, for Weill, who was Jewish, was now seen by them as a danger to the country on the level of Albert Einstein and others, and Brecht was well known for his Marxist politics.

Lotte Lenya, Weill's wife, herself a singer and actress who took part in other Brecht–Weill collaborations, was in the audience, along with Weill's parents. As the performance went on, Lenya recalled, "I was startled out of my absorption by the electric tension around us, something strange and ugly."[1]

The last scene of the piece had actors holding up placards that read,

FOR THE NATURAL ORDER OF THINGS
FOR THE NATURAL DISORDER OF THINGS
FOR THE FREEDOM OF THE RICH
FOR THE FREEDOM OF ALL
FOR THE UNJUST DIVISION OF TEMPORAL GOODS
FOR THE JUST DIVISION OF SPIRITUAL GOODS
FOR PURE LOVE
FOR BRUTE STUPIDITY

Lenya stated that near the close of the opera, "the demonstrations started, whistles and boos; by the time the last scene was reached, fist fights had broken out in the aisles, the theatre was a screaming mass of people." Indeed, the "riot had spread to the stage" by the time the police arrived.[2]

The collaboration between the two young, creative and original artists—Brecht (1898–1956) and Weill (1900–1950)—with Brecht supplying
the lyrics and dialogue, Weill composing the music, and both organizing
the performance, was unusual in that they were very different personalities
from different backgrounds.

Brecht was born in Augsberg, raised by a Protestant mother and Catholic
father, and was well versed in the Bible. He managed to avoid military service
in the First World War, and started writing very early, his first publications
appearing in newspapers at sixteen. He wrote his first major play, *Baal*, in
1918. He then wrote for cabarets, which were often political, and by 1922
was declared the hope of the new German theatre. In 1924 he worked with
the popular and well-known novelist Lion Feuchtwanger on an adaptation of
Christopher Marlowe's *Edward II*, which he said gave him the idea of a new
kind of theatre that he called "epic." From then until his death, Brecht was a
major—for many the major—figure in German theatre. In the mid-twenties
Brecht discovered the works of Marx, and from that time on he was sympathetic to leftist politics and to Communism.

Weill, born in Dessau, was the son of a cantor and grew up in a religious
Jewish household. He started taking piano lessons late, at age twelve, but
by the time he was fifteen he was performing publicly as an accompanist
and soloist. He also started composing early, writing many *lieder*, a string
quartet, a symphonic suite, and his first symphony at the age of twenty-one.
He entered easily into the musical culture of Berlin and Germany, teaching
such later notables as Claudio Arrau and Maurice Abravanel, having his
Divertimento for Orchestra performed by the Berlin Philharmonic in 1923.
In the next few years he wrote many music reviews, an opera, and other
well-received classical pieces. However, like Brecht he was drawn to musical
theatre and held the view that the theatre had a useful social and political
role to play in modern times.

Brecht and Weill began their short, very fertile, sometimes stormy six-
year collaboration in 1927. It transformed modern theatre and opera forever.
As angry as some people were about *Mahagonny*, the German musicolo-
gist H.H. Stuckenschmidt had this to say about what Brecht and Weill were
doing: "If a way out of the present crisis in the realm of opera is to be found,
the only hope lies in the quarter where Brecht and Weill are carrying out
their ideological renovation of the traditional genres…. The work forms a
climax in the operatic history of the present age."[3]

The first collaborative work of the two has come to be called *The Little
Mahagonny*, and was a preparation for the longer, full work to follow in
1930. The occasion was an important annual event, the German Chamber

Music Festival, which took place in Baden-Baden in the summer of 1927. The festival, founded in 1921, attracted major figures in modern music—among them, Paul Hindemith and Darius Milhaud. It also welcomed "experimental" music, including a number of pieces that were atonal, and some that combined traditional classical forms with contemporary popular music, most notably American jazz, which fascinated such figures as Stravinsky and which Weill admired.

The theme for the 1927 festival was the production of one-act operas for a chamber group, fairly simple in style and performance. Brecht and Weill decided to take five of Brecht's poems published the year before in a volume of his poetry entitled *Domestic Breviary*, which mocked prayers and middle-class manners, typical of his work.

The poems together—a sixth was added—make up a sequence about an imaginary place in America called Mahagonny, where a group attempts to establish a utopia. It fails because of the ills of capitalism and the greed of the inhabitants, meant (as in the expressionist drawings and watercolours of the artist George Grosz) to represent the middle class of the day. Brecht was nothing if not someone who loved to shock the bourgeoisie.

The name Mahagonny (ma-ha-GON-ee) was probably a nonsense word invented by Brecht, useful for its poetic value. One version of its origin has it created by Brecht who was living in Munich in 1923, after he witnessed the stormtroopers in the street and the failure of Hitler's Beer Hall Putsch. Mahagonny is close to the German *mahogoni*, mahogany in English, representing the brown-shirted Nazis. This latter tale may have been apocryphal, but it still would have disturbed the Nazi mentality.

The two men decided to call their work a *Songspiel*, an invented term, marking it as derived from the German *Singspiel*, but different from it as well. The *Singspiel* they seemed to be referring to was Mozart's last opera, *The Magic Flute* (1791), for there are at least two musical references to Mozart's work in *Mahagonny*. In his opera, Mozart and his librettist Schikaneder used some dialogue, music from popular melodies, and German religious music rather than the Italian operatic tradition, indicating that the *Singspiel* was designed to appeal to popular culture rather than to the rarefied audience of opera.

The song of *Songspiel* was, of course, derived from the English. First, it was clearly meant to convey that it was not a *lieder*, the German term for a song sung in a lofty manner, very traditional. Also, two of the six Mahagonny songs in the piece were written and sung in English, as it was set in the United States. And Weill himself, like many in Berlin, was an admirer of both jazz and the attempts of the American George Gershwin to bridge the distance between high and popular music. So the *Songspiel* was created, an opera for the cabaret. Song was pronounced the German way—as *zonk*—and the plural was *zonks*. New names were invented for new forms.

There is a self-consciousness displayed by the two new collaborators because they are entering new musical and theatrical territory. Weill's program note, written almost certainly by Brecht, stated,

> In his latest works Weill has been moving in the direction of those who, in all spheres of artistic activity, foresee the liquidation of the arts as social graces. The little epic piece Mahagonny simply draws the conclusion that emerges from the irresistible collapse of the existing social classes. It addresses itself to an audience that unsophisticatedly demands to be entertained in the theatre.[4]

Epic theatre is a term Brecht used from 1927 to describe his new idea of what theatre should do and how it should do it. He first used it on May 16, 1927, several weeks before the production of the *Mahagonny Songspiel* on July 18, in an article in a Berlin publication. He discussed "the creation of a great epic and documentary theatre which will be suited to our period."[5] Later that year he wrote in the *Frankfurter Zeitung*, "The essential point of the epic theatre is that it appeals less to the feelings than to the spectator's reason. Instead of sharing an experience the spectator must come to grips with things. At the same time it would be wrong to try and deny emotion to this kind of theatre."[6]

Brecht, like Woolf for the novel, is moving at this time to the development of a theatrical experience that abandons realism. The purpose of the theatrical piece is not to entertain or provide the audience with an imitation of their lives. In referring to the collapse of the social classes, Brecht is reflecting on his recent discovery of the works of Marx and Engels. He suggests that the theatre should deal with issues of social justice.

Brecht's thinking will evolve by 1930 into a more systematic formulation. *The Rise and Fall of the City of Mahagonny* will see Brecht's theory become far more sophisticated.

On the evening of July 18, 1927, four pieces were performed at the festival. An eight-minute work by Darius Milhaud called *The Rape of Europa* began the evening. Then came Ernst Toch's *Princess and the Pea*, based on the fairy tale. Paul Hindemith followed with a clever ten-minute work, *Forward and Back*, in which the action and music goes forward for five minutes and then reverses itself back to the beginning in the second half. Certainly Brecht and Weill were in good company, and their sense of the experimental was carried through the whole evening.

The longest piece, the half-hour *Mahagonny Songspiel*, came last. No curtain was used at the festival, and the audience witnessed stagehands setting up a boxing ring on the stage for the performance, surely a metaphor for the violence and chaos in modern society. The singers, playing prostitutes and greedy men, were formally dressed, and they climbed through the ropes to perform in the ring. In addition, behind the boxing ring was a screen on which there were projections designed by Casper Neher, who had worked before with Brecht, illustrating scenes of greed and violence, certainly influenced by expressionist and early surrealist images.

No one acted. The six singers, two each of basses, tenors, and sopranos, behaved coolly and detached while performing, more like a concert performance of an opera than a conventional opera itself. Brecht himself, who was also the director, moved in and out of the ring during the performance smoking a cigar, an indication that he saw the piece as a *Songspiel*, a cabaret experience, rather than "high art."

A small chamber group, including violins, woodwinds, percussion and piano supplied Weill's music, which was jazzy and evocative, certainly influenced by the presence of Lotte Lenya as one of the performers, who was said to ooze sexuality in her voice, gestures, and body language. If the German Chamber Music Festival wanted the avant-garde, it certainly got it that evening. This may be opera, but it was not opera as it was conventionally understood.

A pistol shot opened the performance, and the singers told their unhappy story. Lenya performed what became the best-known piece, one of two in English, "The Alabama Song." The song makes reference to the moon of Alabama, but its subjects are whisky, desire, and the power of money. The three verses are about finding the next whisky bar, the next lover, and the next dollar, all part of the promise of the capitalist utopian ideal of Mahagonny.

To an audience who thought opera was something like Wagner's works or *La Bohème*, this must have been jarring, which of course was the intention of its creators. "The Alabama Song" remains part of the canon of Western music. It has been recorded many times, including by Bobby Darin, Ella Fitzgerald, and The Doors.

The *Songspiel* ended with Lenya telling the audience, even mocking them, "For it does not exist, Mahagonny…." The actors then picked up placards with slogans such as "Down with Syphilis," and "Up with the Mortality of the Soul." Lenya's placard read: *"Für Weill"* ("For Weill").

The audience was hardly passive, an indication that Brecht and Weill were succeeding in their intention of getting these people, for whom Brecht had disdain as comfortable bourgeoisie, to think. At the end, even before it was over, people were on their feet, booing, cheering, stomping, even whistling. The singers were prepared by Brecht the director. Lenya remembered that "the entire audience stood to cheer and boo and whistle all at the same time. Brecht had provided us with little whistles of our own, and we just whistled right back."[7] Certainly, the comfortable traditional distance between the conventional audience and the stage was gone.

The reception was a good one, though by no means universal. Some of those at the Festival thought that only atonal music could be avant-garde, and were surprised at Weill moving back to tonality, though his inventive streak and decision to include cabaret music and jazz were praised. The critic Max Marschalk wrote in the *Vossiche Zeitung*, "It is impossible to escape its magnetic attraction.... [O]ne is kept in a state of tension but without knowing why." Another critic said that "this man Kurt Weill does things that others cannot."[8]

In the audience was another young musical genius born like Weill in 1900, the American Aaron Copland. He was ambivalent.

> The chamber opera which aroused most discussion (in Baden-Baden) was Kurt Weill's *Mahagonny*.... A pupil of Busoni's, Weill is the new *enfant terrible* of Germany. But it is not so easy to be an *enfant terrible* as it used to be and nothing is more painful than the spectacle of a composer trying too hard to be revolutionary. Weill, in writing *Mahagonny* cannot escape the accusation. It is termed a "songspiel" and is, in effect, a series of pseudo-popular songs in the jazz manner.... Weill is not without musical gifts, but these are too often sacrificed for the sake of a questionable dramatic effectiveness.[9]

Copland missed the point, for drama is what it was about and effective it certainly was. No longer was this sort of music to be pure sound. It had a political and social underpinning.

The performers and others associated with the *Songspiel* did not know what the response would be as they gathered afterward at a reception in a hotel bar. Lenya remembered that there was "a frenzied discussion in progress." Then, "suddenly I felt a slap on the back, accompanied by a booming laugh: 'Is there no telephone?'" a man asked, quoting a line from the second song sung in English, "Benares Song." The slap, the laugh, and the English came from Otto Klemperer, who was a very distinguished figure in the musical culture of Europe, then the conductor of the Kroll Opera in Berlin. At the Kroll from 1927 until 1931, he championed new music, conducting operas by Hindemith, Stravinsky, Schoenberg, and Janáček. He now voiced his approval of Weill. Lenya further relates: "With that the whole room was singing the Benares Song," probably with wine or whisky in their hands.

The song is a lament made by people in Mahagonny who are not happy with what is there, dreaming about a city called Benares where life might be better. What is missing in Mahagonny? Whisky, money, and prizes. It is time to move on. They ask repeatedly, "Where is the telephone?" But there is no telephone. Simply, said Lenya, "I knew that the battle was won."[10]

The *Songspiel* paved the way for the next collaborative effort of Brecht and Weill, the very popular *Threepenny Opera* they put out the next year, and became the basis of the 1930 masterpiece, the full *Rise and Fall of the City of Mahagonny*.

If in the 1920s Paris could still be viewed as the capital of Europe, certainly the centre of European culture, the city of Berlin had a strong claim to be the capital of European counterculture. In addition to the lively and experimental musical and theatre scenes, Berlin was the centre of the new Bauhaus architecture, begun by Walter Gropius, and had Albert Einstein as the director of its Kaiser Wilhelm Institute for Physics from 1914 until 1933.

The city was the centre of German expressionist art and literature, including such figures as George Grosz, Otto Dix, Hannah Hoch, Jean Arp, and Alfred Döblin. Films were made in and about Berlin, among them Fritz Lang's *Metropolis* and Joseph von Sternberg's *The Blue Angel*. Indeed, there are those who see Berlin and Weimar culture in general as a kind of golden age of creativity, obviously including the works of Brecht and Weill. It certainly has a claim to be the centre of modernism in its time.

Berlin was more than a place of cultural creativity; it was also the scene of social experimentation. Prostitution became open and tolerated, first women, then young people of both genders. The city's cabarets and clubs, in addition to being open to experimentation and sexual performances, included many that catered to gays of both genders and transvestites—guide books were sold describing the erotic culture of Berlin. It also became a centre for drug dealing and use.

Those who opposed its openness called Berlin "decadent." Others were attracted to a city on the edge, where desire was openly cultivated and the boundaries of the middle-class culture of Europe could be pushed back and challenged. There was even the *Institut fur Sexualwissenschaft* (Institute for Sexual Knowledge) founded by the physician Magnus Hirschfeld in 1919, which housed a museum and library. Hirschfeld became a leading advocate in the West for the legal rights of gays and transvestites. Needless to say, the institute, cabarets, and other counterculture places were closed in 1933.

Street violence also began to be part of the Berlin experience as Goebbels became the Nazi Gauleiter for Berlin in 1926. The Nazis had turned into a paramilitary organization, and other right-wing groups became bolder in the late 1920s and early 1930s, challenging both the Communists and edgy Berlin culture. Goebbels claimed, "This city is a melting pot of everything that is evil—prostitution, drinking houses, cinemas, Marxism, Jews, strippers, negroes dancing and all the offshoots of modern art."[11]

Most political parties, including Liberals, Socialists, and Communists, had their own groups to help defend their rallies. Street riots were not common, but no one was surprised that they happened on occasion as the years wore on. Many were injured in what was called *Zusammenstösse* (collisions, clashes), and some died.

In this atmosphere the 1927 *Songspiel* was radical but hardly scandalous. The next year, Brecht and Weill worked together on the *Threepenny Opera*, further developing their new ideas about the theatre and modern music.

The new work was based on John Gay's *The Beggar's Opera*, as both Brecht and Weill were drawn to a subject that not only dealt with the underclass of society but could also depict the social world from the point of view of that underclass. To punctuate this concept, several of the songs, including "The Ballad of the Good Life," were based on German translations of the songs of François Villon. Born in 1431, Villon was a criminal and poet who wrote about thieves and criminals, using their own language, mocking the powerful and the courtly poetry of his time. Brecht was already known for his willingness to borrow from others, something of course done regularly before modern times. Kurt Tucholsky wrote of Brecht,

> Who wrote that piece?
> It's by Bertolt Brecht
> Well, who wrote that piece?[12]

Lenya wrote in 1956, "'Why deny that Brecht steals?' said a Berlin friend last summer. 'But—he steals with genius.'"[13]

The preparations for the production, which opened on August 31, 1928, were a mess. Several engaged actors and actresses withdrew, one because her husband became ill, another refusing to sing what she called obscene lyrics in "The Ballad of Sexual Slavery." Brecht and Weill kept rewriting. A new female lead joined the company only a week before the opening. There were artistic differences between Brecht and the director. The dress rehearsal on August 30 was unorganized, punctuated by disagreements and many vocal arguments.

Still, it opened the next day. The first number was the result of a lucky disagreement. The lead actor, Harald Paulson, who Lenya described as "vain even for an actor,"[14] was not happy with his part. In rehearsal he insisted on a better setting for his entry. So Brecht wrote a poem in one day and gave it to Weill, who the next day came in with the music to the tune that became the signature of the piece, "The Ballad of Mack the Knife."

The stage direction for the opening reads: "Beggars are begging, thieves thieving, whores whoring. A ballad singer sings a Moritat." A Moritat is a medieval song sung by wandering minstrels, dealing with what the term denotes, literally a murderous deed, or the dark deeds of thieves and villains. Weill scored it to be accompanied by a hand organ to emphasize its late medieval origins, but on the first night the organ didn't work. The small orchestra quickly stepped in and the tune that would be sung throughout Europe in the next several years was played:

> And the shark he has his teeth and
> There they are for all to see.
> And Macheath he has his knife but
> No one knows where it may be …

The "orchestra" itself was composed of seven musicians who managed to play twenty-three instruments. They were placed on the stage as part of the experience.

The theatrical and musical experience for the audience was as far from traditional opera as it could be. The music was jazzy, bluesy, modern in instrumentation and tone. The message was radical—turning around convention. Weill argued in a public letter of January 1929 that what he and Brecht were doing was not necessarily redefining opera, but taking it back to its early development and moving it in a different direction. Opera, he argued, began "as an aristocratic branch of art," and it remains part of the social experience of a powerful elite. In a way he is suggesting that it is time to return to the *Singspiel*, to his admired *The Magic Flute*, and move from there to where opera might have gone if it took that as its core. It reminds one of modern philosophers who suggest that what went wrong with Western thinking were the ancient Greeks—it is time to start again, back to pre-Socratic thought. Weill wrote,

> nearly all the worthwhile operatic experiments of recent years emerge as basically destructive in character. *The Threepenny Opera* made it possible to start rebuilding, since it allowed us to go back to scratch. What we were setting out to create was the earliest form of opera.… I had before me a realistic plot, and this forced me to make the music work against it if I was to prevent it from making a realistic impact.
>
> The return to a primitive operatic form entailed a drastic simplification of musical language. It meant writing a kind of music that would be singable by actors, in other words by musical amateurs. But if at first this looked like being a handicap, in time it proved immensely enriching. Nothing but the introduction of approachable, catchy tunes made possible *The Threepenny Opera's* real achievement: the creation of a new type of musical theatre.[15]

The new musical genre complemented a new theatrical experience and message. The themes of *Threepenny* were confrontational from the beginning. Act I opens in the wardrobe room of the establishment of Jonathan Jeremiah Peachum, a businessman who outfits beggars, has a monopoly on begging in London, and who makes a lot of money exploiting others' misery and emotions. He sings a hymn mocking capitalism as fraud, a form of behaviour that would countenance the commodification and sale of one's sibling or spouse.

The music and the content are mocking the audience and the traditional operatic form. Peachum is simply doing what the capitalists are doing, only with the outcasts of society and on the border of legality. Throughout the production, the audience is asked to question whether their lives are much different from those of the underclass. The bourgeoisie know well how to mask their greed with piety, Brecht and Weill are suggesting, but are no better than those marginal people Peachum exploits.

Other societal niceties are challenged. Mack the Knife and Peachum's daughter Polly plan to marry, and the ceremony takes place in a stable, with stolen food, attended by the chief of police who, it turns out, is an old friend of Macheath, leader of the thieves.

At the end of Act II, Macheath and Jenny, a prostitute with whom he gets involved, sing a finale that sums up much of the message of the opera. To punctuate the moment, the curtain drops before the song and the two actors step in front of it. First Macheath sings and then Jenny sings about the need for society to provide for all. They mock those who preach traditional Christian morality while accepting poverty and suffering. Can only those who are wealthy, asks Macheath, "enter in the land of milk and honey?" In the chorus, the two proclaim that in their society, despite the moral façade, people live "by resolutely ill-treating, beating, cheating, eating" others.

Line 8 of the lament reads in German: *"Erst kommt das Fressen, dann kommt die Moral."* First comes food, then morality. It became a famous line that would resonate throughout Berlin and Germany in the next several, very difficult years.

The opera thus challenges much of the self-confident and self-righteous assumptions of the class in power and, to use a metaphor of Marx, wants to strip the halo from the bourgeoisie. For the audience, it suggests that they consider their own piety and morality, something Brecht pursued throughout his life and developed more systematically for *The Rise and Fall of the City of Mahagonny* two years later.

Those who are outside, the Others of 1930, women and the lower class, would challenge the inherited system and insist it be revised.

Near the end of the opera Macheath is in jail, about to be hanged. He speaks to the audience: I represent, he says, a vanishing class, the bourgeois artisans. I was a proper small-scale thief, but we artisans "are being swallowed up by large concerns backed by banks." How can I compete with a bank? "What is a picklock to a bank share?" I am, he laments, a victim of circumstances.

However, Macheath is really accusing the new bourgeois capitalist establishment of being as corrupt as he was. Who can challenge this in an age when banks are bailed out by the middle-class and the poor, and bankers continue to flourish as "banksters"? Of course, the Great Depression that followed *Threepenny* saw the failure of many banks and the loss of savings by the lower classes, a sorry repeat of the hopelessness that began the twenties in Germany with inflation beginning in 1921, culminating in the US dollar being exchanged for over a trillion German marks in 1923.

Macheath is saved at the end by Brecht and Weill announcing to the audience that they are, after all, watching something that is art. "This is an opera," Peachum tells the audience, "and we mean to do you proud." So a royal messenger appears with a pardon from the Queen. Macheath, Mack the Knife, is rewarded by being raised into the nobility with a pension of ten thousand pounds a year. We are given a happy ending for the opera of the poor, though the authors cannot resist having Peachum add, "In reality their end is generally bad. Mounted messengers from the Queen come far too seldom."

From opening night, Lenya remarked, "Berlin was swept by a *Dreigroschenoper* fever." The piece was the most spectacular theatrical success in Germany during the Weimar years. Its music was everywhere in the city and country. The Berlin production ran for over 350 performances over the next two years. In Germany, the opera was produced in more than 100 theatres over the next year, with over 4,000 performances. Recordings were made in eighteen languages, with one edition of the songs going into several printings totalling over 30,000 copies.[16]

The counterculture of Berlin was making an entry into the culture of Europe. Late in 1928, at the request of Klemperer, Weill assembled eight of the numbers into an orchestral piece called the *Kleine Dreigroschenmusik*, which Klemperer conducted to great success in Germany and other countries. By the end of 1929 there were productions in Italy, Switzerland, Hungary, Poland, and Russia. It opened in Paris in 1930 at the Théâtre Montparnasse, as *Opéra de quat'sous* (*quatre sous* then being an idiom in French for something that is cheap, the equivalent of threepenny).

By mid-1929, Brecht and Weill had refined much of their thinking about renewing the theatre and opera. This clearer conception resulted in making a full piece out of the 1927 *Songspiel Mahagonny*, something they had discussed periodically.

In the short period after the opening of *The Threepenny Opera* Brecht began to formalize his concept of epic theatre. He put his ideas together in notes written in 1930 to the published text of *The Rise and Fall of the City of Mahagonny*.

Formerly, Brecht states, opera as theatre was "culinary," a term of derision meant to indicate that it was cooked up to simply entertain, appeal to emotions, and deal with a passive audience. Epic theatre is not only dramatic; first, it has a social purpose. Then it is designed to force the spectator to be active, to query his own assumptions. Like Weill, he cites *The Magic Flute*—as well as *Figaro* and *Fidelio*—as three of the few old operas that were not entirely culinary, as "all included elements that were philosophical, dynamic."

In opera, Brecht goes against the traditional thinking in asking for "a radical *separation of the elements*" (his emphasis). The libretto, the music, and the production are not to be fully integrated, a process that he claims dulls the mind of the spectator, produces "hypnosis … creates fog." He follows by stating that *"Words, music and setting must become more independent of one another"* (his emphasis).

By separating the elements, you create tension and a reflective rather than passive audience. Like many new ideas at the time about understanding reality and commenting on the nature of art, including those of Woolf, the subject—in opera, the spectator—is actively involved in the interpretation of what is going on. Brecht does not comment on the matter, but he probably took the riot that surrounded the first performance of *Mahagonny* as a good thing.

He provided a chart to show the differences between traditional dramatic theatre and the new epic theatre. (See page 79.)

Brecht added an important note to the chart. He asks the reader not to see the two as binary ideas, as opposites. It is more complex—they are not "absolute antitheses but mere shifts of accent." The two concepts are *not* in dialectical relationship with one another.[17]

It is impossible to talk about Brecht's theory of drama in 1930—and he is one of the major theorists of the twentieth century—without referring to the idea of *Verfremdungseffekt*. Though Brecht did not invent the term until 1936, the idea permeates his earlier discussions of the new theatre.

The English translation of the term has itself produced a lot of ink. It began as the "alienation effect," but the baggage—theological, Marxist, later existential—of the term alienation gave it connotations outside of its meaning. Then, *Verfremdung* was translated as "estrangement." These days it is usually interpreted as a "distancing," less often as "defamiliarization." All these descriptions help.

DRAMATIC THEATRE	EPIC THEATRE
plot	narrative
implicates the spectator in a stage situation	turns the spectator into an observer but
wears down his capacity for action	arouses his capacity for action
provides him with sensations	forces him to make decisions
experience	picture of the world
the spectator is involved in something	he is made to face something
suggestion	argument
instinctive feelings are preserved	brought to the point of recognition
the spectator is in the thick of it, shares the experience	the spectator stands outside, studies
the human being is taken for granted	the human being is the object of the inquiry
he is unalterable	he is alterable and able to alter
eyes on the finish	eyes on the course
one scene makes another	each scene for itself
growth	montage
linear development	in curves
evolutionary determinism	jumps
man as a fixed point	man as a process
thought determines being	social being determines thought
feeling	reason

The idea is to have the actors and the whole of the production be one, which is clearly artificial. It is a production, and the actors are not the characters. Realism is abandoned, catharsis plays a lesser role. Rather, the play or opera and the production are to get the spectator engaged; as Brecht said, the actor is to act in a way that shows he knows he is being watched. The audience is no longer an "unseen spectator."

Magritte in 1929 will subtitle his painting of a pipe, called *The Betrayal of Images*, with words written in the painting: "This is not a pipe." At the same moment in 1930, Brecht insists in *Mahagonny* and other works that the audience realize the play or opera are not reality, they are commentaries on human nature and society that require an awake audience.

In a way, what Brecht was doing was abandoning the Ibsenian model of theatre and going back to earlier days. There is now a chorus, people sing or speak poems, there are signs and projections supporting the creation, and there are asides to the audience. After all, we adore Shakespeare, but we know that people do not speak in iambic pentameter; we admire Greek tragedy, but if we have a chorus following us around in life it is only in our heads.

Perhaps *Verfremdungseffekt* is one of those many German concepts that can be properly translated in English only by using several words. (Think of *zeitgeist, schadenfreude* or, post–Second World War, *vergangenheitsbewältigung.*) Something like "marginalizing the experience" or "defamiliarization and reflection" or "distancing for the purpose of engagement" might work better to explain Brecht's intention.

Though not as systematically, Weill also tried to explain what he and Brecht were attempting in *Mahagonny* in a March 1930 article, also calling it epic theatre.

> The content of this opera is the history of a city, its emergence, its first crises, then the crucial turning point in its development, its most scintillating time, and then its downfall. It is a series of "moral pictures of our time" projected onto a broad plane. The content can be expressed in the purest form of epic theatre, which is also the purest form of musical theatre. It is a succession of twenty-one distinct musical forms. Each of these forms is an enclosed scene, and each is set out in narrative form by a title card. The music is thus no longer an element for the developing of the drama; rather it is placed therein as a way of expanding upon the circumstances. The text is so laid out that, from the beginning, it presents an arraying of situations one against the other, and this is given dramatic form in its musically characterized, dynamic action.[18]

Weill's music for the two operas, *Threepenny* and *Mahagonny*, was wonderfully creative and also innovative in how the music related to the text. The music sometimes plays against the words so as to both sharpen the moment for the audience and provide a satiric or ironic comment on society and the events on stage. For example, in *Threepenny* the opening introduction of Mack the Knife, with a recitation of his dark deeds, is accompanied by a jolly little melody on a barrel organ. At Mack and Polly's marriage scene, when they sing of their underclass wedding in a stable, the music is a waltz, then the music of propriety, the bourgeoisie, and social order. In *Mahagonny* cynical lyrics are accompanied sometimes by music associated with romance.

This unusual relationship—not always present, but appearing often enough in both works that it is jarring—between the music and the text is using the aesthetic technique of juxtaposition, in this case putting together elements in a way that is so unusual that the audience should be asking what is going on. It is one used not only in music at the time but in the visual arts, especially in surrealist and expressionist paintings. Brecht and Weill in this case are the opera companions of painters such as Giorgio de Chirico, René Magritte, and Salvador Dalí.

The themes of *Mahagonny* are as radical as those of *Threepenny*, even angrier about capitalism as a political and social system. It opens with three criminals—thieves and forgers—stuck in an imaginary desert in Florida, their truck having broken down on their way to the goldfields in the American west. Lady Begbick tells her two companions, Fatty and Moses, that they should found a town:

> Darum lasst uns hier einen Stadt grunden
> und sie nennen Mahagonny
> das heisst: Netzestadt!
>
> (Let us found a city here and call it Mahagonny, which means "City of Nets!")

The net city is to be a pleasure town, to ensnare those from the West who made money in the goldfields. It is a mock-utopia—people will do as they please. Let's leave this "foul" violent world for a better place, says Lady Begbick. There will be whisky, women, and no need to work: "every day a day of leisure."

Mahagonny is no dull Eden or Eldorado, nor is it the communal world invented by Thomas More (who coined the word utopia), or the socialist paradise envisioned earlier in the nineteenth century by such people as Étienne Cabet or Charles Fourier. It is a utopia of desire, a capitalist world. Money rules.

The net image is important. Obviously, the net is there to trap wealthy prospectors. However, it also signals that Mahagonny is porous, insubstantial, filled with holes, lacking support. It affords pleasure, but it has no foundation. In Auden's fine translation he calls *Netzestadt* Suckerville, an apt term, but the net metaphor should not be forgotten through the whole of the opera.

"The Alabama Song" follows, people flock to what the projection screen calls a "New Jerusalem," and Mahagonny prospers. Jimmy, Jake, Bill, and Joe, four miners with full wallets, arrive and learn that money buys anything: whisky, entertainment, sex. Nothing is forbidden.

This is the fundamental message of the opera. All in capitalist society is commodified, no relationship is authentic. One of the projections, in scene eight of the twenty-one scenes, warns: "Seek and Ye Shall Not Find." The message is that money cannot fully satisfy human needs. We are more than our desire for sex, violence, and drugs. It is telling that Brecht, in one of his theoretical statements about the epic theatre at the time, cites a passage from Freud's *Civilization and Its Discontents* (1930) in discussing human behaviour.

Mahagonny is threatened by nature, which reminds the audience that life has an arbitrary quality to it, even if one has money. A hurricane is moving toward the imaginary town. It forces reflection. Begbick sings, "Bad is the hurricane / Even worse the typhoon / But the worst of all is man." She has, by now, seen everything.

Miraculously—after all, Brecht does this all the time—the hurricane veers away and destroys another city. In the finale of Act I the men then sing, "as you make your bed, so you lie on it." We cannot escape the consequences of our choices.

Act II revolves around the men singing a refrain repeated throughout:

> One means to eat all you are able;
> Two, to change your loves about;
> Three means the ring and the gaming table;
> Four, to drink until you pass out.

Life in this world is superficial, but there are lessons to be learned. Jake is the glutton and he gorges himself onstage until he is dead.

In his 1930 essay on the epic theatre Brecht used this scene to illustrate his intentions. He states that this kind of scene is intended to have a "provocative effect." Why? Because abundance is not ordinary, hunger is more normal in the world of that time. Hence, though he notes that he does not tell the audience others were suffering while Jake eats gluttonously, "It is not everyone who is in a position to stuff himself full that dies of it, yet many are dying of hunger because this man stuffs himself to death. His pleasure provokes, because it implies so much."[19] If the *Verfremdungseffekt* works, the audience, many of whom are themselves metaphorically or actually "gluttons," will reflect actively, not simply be passive.

There follow lovers, and a boxing match in which Moses kills Joe while the spectators enjoy themselves. And then the ultimate sin in a city where money rules and seemingly anything goes. Jimmy orders drinks for all—"Good old Jimmy" they cry—but does not have enough money to pay the bill.

Moses sums up Jimmy's crime by asking: Can there be anything worse than a man who is so broke he cannot pay for his whisky? Jimmy is arrested and sent to prison to be tried.

The trial takes place in a scene mocking bourgeois relationships and justice. Jimmy pleads with his friends to help him pay his bills, appealing to sentiment and their long history of working together. No one responds. Friendship is trumped by money. Other cases—conspiring to murder, seduction, disturbing the peace—get light sentences. Jimmy's fate: "You by law must be sentenced to death in the electric chair." The court scene ends with wild applause after Begbick, Fatty, and Moses sing: "For the penniless man / Is the worst kind of criminal, / Beyond both pity and pardon."

Jimmy, awaiting execution, speaks for Brecht and Weill:

> At last I realize what a fool I've been. I came to this city believing here was no happiness which money could not procure. That belief has been my downfall. For now I am about to die without ever having found the happiness I looked for. *The joy I bought was no joy; the freedom I was sold was no freedom....* (my emphasis)

And then, in Brechtian style, Jimmy turns to the audience and states, "I'm damned and so, probably, are most of you."

Brecht and Weill are arguing that there is no possible utopia in capitalist society, as did Marx. Relationships are artificial, all is commodified, nothing is human and authentic. The family is an economic unit, morality, the law and religion are merely tools the powerful and wealthy use to legitimize their greed. What is the implied solution? It must, in dialectical fashion, be transcended before anything like a good society can be contemplated.

Neither of the two found Bolshevism the answer. Weill moved to a liberal democratic position, and he was concerned in 1930 that *Mahagonny* may have gone too far. Brecht remained a Marxist all of his life, sometimes called himself a communist, but never joined the Communist Party, keeping his independence. Brecht had an outsized ego and a temperament that almost always displayed itself as *un esprit d'opposition*, wherever he was. He would have found it impossible to submit his will to an authoritarian belief system of any sort.

So the riots and scandal surrounding *Mahagonny* can be understood. It was in-your-face criticism of those who came to the theatre and paid for the privilege.

It is unfortunate that Brecht did not have an opportunity in 1930 to read Marx's *Economic and Philosophical Manuscripts of 1844*, which were first partially published in the Soviet Union in 1927 and then in Germany in 1932. In it, the young Marx (1818–1883) provides a profound literary analysis of money in contemporary society, commenting from works by Shakespeare and Goethe.

Marx discusses buying things like bravery and art, the way wealthy people today buy honour by putting their names on public buildings and university faculties, "conscience philanthropy" as it is now called. He then notes in a world that transcends commodification we can "assume *man* to be *man* and his relationship to the world to be a human one." He cites love and trust as two qualities that are offered freely (yes, the young Marx actually used the word love) and that then can be authentic. The only way to get out of the box of capitalist society is to end the commodification of value and behaviour in a new social order.[20]

The reception of *Mahagonny* did not match the wild enthusiasm that greeted *Threepenny*. It was polarizing and highly politicized, much like life became in Germany from 1930. The Nazis regularly demonstrated where it played and in one case, in Frankfurt, they interrupted a performance and threw stink bombs at the stage.[21] The right saw it as further evidence of the decadence of Weimar and the need to challenge communism. Some on the left were unhappy that the main characters, clearly flawed, were from the proletariat.

However, many liked it and praised both its theatrical content and the music. A production in Kassel, three days after the Leipzig opening and riot, was highly successful. And it had a very successful Berlin production in December 1931. *Mahagonny* was given high praise by the philosopher and music critic Theodor Adorno, among other academics and critics. Lenya recalled that the Berlin production came to be thought of by many as one of those special moments to be savoured in memory. "There were those who came night after night," she wrote, "*Mahagonny* addicts, who tell me they would leave the theatre in a kind of trance and walk the streets, Kurt's insidious bittersweet melodies repeating over and over inside their heads."

Both *Threepenny* and *Mahagonny* continue to be performed. Some commentators like the one better, some the other. All agree that both were important mirrors of Weimar society and the state of the West in their time, and they still resonate deeply today.

The collaboration between Brecht and Weill soured after 1930. In the preparations for the 1931 Berlin production of *Mahagonny* there was open hostility between them about matters of emphasis and interpretation. Never friends, they drifted apart as their interests diverged.

Events in Germany also separated the two. The Nazis came to power on January 30, 1933, and from that moment nothing by Brecht or Weill was performed in Germany until after the Second World War. Fearing arrest, Weill fled to France in March 1933 and then on to the United States in 1935. He was well known in both countries and previously had met many prominent musicians, including one he admired deeply, George Gershwin.

For all of the commentary on "America" in *Mahagonny*, Weill never had the antipathy to the country that Brecht displayed. He admired and used its musical forms. As a Jew, he came to realize that the United States was one of the few places he could freely be himself and pursue his musical ideas. Indeed, many of his friends in the United States were themselves exiles. When Weill came to New York, the Gershwin brothers welcomed him and took him to a rehearsal of *Porgy and Bess* shortly after he and Lenya landed. As he stood at the back of theatre Weill was deeply moved by the performance. He turned to Ira Gershwin, who was next to him, and said, "It's a great country where music like that can be written—and played."

Weill remained happily in the United States. He learned English quickly and became part of the very creative musical theatre in New York. He collaborated with, among others, Franz Werfel, Maxwell Anderson, Ira Gershwin, Elmer Rice, Langston Hughes, and Alan Jay Lerner. He contributed to the war effort during the Second World War with his music and became a citizen of the United States. He died fairly young, in 1950.

Brecht followed another course. He too left Germany quickly, in February 1933. He settled in Denmark and continued to be a prolific and creative playwright. In the 1930s he wrote a great deal, including *Fear and Misery of the Third Reich, Mother Courage and Her Children,* and *The Life of Galileo.*

He wound up in the United States in 1941 but was not comfortable there. He and Weill connected, having a discussion about the possibility of a new collaboration based on the classic Czech novel *The Good Soldier Švejk* (1923), by Jaroslev Hašek, a dark satire on war that seemed to complement their earlier works. It never came to fruition.

Brecht left the United States in October 1947, a day after testifying before the House Un-American Activities Committee, having experienced the blacklist, certainly having had a different experience in the country than that of Weill. In Switzerland for a time, he accepted an offer in 1949 from the authorities in East Germany to head his own theatre company, the *Berliner Ensemble*. Brecht tried to keep his independence: he had Austrian citizenship, he kept his money in accounts outside Germany, and he kept control of his copyrights. He walked a bit of a tightrope in relation to the Stalinist authorities. Still, many in the West were critical of his willingness to take a role in the authoritarian, very nasty East German regime. He died in 1956.

The list of exiles from Germany in the 1930s is very long and very notable. Thomas Mann was correct: not only were many Germans forced to leave, traditional German culture itself was in exile from 1933.

5 L'ÂME NOIR
The Black Soul in the City of Light

ON SEPTEMBER 26, 1930, the best-known American and Black in Paris, Joséphine Baker, opened at the Casino de Paris in the review *Paris Qui Remue* (Swinging Paris). Baker was returning to the city where she had enjoyed a great triumph five years earlier, when she became a star performer in the show *La Revue Nègre*, was adopted by the city, felt at home in France, and Josephine became Joséphine. In between she had toured Europe and Latin America and became an international star.

The theme of the 1930 show was related to the Colonial Exposition that was then being constructed in the Bois de Vincennes in Paris, which was to open in May 1931. The show thus had references to many French colonies—including Martinique, Indochina, Algeria, and many parts of sub-Saharan Africa.

Baker played, among other parts, a colonial girl living in a jungle in love with a French colonist. Here, she included her pet, which had taken the city's imagination when she walked it down the Champs-Élysées prior to the opening, a cheetah named Chiquita, for whom she had bought an expensive and gaudy diamond choker. Baker's reputation was such that Parisians joked it was difficult to say which end of the leash held the wild animal. After all, her most famous performance in 1925 was the exotic "dance sauvage."

Other skits had Baker in Martinique, singing "Voulez-vous de la canne à sucre?" (How Would You Like Some Sugar Cane?); in a forest pursued by savage hunters; and in a press conference telling about herself and her love of Paris. In one sketch she sang "J'ai deux amours," a song composed for her that became her signature melody, composed for her by the trio of Vincent Scotto, Geo Koger, and Henri Varna: "I have two loves / My homeland and Paris," she sang in French. Manhattan is praised, but it is Paris that "bewitches."

The critics lauded her, not simply as in 1925 as a sex symbol or someone exotic, but now as an artist. *Paris Soir* said: "Joséphine Baker, quelle surprise, quelle stupefaction."[1] The newspaper *Ami du Peuple* called *Paris qui remue* "incontestably the most beautiful revue presented in Paris since the war."[2]

Baker's second triumph brought some small regret for the Baker of yesterday. Janet Flanner, who wrote the "letter from Paris" for *The New Yorker* for fifty years, had seen the 1925 debut and now commented on *Paris qui remue*:

> If you can get away for a day or so, it might be a good plan to fly to Paris and spend the evening at Joséphine Baker's new Casino show.... It is ... one of the best in years, is as full of staircases as a Freudian dream, has excellent imported British dancing choruses of both sexes, a complete Russian ballet, trained pigeons, a live cheetah, roller skaters ... the four best can-can dancers in captivity, a thriller in which Miss Baker is rescued from a typhoon by a gorilla, and an aerial ballet of heavy Italian ladies caroming about on wires.
>
> Perhaps, however, enough is seen of Miss Baker in the present instance, for she has, alas, almost become a little lady. Her caramel-colored body, which overnight became a legend in Europe, is still magnificent, but it has become thin, trained, almost civilized. Her voice, especially in the voo-deo-doo's, is still a magic flute that hasn't yet heard of Mozart—though even that, one fears, will come with time. There is a rumor that she wants to sing refined ballads; one is surprised that she doesn't want to play Othello. On that lovely animal visage lies now a sad look, not of captivity, but of dawning intelligence.[3]

Flanner's concern, and that of several others, was indicative of the ambiguity surrounding how Black culture was viewed in Paris. Artists like Picasso saw it as exotic and creative in its natural and *sauvage* style. However, there was also in France a sense that what the country could give Black culture (and others) was the gift of the Enlightenment and civilization. It was a paradox: Blacks were to become *évolués* (a term used then), to evolve into Frenchmen; at the same time, they were admired for their honest and straightforward spontaneity, primitivism, and exoticism. Which Baker did they want—the noble savage of 1925, or the civilized and sophisticated performer of 1930?

As western Europe understood Black culture in 1930, it was in Paris that it and the quest for a Black identity was most visible. The city welcomed Blacks from everywhere, and it was there—and in the persons of Paulette and Jane Nardal—that many strands of Black art, philosophy, and creativity came together.

One group was composed of members of what became known as the Harlem Renaissance, including Claude McKay, Langston Hughes, Alain

Locke, and the sculptress Augusta Savage. Not only was Paris a home for the mythical white "Lost Generation" represented by Hemingway, Fitzgerald, Cole Porter, and Gertrude Stein. Black Americans found themselves far more comfortable in the cosmopolitan atmosphere of France than in the cruel and segregated world of the United States.

Another group was composed of members of the French colonies, both Africans and Antilleans. These included Louis Th. Achille and Aimé Césaire from Martinique, Léo Sajous from Haiti, Léopold Senghor from Senegal, and Léon Damas from French Guyana.

However forward-looking the French and other western Europeans thought themselves to be at the time, it must be remarked that their vision of what it was to be Black was a colonialist construction seen through the eyes of mainly white, wealthy elites. They did not acknowledge that there was a rich and varied Black culture—or cultures—in those parts of the world where people of colour lived, worked, and created apart from Western civilization. Hence, the French saw these educated Blacks in Paris as in the process of becoming cosmopolitan, cultured people in the French tradition, a process they called their *mission civilatrice*. Most Blacks soon refused to accept this formulation and decided that their identity was far more varied and complex than anything the French understood.

The whole of Black culture in France had a centre—the Salon Clamart presided over by the three Nardal sisters, Paulette, Jane, and Andrée. For several years starting in 1929, the centre of discussions of Black consciousness was at 7 rue Hébert in Clamart, a suburb of Paris where the sisters resided. Their first cousin, Louis Th. Achille, fondly recalled the atmosphere. The sisters, he said, got together a wide variety of "people of African descent who were émigrés to a new world." They were seen to be "not only a people, a Black *nation*, but a culture, a soul, a Black humanism, a *Black World* (*un Monde noir*)." In using the concept of Black humanism, Achille himself adopted categories of analysis and understanding that borrowed from Western concepts and values.

The salon included members of the Harlem Renaissance, a wide variety of Blacks from the Antilles, and other Black thinkers such as Senghor, who "often saw the Nardal sisters," and stated that "many of his ideas on Negro humanism came out of his discussions with Jane."[4] In a letter of 1960 referring to the influence of American Black writers on francophones from the colonies, Senghor wrote, "We were in contact with these black Americans during the years 1929–1934, through Mademoiselle Paulette Nardal, who ... had founded *La Revue du monde noir*. Mademoiselle Nardal kept a literary salon, where African Negroes, West Indians, and American Negroes used to get together."[5]

In their discussions, Achille said, participants in the salon

> discovered a common way of being, of feeling, of hoping and, soon, of acting! They did not talk about their differences, coming from so many disparate parts of the world, they simply spoke about being "Blacks" (Noirs). The tone and rituals of these convivial afternoons were feminine, as opposed to a corporate meeting or a masculine club. The furniture of the two main rooms, the parlour and the dining room, in no way resembled that of an ordinary bourgeois salon of France or of the Antilles. Several English armchairs, airy, comfortable and light, contributed to forwarding the conversation; which, naturally, was also in English. Neither wine, nor beer, nor French cider, nor whiskey, nor exotic coffee, not even Creole punch refreshed those throats. Only *le thé à l'anglaise* was served at these meetings which never went past the dinner hours and whose ending was regulated by the train schedule to Paris.[6]

They discussed Parisian and world affairs, thought about colonial and interracial matters, reflected on the place of Blacks in French culture, and noted instances of racism in order to counter them. They heard lectures on a wide variety of subjects, had poetry readings, and, as Andrée was a gifted pianist, on occasion sang Black American spirituals or blues.

The Salon Clamart turned out to be the birthplace of that very important movement and philosophy called *Négritude*, whose "fathers" are considered to be Senghor, Césaire, and Damas.

The word *Négritude* was coined later in the decade by Césaire, but its philosophical underpinnings were discussed in the Clamart Salon and, very clearly, in a journal founded and nurtured by Paulette Nardal in 1931 that published material from many participants in the salon, *La Revue du Monde Noir*. It is now clear, after much work by scholars such as Jacques Louis Hymans, Shireen K. Lewis, and T. Denean Sharpley-Whiting, that if the Négritude philosophy and movement had fathers, it had "mothers" before them, notably Paulette and Jane Nardal.

Paulette Nardal was born in 1896 in the town of Le François, Martinique. Her parents were part of an Antillean Black bourgeoisie. Her father was a construction engineer in the Department of Highways and Bridges of the colonial Martinique regime. Her mother was a piano teacher. There were seven sisters, all educated and musical. The family was Catholic, and Paulette retained an association with the social side of Catholic philosophy for the whole of her life.

She was schooled at home and at the Colonial School for Girls in Martinique, and then travelled to the British West Indies to master the English language. In 1920 she sailed to Paris, the recipient of a competitive scholarship to study at the Sorbonne. She received her *licence ès letters anglaises* certificate (equivalent to a B.A.) in the mid-1920s, writing a thesis on Harriet Beecher Stowe's *Uncle Tom's Cabin*. She and her sister Jane, whose *licence* was in Classics, were among the first Black women to receive degrees from what at that time was the most prestigious university in France.

The sisters, including the younger Andrée, stayed on in Paris, becoming involved in the culture of Black society. In the late 1920s both Paulette and Jane wrote for *La Dépêche africaine*, a journal begun in February 1928 sponsored by the *Comité de défense des intérêts de la race noire* in Paris. The journal's motto was *Défendre nos colonies, c'est fortifier la France* (To defend our colonies is to strengthen France). It was of its times in that it was still racist and colonialist, though it made serious advances in its openness to new thinking and ideas. It had a Black editor, Maurice Satineau from Guadaloupe, a board that included both whites and Blacks of many nationalities, brought together Blacks from everywhere, and its policy saw France and assimilation as something positive. However radical the editors of the journal thought it to be—and however radical the French bureaucracy thought it to be—it was a place to begin reflections that would later mature into an ideology.

To the French government *La Dépêche africaine* had a faintly suspicious quality. It was linked to some anti-colonial journals, and thus Satineau was watched and the contents of the journal were reviewed by a government agency.[7] France may have been proud of its openness and commitment to universal liberty, but even then its officials were troubled by what the Other might portend.

Jane Nardal's most important and influential contribution, "L'internationalisme Noir" ("Black Internationalism") appeared in the first issue, February 15, 1928. Jennifer Anne Boittin has remarked, "the political undertones of this essay laid the groundwork for negritude."[8] As well, Senghor was deeply influenced by his discussions with Jane Nardal.[9]

Nardal first notes that the war of 1914–1918 contributed to a lowering of the national barriers that separated countries and peoples. This in itself was a good thing for Black culture because "Blacks of all origins, of different nationalities, customs, and religions vaguely feel that in spite of everything they belong to one and the same race." Indeed,

> Previously the more assimilated Blacks looked down arrogantly on their coloured brothers, believing they were of a different species; on the other hand, certain Blacks who had never left the soil of Africa to be put into slavery looked down as ignoble swine those who had been

enslaved at the whim of whites, then freed, then shaped into the image of the white man.

The war and its aftermath helped Black artists to launch an art indigenous to their culture, one rooted in Black experience and recognized as both profound and distinct by others. Now, there could be "pride in being Negro." Now Blacks could make their contribution to the variety of cultures in the modern world. Nardal was careful to note that having one's own culture did not mean one is hostile to the cultures of others. Rather, the experience and intellectual life of others can contribute to knowing oneself better and to having one's own distinct personality.

Nardal used the terms Afro-Latins and Afro-Americans as positive concepts. The dual identities "are not incompatible," one of the first statements about the importance of multiple identities in understanding the self of the Other. Rather, she argued the Black spirit would be informed and aided by the association with the West, without losing its own core. Nardal refers the reader to Alain Locke's anthology, *The New Negro* (1925), as one example of this new way of thinking.

Blacks could now study their past, write their own history, and in doing so prove "that there does finally exist a Black race, a racial spirit on the path of maturity."

Not only were the ideas important; Jane Nardal contributed a new language in order to deal with Black culture. She had to invent terms to describe what existed but had no way of being articulated, what later, in the context of feminism, Betty Friedan would call "the problem with no name."

Hence, the short essay talks about *esprit de race, conscience de race, l'esprit nègre, Afro-Latins, internationalisme noir,* and *solidarité raciale.* She shaped the discourse that would be at the centre of the Negritude movement.

Another piece in *La Dépêche africaine* by Jane Nardal, eight months later, also contributed to the understanding of where Black culture was going at the time. Its title was "Pantins exotiques" ("Exotic Puppets"). In it, Nardal challenges the stereotype of Black culture, especially Black Antillean culture. If you come from an island and you are Black, she notes, "you will arouse a lively interest, preposterous questions, the dreams and regrets of those who have never traveled: 'Oh! The golden islands! The marvellous lands! With their happy, carefree natives!' In vain you strive to destroy so many legends they hardly believe you."[10]

This, for Nardal, explains the Joséphine Baker phenomenon:

Here it is that a woman of color leaps onstage with her shellacked hair and sparkling smile. She is certainly still dressed in feathers and banana leaves, but she brings to Parisians the latest Broadway products (the Charleston, jazz, etc.). The transition between past and present, the soldering between virgin forest and modernism, is what American Blacks have accomplished and rendered tangible.

And the blasé artists and snobs find in them what they seek: the savorous, spicy contrast of primitive beings in an ultramodern frame of African frenzy unfurled in the cubist décor of a nightclub. This explains the unprecedented vogue and the swell of enthusiasm generated by a little woman of mixed race (*capresse*) who was begging on the streets of St. Louis.

Nardal saw in 1928 what would trouble Janet Flanner and others two years later. They loved the stereotype, but did not realize that it denied Black culture its profundity and humanity. Nardal challenges several writers, most notably the popular work of Paul Morand, a writer who was both elitist and racist, who presents Blacks "as folk destined to serve as amusement," to exist in order to give artistic and sensual pleasure to whites. "[B]ut when it is a question of intellectual, or moral, qualities, when it is a question of no longer being their clown but their equal, that disturbs nature's plan and the viewpoints of providence." The Black always has to have savage qualities, as someone who is in a state of nature. Joséphine Baker may be admired, but only as one admires a "beautiful animal."

Nardal's plea would become familiar in years to come. Treat us, she implores, as human beings, as people who contribute to the human community.

Paulette Nardal's contribution to *La Dépêche africaine* was literary and artistic. She wrote a piece on the Black sculptress Augusta Savage, who was in Paris at the time on a grant. In it, she brought attention to Savage's art and its contribution to both Black culture and the artistic community in general.

A short story written by Paulette Nardal and published in *La Dépêche africaine* in 1929 has received much attention. Titled "En Exil" ("In Exile"), it focuses on the experience of a woman from Martinique named Elisa, a domestic living in Paris.[11]

Elisa is elderly and worn out both physically and emotionally. We find her as she is returning home from her day's labour on a windy, rainy, wintry evening. She reflects, "This land does not truly suit an old Negress already weighed down by age and sometimes weakened by rheumatism." She finds herself rebelling inwardly, never able to accommodate to the icy winds of Europe. Indeed, she wonders what sin against God the Europeans had committed that they should be punished with such terrible natural experiences.

She is mocked by some students—"Oh! The beautiful blonde," they say amid their own laughter, but she is indifferent to such cruelties, for at the end of this day she is living an interior life, an inner space. In the evening she will have no room even for pleasurable conversations with her roommate and other friends, for exhaustion overwhelms them all.

Elisa is especially alienated by "the insufferable regularity of European life, its exactitude an enemy of fantasy." As she walks to the bus stop in order to save a few *sous* by not taking a second bus, she thinks about one of the pleasures of life, the Antillean coffee she makes with punch on Sunday, her lone luxury.

Elisa has a son who went to South America to make his fortune. If only he would send a little money, she thinks. She would escape the "mirage of Paris" and return to sweet Martinique.

The bus arrives. Elisa sits in second class amid the noise of the city. She too is found to be exotic by the other passengers, for "it was especially her patterned madras shawl (*madras calendré*), so unusually knotted, which attracted looks." The narrator remarks that people on the bus did not seem to think that the vulgarity of staring at the "exotic" might bother one. For Elisa it was no matter—she remained in her inner world.

She imagines herself in Sainte-Marie, her hometown in Martinique. It is evening there too, and she is resting after her day's work. She sits on a bench in front of her little house and chats with friends like herself, captivated by the atmosphere of salty air, sultry winds, a moon which gives light and shape to the cheekbones and teeth of the group of talkers.

They gossip and tell stories that are the essence of Martinican folklore—"African tales adapted to the Antillean soul." They play games. One man takes out a homemade drum, an Antillean tom-tom, and "pulls out of it sounds that echo in the distance like an anguished call," sounds of the soul of Africa.

"Rue de Rennes," cries the bus driver; this is Elisa's stop. She comes back to Paris, to the harsh lights of the stores. And around her she sees faces very different from those of her reverie in Martinique, "strained faces, the hard eyes, the closed or indifferent faces of whites." Life again seems hard and heavy.

She goes home and is told by the concierge that she has a letter from South America. She is lifted up. She reads the letter—"with the casualness of simple folk, she immediately opens the envelope...." Elisa reads that her son has earned some money and he will be taking her home. She weeps with a joy that is almost unbearable.

Elisa must tell her roommate, her young friend. As she climbs up the six storeys of stairs, she startles her neighbours, used to hearing her painful steps. Now she is humming a "strange refrain with the jerky rhythm and the guttural and sweet syllables."

Elisa is going home, ending her exile as a poor exotic in a strange and harsh land. She does not want to be French, she already has an identity far more satisfying to her soul.

Out of the Salon Clamart came some the most important and influential early work on Black culture and identity, in the contents of a journal founded by Paulette Nardal and a Haitian dentist, Léo Sajous. *La Revue du Monde Noir* began publication in November 1931. It was to be a monthly, and only six issues were published, yet it resonated widely because of its quality and cosmopolitan policy and content. Paulette Nardal said, "This review, this movement, it was something that had to happen. It happened like that, like a sudden dawning. At that time, people were ready to read such a review."[12]

La Revue was bilingual, written in French and English, with Paulette Nardal and Clara Shepherd doing the translations from one language to another. As well, it was the only publication to include contributions from major figures of the Harlem Renaissance—Langston Hughes and Claude McKay, among others, writers from the Antilles—and others like Léon Damas, René Maran (who had won the Goncourt Prize in 1921 for his novel *Batouala: A True Black Novel*), Louis Th. Achille, Paulette Nardal, and even African writers such as Félix Eboué and Pierre Baye-Salzmann.

La Revue had as its basis the idea that there is something called Black culture and it transcends place, in a way similar to the notion of another Other, the Jews. Just as Jewish culture is universal, so is Black culture. Linguistic and geographic distinctions in the end did not erase this, they only helped to give Black culture greater depth and shape.

The journal was thus guided by cultural and social matters, and it avoided centring itself on the political issues surrounding colonialism and its consequences. In part this may be because it sought some funding from the French Ministry of Colonies. However, Paulette Nardal clearly wanted not to get caught up in the nasty arguments among Blacks about what was the proper political stance at the time. And like *La Dépêche africaine*, the journal was followed closely by French authorities worried that it might contain material considered treasonous. One of those listed as an editor, Louis-Jean Finot, was described in a police report as "a dangerous Negrophile married to a black violinist."[13] Hence, *La Revue* was cosmopolitan and universal in the French Enlightenment tradition.

The first issue opened with a statement of purpose:

> To give to the intelligentia [*sic*] of the blak [*sic*] race and their partisans an official organ in which to publish their artistic, literary and scientific works.

To study and popularize … all which concerns **Negro civilization** and the natural riches of Africa … sacred to the black race … to create among the Negroes of the entire world, regardless of nationality, an intellectual and moral tie, which will permit them to better know each other, to love one another, to defend more effectively their collective interests and to glorify their race. (emphasis in original)[14]

Hence, it continued, the Negro race will contribute to the progress and betterment of all of humanity. The motto echoed that of the French: "For Peace, Work, and Justice. By Liberty, Equality and Fraternity."

In the early 1930s, as we know, the category of race was one used by many as a way of understanding how humanity was divided. It was part of the ontology of the times and sinister at the same moment. There was neither the idea that it is a social constructed concept, the invention of a society related to values, ideology, and issues of power, nor the evidence from DNA that it is not at all based on biology. Black culture in Paris accepted race as a category that described reality, as did European culture, and Blacks used it to give credence to their own traditions, history, and intellectual creations.

Contributions to *La Revue* covered broad social and intellectual territory. The lead article in the first issue was by the "dangerous" Louis-Jean Finot, on "Race Equality." Finot quickly associated the concept of race with matters related to patriotism and nationalism in the world of 1931. He writes, as do so many public intellectuals in that decade, of the crisis of the times, citing the economic Depression, severe unemployment, and the crisis of confidence. "Only a very real solidarity between the nations," he claims, "can preserve us from … a deluge." We are witnessing "the failure of an epoch."[15]

Finot argues that only a humanistic stance with regard to the question of race will enable the world to avoid a cataclysm. First, he challenges the notion of the purity of the nation. France itself, he claims, is the product of a wide variety of races and change occurs constantly. We live in a dynamic, developing world, not a static one. Second, no particular people has a monopoly on intelligence or progress; all have individuals who contribute to the betterment of humanity. Hence, a notion of the superiority of some races will lead to catastrophe. Those who think themselves superior must abandon their "mediaeval prejudices" in order to create solidarity among all humankind. In short, the concept of superior and inferior races must be transcended and abandoned or tragedy will occur. Prophetic words.

La Revue also contained a continuing discourse on the question: "How should the negroes living in Europe dress?" Clothes, as was noted by Paulette Nardal in her short story "In Exile," are politicized, as is food, in terms of understanding the Other. How, then, should the Other appear? Responses referred to the fact that in Europe the Black was stared at, sometimes laughed at, was always on public display—no Black men and women were invisible in the Europe of the day. How to dress? Louis Achille gave the answer: "dress with taste, and if your type permits it, with art, and let them laugh who will!"[16]

One contributor, the Senegalese Pierre Baye-Salzmann, dealt profoundly with the topic "Negro art, its inspiration and contribution to Occident." Baye-Salzmann notes that Black art has its origin in the material conditions of Black life. Black artists want to translate "the morose and fettered underpart of (their) existence into food for the soul." Hence, what occurs is a move into an alternate world, what Baye-Salzmann calls "the creation of a spiritual cosmos"[17] where the soul can flourish, free from the constraints of an existence that can bring only unhappiness and despair.

Baye-Salzmann thus explains the nature of African art as abstract, referring to an inner world rather than conforming to outer perceptions. The result, he rightly claims, is that African art is "fitted to satisfy the contemporary disquietude." It suits the contemporary moment. This is why Picasso, Derain, Matisse, and many other artists, Apollinaire and many writers, Eluard and many other poets are influenced by Black art, an aesthetic that speaks to their own inner life.[18] The inversion is subtly made—Africa has much to teach Europe. Baye-Salzmann makes it clear he is not proposing that African art is superior, merely that Europe can use some of African aesthetics for inspiration without losing its own individuality. Of course, what is unsaid is that the opposite would also occur.

La Revue also discussed dance and music. "Negroes are essentially artists," claimed Louis Th. Achille in the first of two articles on Blacks and art. And it is in dance that the Black can most readily express himself in the modern world. Indeed, it is by examining dance forms that one can most easily see the connection between African, Antillean, and American Blacks.[19]

Achille did not cite Nietzsche, Matisse, or Duncan, but his ideas echo much that came to be part of the idea in the twentieth century of dance as a primal art. It is in dance that there is free expression, the "nervous and rapid execution" of dance in Africa, the "voluptuous suppleness" of the beguine in the Antilles, the "noisy buoyancy" and "proud strutting" of the Americans, all united by rhythm, syncopation, and emotions of joy and identity.[20]

Achille's ideas were elaborated on by authors of other articles, including Félix Eboué on the music and language of the Banda. He argued that the Banda language is itself musical, and it can be both spoken and whistled. As he concluded, "singing and speaking are one and the same action under a different guise."[21] Another piece in La Revue studied the tom-tom as a language of communication, both articles indicating how music is central to the life of Black culture.

The contributions of members of the Harlem Renaissance included poems by Langston Hughes and Claude McKay. Hughes's poem, titled "I, Too" (*Moi Aussi* in the French translation) was highly political, recalling Walt Whitman. The opening line—"I, too, sing America"—foreshadows its optimism. Hughes calls himself the "darker brother" who, while now being the object of bigotry and separation, will in the future be recognized as handsome and attractive, to the shame of those who looked down on him in the past. As he ends, "I, too, am America."[22]

The journal was rich in its contents. It also included articles on Liberia, Haiti, Cuba, and other places, on race equality, on Black magic, fables, spiritualism in Central Africa, and much else on Black experience, ontology, epistemology, and identity.

The most influential piece was in the last issue, an article by Paulette Nardal titled "Awakening of Race Consciousness."[23] She begins with the statement that among Antillean Blacks something very new is occurring. Issues not discussed only a few months ago, regarded as taboo, are now part of the discourse. These relate to "race consciousness." Heretofore an Antillean Black "could not speak about slavery or proclaim his pride of being of African descent without being considered as an overexcited or at least as an odd person."

What changed was the "exile" Nardal discussed earlier in her short story. Being uprooted from home resulted in "estrangement" in Paris, where they were outsiders. Antilleans were forced to confront their true selves, rather than to view themselves as *évolués*, Blacks being transformed into Frenchmen. Most Antilleans are of mixed race, of both Black and white descent, but they had been nurtured in European culture and were ignorant of Black history. Now that was changing rapidly.

Nardal contrasts the Antillean development with that of American Blacks. They, too, are often of mixed race, but the American context is different from that of the French colonial one. They were slaves and were treated with "deliberate scorn" by white America, even after the abolition of slavery. Hence, the race issue as part of identity and history was always a concern.

The American experience is thus important for all Blacks because it is they who have experience in the study of African and Black history. Nardal organizes the experience into three periods.

The first is the period of "acquisition," when Black culture, being erased by the conquerors and slave masters, disappears, and "the Negroes imported from Africa had to master a strange language and adapt themselves to a hostile environment." Blacks were "imitators," and "only certain slave narratives retain all their original freshness and genuine emotion because they were written in dialect." Interestingly, Paulette here echoes her sister Jane in describing the importance of language as a way of constructing reality. She also has clearly absorbed modernist ideas used by Woolf and Brecht.

Then Black writers entered into a period when they developed "a literature of controversy and moral protest" in opposition to slavery and the general condition of Blacks throughout the United States. Here, there is some "real success" in literature and oratory.

From 1880 on, says Nardal, "we witness the accession of Negroes to real culture" (à la culture réelle). There grows a literature that uses both the accepted norms of the English language and dialect, a realism. And there also grows a sophisticated literature of protest that used ordinary English to discuss racial issues with great emotional commitment. Now, giving as examples the poetry of McKay and Hughes, published in earlier issues, young Black writers can discard whatever inferiority complex is imposed socially upon them and "express their individual dark-skinned selves without fear or shame."

Nardal returns then to Antillean writers, noting that they are not merely imitating European French writers, but themselves quickly became French, producing works of excellence valued by French culture, including those of Dumas père and fils. Nardal brings the Antillean discussion to the present, citing a number of Antillean authors and publications, including La Dépêche africaine. However, "in none of these publications are the racial problems studied for themselves." They remain part of European culture.

Nardal then introduces another factor in understanding the current change in attitudes, that of gender. "However, parallel to the isolated efforts ... mentioned, the aspirations which were to be crystallized around The Review of the Black World asserted themselves among a group of Antillian [sic] women students in Paris.... They were ... aroused to race consciousness." Women were in a different position from men. They were made conscious not only of their African ethnicity and their colour, but also of their gender. Some began to study. And they pioneered the study of Black literature in France. Nardal notes, modestly, without telling the reader she is referring to herself, that for the first time, one of them took "The Life and Works of Harriet Beecher Stowe ... as a subject for the Diplôme d'Études supérieures d'anglais." Others followed.

Nardal continues with the hope that students in history and geography will now "avail themselves of the riches which the black race and the African continent offer to them." A new field of consciousness and study has opened.

The last paragraph reconciles and clearly depoliticizes the matter. Nardal asks whether her plea might be seen as an attack on European culture. That, she clearly states, is wrong.

> We are fully conscious of our debts to the Latin culture and we have no intention of discarding it in order to promote I know not what return to ignorance. Without it, we would have never become conscious of our real selves. But we want to go beyond this culture, in order to give our brethren, with the help of the white scientists and friends of the Negroes, the pride of being the members of a race which is perhaps the oldest in the world.[24]

The concept of "real selves" articulated by Nardal was a leap and a very complex construction. It was something very difficult to articulate for Black people with European educations living in white bourgeois society, unable to represent the cultures they were born into without being exoticized. In the context of the times, when official French culture and its educational establishment had a very clear sense of identity, it was a struggle on the part of people like the Nardals and others—Jews, for example—to come to a determination of identity. They needed, at minimum, to deal with the issue of multiple identities. They had an alternative history from that of anyone who was white and born in France. Hence, they needed to attempt to get to a far more complex concept of self, one deeper and richer than those in the majority and the mainstream.

Once knowledge of Black civilization is part of the general intellectual scene, thought Nardal, there will be a new confidence in the future of the race. Blacks who contribute to this "will tender to their retarded brothers a helping hand and endeavour to understand and love them better."[25]

In her article, Nardal explains why it is that race consciousness arose first among Black women in Paris. Black men "are content with a certain easy success"[26] at the time, a success not open to Black women living alone in the city. Hence, women felt a greater need, earlier than men, for a racial solidarity that was spiritual, not simply material.

Nardal directs the reader to a short story by Roberte Horth, a moral fable, in an earlier issue of *La Revue*. Horth entitled her tale "A Thing of No Importance" (*Histoire sans importance*).[27]

Horth tells the story of Léa, a woman with "a name like any other" who was special. On the island where she was born and raised she was given a nickname that evoked the tastes, scents, and dances of the islands. Léa often gazed into the horizon, imagining the wondrous place whose people "were polished, courteous, and friendly to all intelligent strangers."

Léa travelled to the land of her dreams and went to a Catholic school, where she was taught by devout and devoted women, and where she excelled. She developed a fine logical mind and immersed herself in the tradition of Western literature. She then entered a prestigious university where "her studies revealed to her the originality of thinkers, of scientists, of artists, and the variety of the great currents of thought, the inappreciable richness of the country in which she lived." Léa found happiness, though it was the happiness of intellectual challenge and joy, and she was valued by her professors and fellow students.

The narrator then asks: "but what of the world and its pleasures?" Léa dressed with discreet taste, and she was looked at as interesting and exotic. She loved music and danced like someone in a Matisse painting. She was a talented intellectual, and she was also "all feeling, all spirit." She was invited to smart social events where she found herself as "a doll to be proudly exhibited to guests, a strange fruit that flattered the taste of its discoverer."

In this country of her dreams, where she was successful and admired, Léa found that though she had friends, she was denied intimacy. She was taken to social events, but not invited into people's homes, as were other young women born in the cultured and refined country of dreams. She was praised, but as an exotic, not taken into people's hearts.

She came to realize that in this country "she will never be a woman like the others … because she will never be able to blot out, for the others, the absurdity of her soul fashioned by Occidental culture but concealed by an objectionable skin. She sighed; she had only overlooked one little fact, a thing of no importance, the simple irony of her mixed blood."

Horth's tale might well have been modelled on the life of one or more of the Nardal sisters. It could easily be Pauline's or Jane's story. Nardal remarks in her last article that the experience of being uprooted was well told by Horth. This feeling led to women being especially sensitive about their differences and to the study of their own origins.

Black women, like many females, are a double Other, and this makes them different not only from whites but from Black men as well. Both the fictional Léa and the real Paulette Nardal realized that the promise made by French Enlightenment cosmopolitan culture would not be realized for them. However much they became évolués, they would not be fully accepted as French; there is an invisible curtain always in front of them. Also, Paulette Nardal came to believe the Black culture in Europe, with its base in Africa and the Antilles, carried with it a gender issue: as a woman she would be put in the background, in much the same way that Virginia Woolf believed that this was so in her own land.

It should be noted that both Paulette Nardal and Roberte Horth were quite young in 1932, when they were articulating this new insight. Nardal was 36, and Horth is reported to have died at 27, shortly after writing the fable.[28]

Nardal's and Horth's perceptions have a long history in the context of the influence of the West on so-called less developed areas. For example, Russian aristocrats sent their children to France and Germany in the eighteenth and nineteenth centuries to be educated, only to have them return alienated from the very society they had been born into. The Russian intelligentsia, from the fictional Bazarov of Turgenev's *Fathers and Sons* (1862) to the rebels of 1917, became the group that transformed their society in place of the bourgeoisie of western Europe. Similarly, Chinua Achebe's *No Longer at Ease* (1960) reflects on the African experience in the twentieth century.

So Nardal's *La Revue* had articles that noted that, especially for Black women, their education in France simultaneously enlightens and alienates. Young women (and many men) bought the rhetoric of Paris as cosmopolitan and enlightened. Their experience conflicted with the rhetoric—they were still different. Hence, their identities began to be transformed in the late 1920s and 1930s into ones that included their gender and colour in addition to their education.

Funding for *La Revue* was withdrawn by the French government, and Nardal's essay was thus the major piece in its last issue, April 1932. Achille later remarked that the government's action resulted in "the brutal stoppage" (*l'arrêt brutal*) of the journal. However, it had great success. Many have commented on its influence, including Jacques Louis Hymans, one of the major biographers of Léopold Senghor, who states: "By April 1932, when it ceased publication the *Revue du Monde Noir* had introduced the themes that the *négritude* movement later developed." And "the *Revue* ... proved to be an intellectual mine for Senghor."[29]

The issue of being a woman arose three decades later in the history of Negritude. Paulette Nardal wrote a letter to Hymans in 1963 in which, reports Hymans, she "complained bitterly" about what she called the "silence (that) was maintained for a long period" about her contributions to Black identity and culture. Paulette gave credit to her sister Jane as the "promoter of this movement of ideas, so broadly exploited later." Nardal stated that Senghor and Aimé Césaire "took up the ideas tossed out by us and expressed them with more flash and brio." Nardal continued, "we were but women, real pioneers—let's say that we blazed the trail for them."[30]

To be fair, Senghor acknowledged early on that the Nardal sisters had a role in his intellectual development and in the raising of his consciousness. Still, the fathers of Negritude did ignore the contribution of the mothers once they gained fame. Black culture has its own gender issues, different from that of white culture in the West, but as profound.

The Colonial Exposition, *L'Exposition coloniale internationale de Paris*, opened on May 6, 1931, lasting six months. Its purpose, stated by its organizing head, Maréchal Hubert Lyautey, was to prove that "colonial action, so long misunderstood … is a constructive and beneficial action."[31] France was seen to have what many called a *mission civilisatrice*, the equivalent of the English "white man's burden," which was believed to benefit both the central country and the colonies.

The idea for the exposition, even some of the planning for it, went back before the Great War, when colonialism was ordinary and expositions were considered both educational and entertaining, much like World Fairs. By the time it came to realization in 1931, there was ambivalence on the part of many about its purposes and depictions of the Other as a result of the reflections and efforts of the Nardal sisters and their colleagues.

Even so, the exposition was a popular and commercial success. Over thirty million tickets were sold, more than any other event since the Universal Exposition in Paris in 1900. Many were pleased with the variety of pavilions, amusements, and artistic performances. There were lectures, film presentations, and parades on the grounds.[32] The architecture was carefully constructed to show the variety of colonial enterprises and the lives of those abroad.

Not everyone was happy with the portrayal and the message. Colonialism had a cost and an underside that could not be ignored. Léon Blum, an assimilated Jew, was at the time the representative from Narbonne in the National Assembly, and leader of the Socialist Party. It was made clear to him throughout his political life, which later would include his being prime minister of France three times, that he remained a member of the third Other in France, just as the fictional Léa would forever be an outsider. He commented on the inherent inequality that is part of the colonial enterprise:

> The colonial Exposition is doubtless a beautiful spectacle, fertile in instruction and insights of all sorts. We do not object to the people of Paris, of France, of the Universe taking pleasure and profit from it. Except that we must not forget what reality hides behind this décor of art and of joy. We must not forget that everywhere conquered or subject peoples begin to reclaim their liberty. We have imposed on them our "superior" civilization; they recall against us its first principle: the right to dispose of themselves, of the fruit of their labor, of the riches of their soil. At the Exposition, we reconstitute the marvellous stairway of Angkor and make the sacred dancers twirl, but in Indonesia we shoot, or deport, or imprison. That is why we do not take part in

it with enthusiasm. We would like less festivity and talk, more human intelligence and justice.[33]

The Surrealists, along with a Communist organization, the *Ligue anti-impérialiste*, constructed a small counter-exposition in which they attacked the idea that colonialism could be seen as beneficial. In effect, they accused the exposition of being propaganda that justified oppression and violence against those France claimed to be civilizing. One of their manifestos opposing the event was titled *Ne visitez pas L'Exposition Coloniale*.

Like Pierre Baye-Salzmann in *La Revue*, the Surrealists and others opposed to the portrayal of the colonial in the exposition noted how French culture appropriated some of the art of the colonies. The primitive was valued by them far more than what they thought to be the over-sophisticated and formal works of a dying Western culture.

In our post-colonial era, where we now study the legacy of Western global domination and the many social, economic, political, and psychological effects of that colonial domination and exploitation, some of the images we have of the relationship between the spectators and those engaged in displaying their colonial way of life and forms of creativity are very disturbing. Often, there are many white well-dressed anonymous spectators, part of a crowd, gazing at a small number of Black colonials wearing as few clothes as possible. The iconographic subtext has the white culture going to something like a zoo. Indeed, human zoos had been extremely popular entertainments across Europe before the Great War.

It is no small irony that the French would see themselves as having a *mission civilisatrice* in 1931. France, along with the rest of the great European powers, stumbled into a senseless war in 1914, only to lose much of a generation of young men in a barbaric endeavour that resulted in 16 million dead and 20 million wounded. By 1931, France and the rest of the West were embroiled in the worst economic depression of the industrial era, which caused great suffering for millions of people around the world.

In every French village central square, there are three structures that tell much about the country's history: a Roman Catholic Church, still ringing its bells; a *mairie* (town hall) with republican symbols and the slogan "Liberty, Equality, Fraternity" over its portal; and a monument to those lost in the Great War, listing the war dead's names, dedicated *À nos infants* (To Our Children), in order to remind every family of their loss and enjoin all that the foolishness of their elders resulted in sending a generation of young men to their deaths.

Further, as is documented in this work and elsewhere, the most prominent humanist minds of the time—from Mann to Woolf, Ortega, Einstein, and Freud—believed Europe was in crisis, several predicting hard times, none managing to conjure up what would happen shortly in the unprecedented horrors of the Bloodlands and the Second World War. If Europe in 1931 thought itself the most advanced and progressive civilization ever, a model for all others, it was self-deluded.

The work that began in the Salon Clamart yielded the ideas related to Négritude, and thus made important contributions to post-colonial thought in France and in the wider discourse after the Second World War. Frantz Fanon (1925–1961), a Black French psychiatrist and revolutionary, published his groundbreaking *The Wretched of the Earth* in 1961. In it he insightfully and bitterly attacked white concepts and white domination. On a psychological level, said Fanon, "the native discovers that his life, his breath, his heart are the same as those of the settler. He finds that the settler's skin is not of any more value than a native's skin."

Fanon made a monumental inversion that illuminated the economic exploitation of the imperialists and colonialist.

> [I]n a very concrete way Europe has stuffed herself inordinately with the gold and raw materials of the colonial countries.... From all those continents, under whose eyes Europe today raises up her tower of opulence, there has flowed out for centuries toward that same Europe diamonds and oil, silk and cotton, wood and exotic products.... The wealth which smothers her is that which was stolen from the underdeveloped countries. The ports of Holland, the docks of Bordeaux and Liverpool were specialized in the Negro slave trade, and owe their renown to millions of deported slaves. So when we hear the head of a European state declare with his hand on his heart that he must come to the aid of the poor underdeveloped peoples, we do not tremble with gratitude.[34]

"Europe," he concluded, "is literally the creation of the Third World."

Jean-Paul Sartre (1905–1980) wrote the preface to Fanon's work. Read this book, he urged his fellow Frenchmen. Read it to realize that though you think yourself liberal and humane, many were "massacred in your name." And read it to feel shame, for, as he claims, shame will help to cause a revolution in thought and action.[35]

Paulette Nardal lived a long and useful life until her death in 1985. She was in Martinique when the Second World War broke out, doing some work for the French Minister of Colonies. In September 1939, she attempted to return to France. However, the ship she was on was torpedoed by a German submarine. Injured, Nardal was rescued by a British destroyer, suffered serious leg injuries, and was taken to Britain for treatment, where she spent a year recovering.

In 1940 the world was different. Nardal decided to return to Martinique rather than to Vichy France. She became part of the Martinician resistance, teaching English to young people who wanted to leave the island to join the Free French.

Nardal devoted much of the remainder of her public life to feminist issues in Martinique. In 1945 she founded a new journal, *La Femme dans la Cité*, dealing with raising consciousness about women's place in society, providing social support to women, and encouraging women to play a role in the social and political life of their country, especially now that French-women had the vote, given to them in 1944.

La Femme dans la Cité was associated with the *Rassemblement féminin*, founded by Nardal in Martinique, a branch of the French women's organization *l'Union feminine civique et sociale*. This gave Nardal a larger influence because she now had access to international conferences and associations for women. She went to New York in 1946 for a year and a half as a delegate to the United Nations, and she had a position on the Division of Non-Autonomous Territories of the Secretary of the United Nations.

Nardal's work for women and justice continued. Her contributions to both Black consciousness and culture and to women's rights and identity are now being appropriately recognized as vital and central to both areas. The world several score years after her work on *La Revue du Monde Noir* is different and better because of her intelligence, dignity, tenacity, and devotion to social justice. Her contributions to Black culture are also an important part of French and European intellectual history.

6 L.H.O.O.Q.
Painting in 1930

THE WORLD OF the visual arts in 1930 in the West was near the end of its greatest transformation since the Italian Renaissance of the fifteenth century. In the last decade of the nineteenth century and the first of the twentieth there grew a set of inquiries and experiments that overthrew what had been assumed for centuries. The new painters and images had unusual names: Cubism, Fauvism, Expressionism, Futurism, and the Nabis among them.

The most transformative shift was the abandonment of mimesis, the idea that a work of art was supposed to represent external reality. This came about for many reasons. First, a new view grew that so-called external reality was just appearance, not reality at all. Now it was necessary to go through or beyond appearance to investigate what was real.

The developments in other intellectual pursuits contributed to this change. In science, especially the new physics, there was a major epistemological shift. In the world of Albert Einstein or Henri Poincaré, the notion of what was real became one that involved taking into account the frame of reference of the observer, the subject. Now there was negotiation between the observer and what was being observed, an end to the idea there is an objective reality. As the physicist John Wheeler said, "there is no out there out there." What is out there is partly determined by our own perceptions and our conceptual frame of reference. Maurice Denis reported that Gauguin instructed Paul Sérusier with regard to his breakthrough painting *The Talisman* (1888): "How do you see these trees? They are yellow. Well, then, apply some yellow. That bluish shadow, paint it with pure ultramarine blue. These red leaves? Try vermilion."[1]

Two other developments contributed mightily to the end of the tradition of mimesis in the visual arts. Photography developed in the 1830s. The first war to be photographed was the Crimean War (1853–1856), and by the end of the nineteenth century it was both a journalistic technique and an art form. For the first time, visual artists no longer had a monopoly on the representation of external reality. And if anything could claim to do mimesis well, photography was the mode.

The other change was part of a clear intellectual reversal. One of the fruits of the world of imperialism in the last half of the nineteenth century was the encounter with cultures different from that of the West. In its arrogance, the West thought it was bringing knowledge and culture to the rest of the world. The irony in the art world was that major artists in the West would adopt styles and techniques from others because they became excited about new modes of seeing and representation.

Examples of the reversal abound. They include the influence of Japanese art on the work of Van Gogh and many others, especially in the area of perspective; the change in the palette and notion of beauty in the land of Tahiti and the Caribbean islands in the work of Gauguin and Matisse; and the deep impression African masks made on Picasso, which led him to cubism. Hence, in the case of the visual arts, a rare one, the West bowed before the Other. By 1930, most of what was being painted would not have been conceived of as art fifty years earlier.

Artists now paralleled what was happening in literature, represented in 1930 by Woolf's *The Waves*. There are multiple realities, and there is a whole, deep world of the unconscious guiding us. Hence, many writers and artists argued that we need new ways of representation. It opened what had been thought closed, it enabled some to break the old rules in order to develop new forms for new content.

This metamorphosis in the visual arts began before the Great War and continued into the 1930s. Some say it is still being played out; others argue that it has ended, and not much replaced it after the 1930s. The latter suggest that Picasso's *Guernica* (1937) is the last great work of art in the Western tradition.

The year 1930 was a vital and active time in the development of the art world. In some cases, as with Woolf's novel, art and meta-art coexisted. René Magritte's *The Key to Dreams* (1930) is a painting that is about painting as well as about how we construct reality. (See Figure 1.)

The six objects in the image, in frames, are accompanied by nouns, but the words do not correspond to the images. Magritte had done this before as a way of suggesting visually what philosophers of language were themselves discussing: words are arbitrary, they do not denote the object unless we have

Figure 1 René Magritte, *The Key to Dreams* (1930). © Estate of René Magritte/
SODRAC (2018). Photo: HIP/Art Resource, NY.

a convention (the *Oxford English Dictionary* in the case of those of us who
use English) that is generally agreed upon. Moreover, the designation is not
the object itself, as Woolf reflected on when she had one of her characters
resist using words for fear of them getting in the way of experience.

Indeed, in 1928–1929, Magritte painted *La trahison des images*, a painting of a pipe with the statement in the image, *Ceci n'est pas une pipe* (This is not a pipe). It clearly argues that the painting of a pipe is just that, a painting. The painting can refer to an object, but certainly is not the object itself. Language and images help us to negotiate reality, but reality itself is still somewhat elusive. As Maurice Denis famously said in 1890 about art, "remember that a painting, before being a horse, a nude, an anecdote or whatever, is essentially a flat surface covered with colours assembled in a certain order."[2]

In *The Key to Dreams,* Magritte goes further. He is noting, as everyone in the West understood after Freud's *Interpretation of Dreams* (1899) and other works, that the code of dreams is different from the code of experience. Hence the words in the image no longer correspond to the objects because our dreams are coded symbolically. Is the shoe really the moon? Of course not. But in some dreams—and this is a problem because there is no universal code or agreed-upon conventions in dream language; context and personality matter a great deal—a shoe might refer to the moon. The key to dreams is to understand the code, not to work literally. Normal denotations and connotations do not work.

Magritte's paintings, and many others, are at the same time art, meta-art, and reflections on how we negotiate our experiences, both conscious and unconscious.

Magritte also used the technique of juxtaposition beloved by surrealists. In *On the Threshold of Liberty* (1930, a second version painted in 1937) he shows eight different panels, with a cannon very prominent, dominant really, on the right. (See Figure 2.) The panels themselves are of a variety of images, including a woman's bare torso, fluffy clouds, an urban apartment building, a forest, two panels of different kinds of wood, a brick wall, and one with the texture of metal with balls attached, the latter used by Magritte in other works.

On the Threshold of Liberty might or might not be political—it could simply, like *The Key to Dreams*, be asking the viewer to reflect on the meaning of the title, using the variety of panels. The cannon itself, however, makes a clear statement: liberty is often not gained without struggle and violence, sometimes destroying serenity and stability.

Marcel Duchamp also entered the discussion of the nature of art in 1930. Duchamp was well known and had earlier helped to shape modern art with his *Nude Descending a Staircase, Number 2* (1912), and his ready-mades, including *Bicycle Wheel* and *Fountain*, meta-art that challenged the whole conception of what art was thought to be. (See Figure 3.) He was associated with the Dada group, a movement that began during the Great

Figure 2 René Magritte, *On the Threshold of Liberty* (1930). © Estate of René Magritte/SODRAC (2018). Photo: Herscovici/Art Resource, NY.

War to critique Western culture. The Dadaists seemed absurd—they spouted nonsense words, they suggested that common objects be considered as works of art, they created found poetry from newspaper cuttings.

However, the Dada artists, performers, and poets made their mocking of Western culture a critique of the West itself, for they were calling attention to the violence and injustice that culminated in the most savage war in history. The point is that their nonsense made sense. For them, nonsense was not the opposite of sense, it was the opposite of common sense.

In 1930, Duchamp presented his *L.H.O.O.Q.*, sometimes called *Mona Lisa with a Moustache*, a copy of the *Mona Lisa*, now large scale (he created an earlier, smaller one in 1919, but did not make it public until 1930 along with the larger version). The copy had Mona Lisa with a moustache and beard, and the title *L.H.O.O.Q.* written below. (See Figure 4.)

This is very close to Brecht's *Verfremdungseffekt*, presented the same year *Mahagonny* opened. Duchamp wants to get the viewer to reflect on the image, not simply to look at it. He wants the audience to be bothered, to do more than boast they have seen the most famous painting in the Western canon.

Figure 3 Marcel Duchamp, *Nude Descending a Staircase, Number 2* (1912).
© Association Marcel Duchamp/ADAGP, Paris/SODRAC, Montréal (2018). Photo:
Philadelphia Museum of Art, Arensberg Collection, 1950-134-59.

Figure 4 Marcel Duchamp, *L.H.O.O.Q.*, sometimes called *Mona Lisa with a Moustache* (1930). © Association Marcel Duchamp/ADAGP, Paris/SODRAC, Montréal (2018). Photo: Cameraphoto Arte, Venice/Art Resource, NY.

First, he desecrates the image. He challenges the notion that it cannot be tampered with, that it is sacred. Further, Duchamp asks about the Western cult of the original, something that was not part of the artistic tradition in the West until the eighteenth century. Can we make copies of the *Mona Lisa* that are "as one" with the original? Why are they not valued? Do we value the Mona Lisa—and by extension, other canonical works—because we have commodified them? The original is worth everything, the copy nothing.

L.H.O.O.Q. is Duchamp's clear challenge. If you say the letters as they are spoken in French, they come very close to "Elle a chaud au cul," variously translated as "She has hot pants," or "She has a hot ass." The painting mocks the relatively new Western idea of turning paintings into objects we worship in a museum, a substitute for the decline in the worship of traditional religious icons.

Magritte was a favourite of André Breton, the French philosopher often referred to as "The Pope of Surrealism." Breton's *Second Manifesto of Surrealism* was published in the journal *La Révolution Surréaliste* in December 1929. The publication was one organized by Breton. It came out from 1924 to 1929, though not regularly, and this was its last issue. Signalling what was inside, Magritte's painting *The Hidden Woman* was on the cover. As well as the *Second Manifesto*, the issue included the script for the surrealist film *Un Chien Andalou* by Salvador Dalí and Luis Buñuel.

In his first *Manifesto* (1924), Breton provided his influential definition of Surrealism:

> SURREALISM, *n.* Psychic automatism in its pure state, by which one proposes to express—verbally, by means of the written word, or in any other manner—the actual functioning of thought. Dictated by thought, in the absence of any control exercised by reason, exempt from any aesthetic or moral concern.

> ENCYCLOPEDIA. *Philosophy.* Surrealism is based on the belief in the superior reality of certain forms of previously neglected associations, in the omnipotence of dream, in the disinterested play of thought. It tends to ruin once and for all other psychic mechanisms and substitute itself for them in solving all the principal problems of life.[3]

The *Second Manifesto* elaborated on the philosophy of the first. For example, Surrealists "are especially interested in the Freudian concept which affects the greater part of their deep concerns as men—the concern to create, to destroy artistically—I mean ... sublimation."[4]

It also served to give Breton an opportunity to praise some, and in effect excommunicate some others from the movement. Moreover, Breton himself joined the Communist Party in 1927 and wanted his Surrealist group to take part in the politics of the day. Hence, the *Second Manifesto* also included an attempt—wildly unsuccessful—to put what he understood as Communism together with the spontaneous and inner-directed ideas of Surrealism.

Surrealism was enormously influential. It even touched Pablo Picasso, whose reputation and influence exceeded that of Breton. Picasso's *The Crucifixion* (February 1930) is the closest image of his to the Surrealist style and intent. (See Figure 5.) The distortions and exaggerations are Surrealist in style, far different from the Cubist usage. As well, the painting is interested

Figure 5 Pablo Picasso, *The Crucifixion* (1930). © Picasso Estate/SODRAC (2018). Photo: Mathieu Rabeau, Musée national Picasso, Paris, France. © RMN-Grand Palais/Art Resource, NY.

in the power of myth and can certainly be interpreted to have some of the Jungian elements favoured by the Surrealists. Some commentators see it as being a forerunner of *Guernica* in some of its symbolism.

The rising star of Surrealism in 1930 was another Spaniard, the young Salvador Dalí (1904–1989). Dalí, first, was an extraordinarily talented artist technically. His early drawings are as accomplished as his oils. But he also mastered a combination that few others in the Surrealist movement could muster: his paintings were at once provocative, mythic, and phallic, while also using juxtaposition to great effect. Even his titles were inventive and suggestive. Some of his 1929 and 1930 paintings are called *Paranoiac Woman-Horse*, *The Bleeding Roses*, *Oedipus Complex*, and *The Great Masturbator*. (See Figure 6.)

The last is placed in a strange landscape, with a central image filled with phallic shapes. It is dream-like, an important Surrealist tenet, and it suggests an exploration of our inner desires and fantasies. As with Magritte, the code of understanding is closer to Freudian psychotherapy than it is to "reason." In the image are an army of ants, several people, a locust, and an egg. One of the people is a female nude, another is a male body, bleeding, seen only from below the waist.

Figure 6 Salvador Dalí, *The Great Masturbator* (1929). © Salvador Dalí, Fundació Gala–Salvador Dalí/SODRAC (2018). Photo: Alinari/Art Resource, NY.

The themes of *The Great Masturbator* and others are clearly set out in two 1931 Dalí images. His *The Dream* is hardly the *Mona Lisa*, though it, too is a portrait of a woman with a landscape in the background. Here, the woman has her eyes closed, dreaming, rather than looking at us with that enigmatic smile. Dalí's woman has hair that is wild, and that by now recognizable army of ants is on her mouth. She is artificial, as if her external features have no meaning in a world where, as Freud said, a dream is a "fact," though a different fact from the conventional understanding of reality.

Dalí also painted his "signature painting," *The Persistence of Memory*, in 1931 (it was also very small, 9½ by 13 inches). (See Figure 7.) Here, the landscape goes on forever, with craggy rocks in the right background giving it some substance. Two main symbols are immediately evident. The creature on the beach has been variously understood, with those fond of biographical interpretations noting that the face in profile might resemble that of Dalí. But the creature could also (or even at the same time, using a multiple interpretation) be the beginnings of human history as we come out of the sea, or an indeterminate being of our dreams and dream-memory.

The Persistence of Memory was the first of Dalí's images to have in it the symbolic melting watch, which in this painting represents the introduction of psychological time in place of the objective, artificial, mechanical time

Figure 7 Salvador Dalí, *The Persistence of Memory* (1931). © Salvador Dalí, Fundació Gala–Salvador Dalí/SODRAC (2018). Credit: Gala–Salvador Dalí Foundation/Artists Rights Society (ARS), New York Digital Image. © The Museum of Modern Art/Licensed by SCALA/Art Resource, NY.

introduced by modern Western culture. Time bends, it melts, it is in our heads, especially when we deal with memory, for surely some pieces of our lives are more significant than others, a notion reinforced by the Freudian concept of the importance of trauma. The tree with no leaves is rarely mentioned in discussions of the image, but it does have a role. It makes the painting bleaker than it otherwise might be, more of an essence of things than a developed growth.

The melting watch has become part of our symbolic world. Dalí used it regularly, and it would be borrowed by others. Interestingly, in 1969 Dalí did a series of illustrations for Lewis Carroll's *Alice's Adventures in Wonderland* (1864), a classic work about a young girl who voyages via a dream to an alternate world, a book beloved not only by children but by philosophers of language and surrealists. In the illustrations, which are very fine, the melting watch is ever-present as Alice explores her inner world.

The Surrealists, as bizarre and contentious as they sometimes were, made important, lasting contributions to the world of the visual arts. They and the Expressionists opened up the canvas to an inner world that came to be explored by others in literature and psychology. Some even suggest that they were influenced by Einstein's idea of relativity and the importance of taking into account the observer's (inner) frame of reference in the understanding of the world.

Cubism, or at least its offshoots, continued in 1930 to be a major mode of visual representation. It began 1907, and its two founders were Pablo Picasso and Georges Braque. Both continued to develop their ideas into their later years.

The name was given to the style by the critic Louis Vauxcelles in 1908 when he called the new development, insultingly, "*bizarre cubiques.*" It stuck.[5]

Braque's *The Blue Mandolin* (1930) is a good example of what the cubists were attempting. First, they took from Cézanne the idea that what we see are not objects, but shapes and forms. That is, the eye simply sees what is out there, and that can be organized into geometric forms. It is the brain that distinguishes what is seen, and through cultural convention interprets it. Hence, in a room full of people at a table what we see is shape, form, and colour. We interpret it according to social norms. Someone from Mars might not do the same.

The cubist also suggests that we abandon conventional perspective. Rather, the eye moves, and there are multiple perspectives visually, just as philosophers were suggesting there are multiple perspectives socially and culturally. Hence, the image combines several perspectives at once, rather than giving us the accepted norm of the illusion of three-dimensionality practised by Western artists since the Renaissance.

Cubists, like many at the time, do not deal in mimesis, but there are many references to mimesis in their works. In Braque's painting, we have reference to a mandolin, a cup, fruit, a chair, a music score, the word *valse*, and so on, though they are not portrayed in any photographic manner. We, the viewers, are expected to actively put this together. Indeed, in the most famous of "Cubist" paintings (though some art critics see it as pre-Cubist), Picasso's *Les Demoiselles d'Avignon* (1907), the artist purposely moved the table in front of the women, placing it in an unusual position in order to bring the viewer into the image as a participant.

The Blue Mandolin, like many Cubist works, uses the technique of collage. There are layers of things and references. This relates to a new idea about how we put the external world together, how we perceive it before it is organized for us by authority or society. We do not see it as coherent and orderly; instead we have a number of perceptions, some of them coming all at once.

It should be remembered that these artists, unlike their Western predecessors, often wanted a painting to be seen holistically before being analyzed in its parts. They are part of a movement that began before the First World War and that consciously desired to transform what it was that artists were doing and how they were doing it. They rejected the notion that the artistic tradition begun during the Renaissance laid out forever an agenda to be completed and followed by all others. Mimesis, the illusion of three-dimensionality, the golden triangle—all from the Renaissance—were now viewed not as *the* way of doing art, but as *a* way of doing it. The artist has many choices. They were the second generation (some, like Picasso and Braque, were also part of the first) who changed the art world in the West as deeply as Einstein did in science and Freud in our considerations of the human personality.

Hence, unlike music, a novel, or a work of history, their art often does not function temporally in its presentation. The collage is thus a way of getting at what we experience at any given moment rather than a temporal discussion of our experience. An example of how reality gets distorted in temporal modes would be reading a history of a revolution. It is presented as coherent, a series of happenings and perceptions that follow one another, when in actuality this would have been very different—incoherent, disorderly, even anomic—for those who experienced it. The cubist painting can juxtapose the jumble of our perceptions all at once. In the West we are trained to understand life temporally, though we experience it as a collage.

Cubists and some of the other groups of artists, including the Surrealists, also often present a work of art as autonomous. As Derain remarked, painting in the West from the Renaissance was representative; it told a story and therefore had a literary function, was didactic, and sometimes allegorical. A person could go into the Louvre or another major museum with a copy of the Bible in one hand and Ovid's *Metamorphoses* in the other and these will explain a lot about works of Western art from 1450 to about 1890.

Not so for many artists in 1930. The painting is a painting, it is a thing-in-itself, an autonomous work. What does it refer to? Itself. What does it present? What the engaged (and this is very important) viewer makes of it.

In reflecting on what Woolf was doing with the novel, what Brecht was doing in the theatre, and what many artists were trying to accomplish, it appears that by 1930 there was some agreement from several quarters about what art should be doing. It does not depict an objective reality, it does not expect to entertain or to reveal something to a passive audience. It interprets reality. "There is no out there out there."

In *Tonio Kröger,* Thomas Mann had Tonio reflect in a letter to his artist friend that ends the novella,

> As I write, the sea whispers to me and I close my eyes. I am looking into a world unborn and formless, that needs to be ordered and shaped. I see into a whirl of shadows of human figures who beckon to me to weave spells to redeem them: tragic and laughable figures and some that are both together.[6]

Mann's sea, Woolf's waves, Brecht's distancing, Braque and Picasso's deconstruction of perception. This is a world far different from that of the Victorians.

Picasso in his *Crucifixion* and *The Acrobat*, both of 1930, flirted with Surrealism for a short period of time. His talent was so remarkable that no style was beyond his grasp. However, he found that it did not satisfy. The idea of automatism, of presenting a symbolic dream world, of even shutting off one's critical senses did not capture him, and he shortly moved back fully to a more natural way of painting, influenced by his Cubist experiments, and sometimes going beyond them.

Picasso's *The Dream* (January 1932) can be contrasted with Dalí's painting of the same title to demonstrate his movement away from Surrealism. The woman is recognizably a person, the colours are bold, the perspective far different from Dalí's immense landscapes. It is indeed erotic, with an erect penis as part of the face of the dreamer (biographical note: the model is the fifty-year-old painter's new twenty-two-year-old mistress), but far different symbolically from the Surrealist prescriptions.

Two months after painting *The Dream*, Picasso dug far deeper into the psyche of his subject with *Girl Before a Mirror*, accomplishing what was part of the agenda of Surrealism—the examination of inner life—but doing it in his own style. (See Figure 8.) The girl is different from the girl seen in the mirror, with the mirror serving a multiple symbolic purpose—revealing inner reality, unveiling one's thoughts, asking about the inevitability of the end of youth and our own fragile lives. The colours in the image also have symbolic meaning, from that of youth to old age. The shapes are themselves suggestive of the meaning and understanding of the body, and the flattened background heightens both the woman and the woman in the mirror in the foreground.

Artists themselves had a different stature in 1930 than they might have had before the Great War. Important artists were viewed as culture heroes, to be lionized and courted. The October 20, 1930, issue of *Time Magazine*, the popular tastemaker of the United States, had on its cover a photographic portrait in profile of Henri Matisse (1869–1954). The occasion was the 29th Carnegie International Institute of Modern Painting in Pittsburgh, regarded as the most important painting exhibition of living artists in the country at that time.

Matisse had won first prize in 1927 ($1,500 USD) and he agreed to join the jury in 1930. That prize was awarded to Picasso for a portrait of his wife. Showing how much the reporter and the magazine knew about modern art and artists, the story noted that "the two heroes of the Pittsburgh show were French … Henri Matisse and Pablo Ruiz Picasso" [*sic*].

Figure 8 Pablo Picasso, *Girl Before a Mirror* (1932). © Picasso Estate/SODRAC (2018). Photo: Digital Image. © The Museum of Modern Art/Licensed by SCALA/ Art Resource, NY.

Matisse was interviewed and indicated that he liked New York and the landscapes of the United States, but he was wisely mainly silent. "Who in his opinion were the greatest US artists? M. Matisse didn't know. What were his views on US art? M. Matisse had none. Were there any signs of a return to classicism in France? Matisse declined to comment." Celebrity clearly was not his milieu.[7]

In the early part of the century Matisse was a member of a group of painters called the Fauves. They too were given their name by Louis Vauxelles when he attended an exhibition in 1905 that had many paintings by the group, all with bright colours not necessarily in a realistic style and using strong brushwork. Also present in the room was a piece of sculpture in the classical style. "Donatelli parmi les fauves" ("Donatelli among the wild beasts"), said Vauxelles in derision.[8] The group, in the tradition of the Impressionists, proudly adopted the insult as their name.

The Fauves group, including Matisse, Derain, Dufy, Marquet, Vlaminck, and others broke up soon thereafter as each artist developed his own style and following.

Of all of the major artists of the first half of the twentieth century, certainly of all those who were major in 1930, Matisse was the one most concerned with an issue central to aesthetic philosophy—the beautiful. He rarely commented on social matters, and only a few of his very large numbers of paintings have any direct psychological import. Matisse was the painter most directly connected to the classical idea that art dealt with the beautiful.

He, too, was deeply influenced by Cézanne, who turned out to be the grandfather of much of modernist art, but it was not the Cézanne who deconstructed Mont Sainte-Victoire and was beloved by the Cubists. In 1899 the young Matisse purchased Cézanne's *Three Bathers* (1879–1882) for 1,200 francs (which he paid in installments), a work he admired greatly. Cézanne painted several "Bathers" over the course of his life, all of which have figures that are clearly women, but not mimetically so. As well, the colours reflect light and nature. Matisse in 1936 said of the work on the occasion of his donating it to a museum in Paris: "In the thirty-seven years I have owned this canvas, I have come to know it quite well, though not entirely I hope; it has sustained me morally in the critical moments of my venture as an artist; I have drawn from it my faith and my perseverance."[9]

It is this Cézanne who liberated Matisse from his early semi-realistic style. He realized that the beautiful could be combined with modern aesthetics and perception. Hence, Matisse's paintings use a variety of colour, his palette is as various as that of any artist, and his paintings often treat space as perceptual rather than as three-dimensional. Matisse is relentlessly modern in his techniques, style, and modes of artistic discourse. He is, however, traditional in his purpose. No Western painter matches him for his ability to get us to reflect on beauty in the modern world.

In 1930 Matisse, then in the United States, was offered and accepted a major commission. He met with Albert Barnes, the head of the Barnes Foundation in Merion, Pennsylvania, near Philadelphia. Barnes was a great collector of modern art, including Matisses, and his foundation (now moved

Figure 9 Henri Matisse, *The Dance*, Summer 1932–April 1933 (oil on canvas), three panels. Overall (left): 133¾ x 173¾ in. (339.7 x 441.3cm), 2001.25.50 a,b,c. © Succession H. Matisse/SODRAC (2018). The Barnes Foundation, Philadelphia, Pennsylvania.

to the city of Philadelphia) then had one of the finest collections of "avant-garde" paintings in the world. Matisse agreed to create a triptych, really a mural, for the main hall of the foundation's building, above some windows.

The result is what has become known as *The Dance*. (*Dance I* and *Dance II* now refer to two of Matisse's earlier works of 1909 and 1910.) (See Figure 9.)

Dance II flows as the three pieces of the mural are connected by small extensions. The colours are pale—blue, pink, and gray, along with some black, the dimension is flat, and there is simplicity in the execution. Some critics remark that the dancers, very Cézanne-like, are engaged in modern movement. They are not doing a minuet or a waltz; rather they are in a kind of flow that celebrates the body and its possibilities. It is more Isadora Duncan (1877–1927) than any formal, classical dance, a dance that is natural, celebratory, and part of folk ritual.

The mural has a Dionysian flavour, but a different one than most modern interpretations of the Dionysian. The Dionysian has come to be equated in the West with a *Walpurgisnacht*, a Bacchanalia, a releasing of libidinal repression often depicted as an orgy, sometimes associated with either the coming of spring and/or witchcraft.

Not so in the Matisse. His dancers are indeed engaged in elemental movement, but it is associated with joy. It has a freedom, but one that gives pleasure without the dark shades of the modern Dionysian in it. Mann rightly feared what would happen if the Dionysian came to be directed in destructive ways. Matisse's dancers, filled with energy, celebrate life, a rare moment in the dark times of the thirties, years rightly described by Auden in 1939 as "a low, dishonest decade."[10]

There were still artists who saw their main role as commentators on the contemporary social and political world. The German Expressionists were the artistic complement to the work of Brecht and Weill, especially George Grosz and Otto Dix. Both men spent part of their formative years as soldiers in the Great War. Both, like many of their peers, were deeply wounded, not simply in body, but in mind and soul.

The result was the use of their formidable artistic talents in the 1920s to comment on society. Grosz stated, "I considered any art pointless if it did not put itself at the disposal of political struggle … my art was to be a gun and a sword."[11]

Their critique of Western culture and society has the flavour of raw anger. Grosz was especially concerned to reveal what he saw as the hypocrisy and unfairness of contemporary life. His drawings and other works often portray a middle class of self-satisfied, superficial beings practising a Christianity with no care for social justice, unconcerned with what they refuse to see around them: veterans with artificial limbs, poverty in the streets, open sex, and a city—Berlin—represented as a place on one of the levels of Dante's inferno.

For Grosz, the grotesque and the horrific are part of everyday life in the failed culture of the West. His use of satire spurred him to develop techniques that used distortion, inversion, and exaggeration to great effect.

Grosz's *Berlin Street Scene* of 1930, painted after more than a decade of bitter and insightful commentary on social matters is, for him, relatively low-key and more subtle than many of his drawings. Still, the street is a study of contrasts. (See Figure 10.) The middle class, well dressed and smug, are at the centre of a street in late fall, with decorative lights anticipating the coming of Christmas. On the side, ignored, is a beggar, someone who has fallen on hard times.

The social commentary is subtle and prophetic, for the begging man, in darker hues than those at the centre, is dressed in the fraying clothes of the middle class. In better times, he may have been one of the friends of the two well-off people in the middle of the street, even attended their parties. Now he is ignored, treated as if he were invisible.

The painting suggests that bourgeois society does not concern itself with those who fall into poverty, that the bourgeoisie are insensitive to the possibility that, as the saying goes, "there but for the grace of God go I." There is no room for empathy. That generation experienced much in war and throughout the decade of the 1920s, Grosz says, but it learned very little.

The prophetic side of the image is Grosz's insight that German (and Western) society in the Depression is going to produce very many people who will go for help? Soon thereafter, in the German presidential campaign of early 1932, there appeared a poster of a number of unemployed, all grey, with clothing and faces like those of

Figure 10 George Grosz (1893–1959), *Berlin Street Scene* [Berliner Strassenszene] (1930). © Estate of George Grosz/SODRAC (2018). Black ink, watercolour, and thinned oil on paper. Executed in 1930. 59.7 x 45.7cm. Christie's Images Ltd./ SuperStock.

Grosz's beggar. The words on the poster: "Unsere lezte Hoffnung: Hitler" ("Our last hope: Hitler").

The Great War did not disappear from peoples' consciousness by 1930. The novel *All Quiet on the Western Front* by Erich Maria Remarque was first

Figure 11 Otto Dix (1891–1969), *The War* (1929–1932). © Estate of Otto Dix/ SODRAC (2018). Photo: bpk Bildagentur Gemäldegalerie Neue Meister/photo: Jürgen Karpinski/Art Resource, NY.

published in November and December 1928 in the newspaper *Vossische Zei-tung*, then in January 1929 in book form. It quickly became an international bestseller, with over two million copies in twenty-two languages sold in the next eighteen months. The novel's depiction of the life of individual soldiers in war made it the most powerful anti-war literary statement of its time. It was made into a Hollywood movie in 1930 that won two Academy Awards.

Otto Dix at this time worked on his *The War* (1929–1932), a large and important triptych. (See Figure 11.) The form chosen by Dix was significant. The triptych had its origin in Christian art in the Middle Ages and was the form that many religious images took, especially those designed as altar-pieces for a church. In three panels, a large middle panel and two smaller side panels, it usually depicted the lives of Jesus and/or Mary, sometimes some of the saints. It was didactic, designed to teach the faithful the basic tenets of the faith.

Now, Dix uses the triptych form to challenge the tradition. His work makes direct references to other triptychs, mostly to the *Isenheim Altarpiece* triptych (1512–1516) of Matthias Grünewald, which adds a fourth, small panel below the centre image, as does Dix.

Dix's work, like many triptychs, is to be "read" from left to right. The left panel has soldiers marching to war, their backs to the viewer. In the centre, similar to an earlier work by Dix, *The Trench* (1923), there is the horror and total devastation of the battlefield, the sole survivor in the hellish landscape being a soldier wearing a gas mask. Corpses and skeletons litter the scene, depicting something apocalyptic that would have been imaginary in earlier centuries but has become real. The war now imitates the visions of hell of someone like Hieronymus Bosch.

On the right, two soldiers strive to survive. The soldier who is dragging his comrade to safety is a self-portrait of Dix, not only his way of signing the image, but a statement about his personal experience. The soldier being aided has wounds that some commentators liken to those of Christ. The fourth panel, below, shows soldiers either asleep or dead in a bunker.

What is missing from *The War*, purposely, is hope. Unlike other triptychs, Grünewald's included, in its fourth panel there is no suggestion of resurrection. Dix's generation experienced Good Friday, but no Easter followed.

One of the issues that modern theology and philosophy will grapple with is that of the meaning of our suffering. Traditional Christianity had an answer. Dix, much bleaker, insisted that the suffering of the Great War was meaningless. Dix worked in the tradition of Goya's etchings in his *Disasters of War* (1810–1820). One of Goya's images has the title, "Was It for This That We Were Born?" Dix asks us to contemplate the void.

The visual arts in 1930 were vital, very much a part of the culture of Europe and the West. They dealt with the meaningful issues that Mann, Woolf, Ortega, Freud, and others grappled with at the time, problems of human nature, ethics, knowledge, social justice, and meaning.

This was, however, near the end of a very long period during which Paris and France could claim to be the home of painting in the Western world. This generation of artists was the last in which every important figure would be seen as French by the wider world. France, as we know, fell to Germany in 1940, beginning a difficult period in the life of the home of the Enlightenment. By 1950, the centre of the art world in the West moved to New York, and a wholly new era in what was seen as the task of the visual arts would begin. What became contemporary in New York was very different from the work of Picasso, Matisse, and the world of 1930.

7 HUXLEY
Fearing the Future

IN 1842, THE YOUNG Friedrich Engels was sent by his parents to the city of Manchester in northern England to work for the family firm, the Ermen and Engels's Victoria Mill. Engels was horrified by the state of the growing industrial city and the squalid treatment of labour in the textile industrial plants. He published a number of articles that in 1845 became the insightful and angry book *The Condition of the Working Class in England*, one of the most important documents on the social conditions of the first generation of the industrial revolution, an impetus to reform.

On October 10, 1930, the British novelist and essayist Aldous Huxley gave a lecture to workingmen in Durham, a mining town in the north of England, titled "Science and Poetry." He reported the event in a letter of October 18, remarking that he also had a "look at mining villages—than which nothing can be much more frightful."[1]

Huxley returned to the north the next February. He then made his first trip into a coal mine and visited the ICI (Imperial Chemical Industry) plant in the town of Billingham, a manufacturing colossus associated with the name of its founder, Sir Alfred Mond. He noted that conditions of labour were somewhat improved from the world of the 1840s. Yet he still found the work in the mines difficult and dehumanizing—that is, for those who could get work, since there was a high rate of unemployment at the time.[2]

In an essay titled "Sight-seeing in Alien Englands" (June 1931), Huxley reported on his experience at ICI. "Billingham is a triumphant embodiment of particular planning. The great ICI factory is one of those ordered universes that exist as anomalous oases of pure logic in the midst of the larger world of planless incoherence." He described the complex and ordered technique of producing ammonia and other chemicals with some admiration, and noted that "merely as spectacle ... the process is wonderfully impressive."

He described the tone of rapture that many technicians and industrialists used when discussing their work. Huxley also visited ironworks in Sheffield and a factory in Birmingham making parts for automobiles, "a very efficient, up-to-date factory."[3]

Huxley was searching for an inspiration for his next novel. He found it in the north of England, with the introduction of the new machine age that introduced to factory work the assembly line invented by Henry Ford, the worker turned into a cipher, doing "low-level routine work."[4]

He saw the future, and the result was a new kind of novel, a work of dystopian speculative fiction, *Brave New World*, still one of the most widely read novels in the English language. He finished the book in August 1931 and wrote to his father, "I have been harried by work—which I have at last, thank heaven, got rid of—a comic, or at least satirical, novel about the Future, showing the appallingness (at any rate by our standards) of Utopia."[5]

Huxley, like Woolf, came from a distinguished family. His grandfather, Thomas Henry Huxley (1825–1895), known in Victorian England as "Darwin's Bulldog," was a prominent biologist and essayist who invented the term "agnostic" and bested Bishop Samuel Wilberforce in the famous debate on evolution in 1860. On his mother's side, he claimed Matthew Arnold, poet, educator, and essayist, as an uncle. His parents were notable educators, and one of his brothers, Andrew, won the Nobel Prize in Physiology or Medicine.

Huxley was good at science and understood more about the world of natural philosophy than did most humanists. However, his career was in letters, as a novelist, playwright, poet, and essayist. His first novel, *Crome Yellow*, a witty satire of society, appeared in 1921. He soon became a major public intellectual, commenting on social mores and the quality of modern life.

Brave New World, like many important novels, signals much in its opening few sentences. First: "A squat grey building of only thirty-four stories." The architecture is monumental and dull, signalling the power of the state. It uses what would soon be called the "fascist aesthetic," and prefigures the dreadful and dehumanizing Soviet style.

Then a longer sentence with three main ideas. "Over the main entrance the words, **Central London Hatchery and Conditioning Centre.**" Something unusual is happening here. The title seems odd, and the implication is that more than birth occurs there, as though beings are developed in directed ways.

"[A]nd, in a shield, the World State's motto"—there is a World State, a single entity of authority, uniform for the whole planet—which is "**Community, Identity, Stability.**" This is clearly in contrast to the motto of European modernity: the French Revolution's Liberty, Equality, Fraternity.

Community trumps liberty—the collective is very important; the individual is expected to subordinate his will to the group. Clearly, identity is more important than equality—know your place and who you are in the organized World State. Stability is cherished—your fraternity is not expected to be an agent of change, as it was and is for so many reform and revolutionary movements.

We are in an alternate world. Not the usual one of "once upon a time," but a world of the future. Huxley is critiquing utopian thought, but doing so by working in a genre, the dystopia, that is relatively new.

The utopia has a long history in the West, from Plato and on through Christian theology to More (who coined the term in 1516), to the opening of the twentieth century. Utopias were especially prevalent in the eighteenth and nineteenth centuries, as the genre was linked to the idea of progress and the notion that the future could only be much better than the present.

The world after the Great War was not one conducive to the writing of utopias, and the genre went out of style during the interwar years. In fact, it was turned around. Now the dystopia, a fear of the future, replaced it.

The term dystopia, like agnostic, was coined in Victorian times. On March 12, 1868, John Stuart Mill, then a Liberal member of Parliament, responded to the Irish land policy of the Conservative government: "It is perhaps too complimentary to call them Utopians, they ought rather to be called dys-topians or caco-topians. What is commonly called Utopian is something too good to be practicable; but what they appear to favour is too bad to be practicable."[6]

Indeed, the idea of progress was inverted. We are now, in 1930, in the more ordinary world of the idea of regress. Traditionally in the West, the two main sources of myth, Greco-Roman culture and the Judeo-Christian tradition, placed utopia at the origin of the world: in the former it was the golden age, replaced by ages of silver, bronze, and according to Ovid, our own nasty iron age; in the latter, utopia was Eden, a perfect garden replaced by the sinful and harsh world in which we dwell, waiting for the Second Coming.

Scholars see the first dystopia as Book Four of Jonathan Swift's *Gulliver's Travels* (1726), Houyhnhnmland. By Huxley's time several other dystopias had been written, most in the twentieth century, including those of H.G. Wells and Yevgeny Zamiatin. Still, the term was not common currency, as we can see when Huxley describes his work to his father as one that uncovers "the appallingness ... of Utopia."

By the end of the Second World War, the term was in common use, and as the twentieth century unfolded there were more dystopias written each decade—totalitarian, nuclear, environmental, and those warning of a state that, in the name of security, ended liberty and privacy.

Most utopias are perfect alternate worlds, often located on an isolated island, meant to stand in contrast to our imperfect, primary world. They are written as works of reform, intended to get us to think about how we can make ourselves and our communities better. The first, Plato's *Republic*, was written not to be implemented, but rather to show Athens how to reform. The *Utopia* of Thomas More was a plea for justice in the society of Renaissance England. Utopians are not tinkerers. They want big transformation, a change in kind, not degree.

The dystopia, however, is an alternate world that overlaps our primary world. It suggests that we are headed in a certain direction, and that direction should be feared. Like many of the artists of the time, Huxley's dystopia resembles the modern world, for as speculative fiction it is a cautionary tale that asks what might happen next. It is science fiction, political philosophy, ethics, and a reflection on human nature all at once.

What is soon revealed in the novel is that we are in an imaginary future, in the year A.F. 632. "A.F." stands for After Ford, the beginning of the new era being the introduction of the assembly line by Henry Ford in 1913. Now the world can have order. Now science can be used for the control of life and society.

In this world, humans are made in laboratories under highly controlled conditions. There are no births, no mothers or fathers, no families. Humans are divided into five basic groups—Alphas, Betas, Gammas, Deltas, and Epsilons, each with its own intelligence and social purpose. As the Director of the Centre says: "standard Gammas, unvarying Deltas, uniform Epsilons.... The principle of mass production at last applied to biology."

Not only are humans "hatched," they are nurtured into a specific personality. "We also predestine and condition. We decant our babies as socialized human beings." Using the ideas of the Russian physiologist Ivan Pavlov about behaviour control and conditioning (no need for modification), Huxley has the Centre prepare the embryos and babies for their place in the world. Epsilons are given only so much oxygen and intelligence; those destined to work in tropical climates are conditioned to love heat and hate cold. All are given the belief that their social position is wonderful. They will cherish their "inescapable social destiny." All will be happy as they live out their scripted lives.

Another element introduced by Huxley is "the principle of sleep-teaching, or hypnopaedia." Young children are taught by recordings that work on their unconscious minds while they are sleeping. Hence, they absorb the values of the society.

Huxley thus uses both science and psychology to create a future world where all are happy, there is stability, and conflict is ended. Of course, what he fears is that much of what we regard as being human would disappear.

Huxley's world was only a few steps from what was being proposed in several quarters in 1930, represented by the new science of eugenics.

The term eugenics (from the Greek *eu*, "good" or "happy") was also invented in the Victorian period. It was coined by Francis Galton, a cousin of Charles Darwin, in 1883. He used it to describe his idea of taking a Darwinian category, Variation under Domestication, and applying it to human heredity. In effect, he proposed that humans now had the opportunity to shape human society and intelligence in progressive ways. Hence, as he defined it, eugenics was "the study of all agencies under human control which can improve or impair the racial quality of future generations."[7]

In the 1920s, eugenics was considered a legitimate branch of science and social philosophy. It became an academic discipline. Some universities had departments of eugenics, and many offered courses on the subject. International Eugenics Conferences were held in London and New York in 1912, 1921, and 1932. Many important figures and groups associated with progressive politics were interested in its possibilities, including Havelock Ellis, Margaret Sanger, H.G. Wells, John Maynard Keynes, Theodore Roosevelt, and many Swedish social democrats. Another of Huxley's brothers, Julian, a prominent evolutionary biologist, was a member of the British Genetics Society and served as its vice-president from 1937 to 1944 and president from 1959 to 1962.

Genetics was hardly just an ivory tower pursuit in 1930. Governments saw it a way of dealing with undesirables in their population, especially those they regarded as unfit. This included the deaf, blind, mentally unstable, homosexuals, prostitutes, alcoholics, even sometimes the poor. The remedies included sterilization, euthanasia, abortions, even proposing genocide in the case of outsiders such as the Roma. Lawmakers passed the first laws related to eugenics in the United States in the early twentieth century. They were followed by Belgium, Sweden, Canada, and Brazil, among others. In the West, government agencies used sterilization on certain groups, and scientists who adhered to the movement performed experiments on individuals. Inevitably, eugenics bled into what was being discussed as "racial science," a kind of combination of eugenics with social Darwinism.

Hence, one of the things that Huxley was doing in *Brave New World* was to open the question of the ethics of genetic engineering. Bioethics was not a field in 1930, but Huxley's work made a contribution to its founding. His work still suggests that it is as serious an issue today as it was in 1930. Science is natural philosophy, but it also raises profound issues in moral philosophy.

Another important feature of the World State is its attempt to stop change, providing what it calls stability in its place. Henry Ford hardly uttered many quotable statements, but the one most used in the society that reveres him is "History is bunk."

Change is menacing. It creates unhappiness and conflict. Hence, the World State exists in an eternal present and works hard to keep it that way. No one is permitted to study history. These new human beings are like Ortega's mass man who is parachuted into the world. In this case, they have no ancestors, no parents, and no past. They have only the World State and the desire to be happy. Humans are standardized products. If there is an "end to history," it is to be found in the brave new world.

Two other important elements are part of the lives of the people living in A.F. 632. They are soma and a new sexual ethics and practice. Soma is a drug designed to elevate the mood and produce a condition of euphoria in those who take it. "[T]here is always soma, delicious soma, half a gramme for a half holiday, a gramme for a weekend, two grammes for a trip to the gorgeous East, three for a dark eternity on the moon." The drug is used by all, an integral part of being. It has, says one character, "all the advantages of Christianity and alcohol; none of their defects."

"Everyone belongs to everyone else" is one of the many sayings taught to all. Simply, sexual pleasure is encouraged as personal freedom no longer exists. There is no commitment or social sanction regarding who you copulate with or how often you do so with any number of partners. Libido is looked after in the World State, but it has no meaning at all. Love, of course, if there is such a thing, is directed to the authorities and to conforming behaviour. There are no serious relationships.

In this world, one of the great fears is that of being alone. All is done in concert and in tandem with others. Being alone creates enormous tension and a sense of feeling outside society.

Huxley also sees the future as one that is directed to consumption and the furtherance of production in balance with need. "Ending is better than mending" is the commandment. It is necessary to have production as a way of giving the population something to do, and to keep balance, order, and stability.

The cult of youth, or at least the appearance of youth, is made into a fixed belief. People look youthful, carefully look after their bodies, use creams and balms, until they are sixty. Then, "crack! the end."

There are rituals designed to reinforce the system. Solidarity Service Days are in place, slogans have the status of religious dogma, games are designed to both entertain and produce social conformity, songs, extraordinarily banal, are sung. In one ritual for twelve people,

> Ford we are twelve; oh, make us one,
>   Like drops within the Social River;
> Oh, make us now together run
>   As swiftly as thy shining Flivver.

There is no poetry, just as there is no history. Rhyming is used only in the service of the World State.

Huxley does introduce some persons and personalities into this regimented and orderly society. Bernard Marx is an Alpha who has feelings, even guilt, and who reflects on his condition. His Alpha friend, Helmholtz Watson, has a desire to be creative. Both were different. Marx was physically small, said to be the result of an error in the laboratory during his creation. Watson was excessively smart and able. Both were somehow aware that they were individuals and could experience a wider range of emotion than others; indeed, they had emotions.

There are other societies on the edge of the World State. Bernard takes Lenina Crowne, a vaccination labourer at the Hatchery, a normal, beautiful woman, to visit a Savage Reservation in New Mexico. The reservation is regarded as primitive and ugly, a place that offers no threat to the stability of the world, but has customs and manners from the ancient days. If anything, the reservation and its peoples are regarded and treated as freaks by those who are "civilized." Safety is provided to them by an electrified fence around the reservation.

The Savage Reservation immediately terrifies Lenina. Some who live there look old, others practise rituals that seem horrific, such as self-flagellation to ask the gods to bring rain in order to grow corn. It is an experience in moving backward in history: families, strange extinct languages, disease, wild creatures, religion.

They meet John, a strange young member of the reservation. He is blond, blue-eyed, and speaks English, though some of his English is archaic. "Good-morrow," he says as he greets Bernard and Linda, "you're civilized, aren't you? You come from the Other Place, outside the Reservation?"

John explains that his mother is also from the Other Place. She fell while visiting the Reservation some years ago. Her companion abandoned her, returning to the World State.

His mother, Linda, appears. She smells of alcohol, is overweight, dirty, and ugly, and is thrilled to meet "civilized" people. She had been pregnant when she was rescued by the Indians on the Reservation because the contraceptives she had used were faulty. The Reservation had no abortion facilities, so she gave birth to John. As well, there is no soma in the Savage Reservation, but there is mescal and alcohol, and Linda is addicted to both.

Linda and John are treated badly by the reservation's inhabitants. Linda was regarded as a prostitute who could not accommodate or even understand (she was a Beta-minus) the savage practice of monogamy. John is an outsider, denied the opportunity to participate in important rite of passage rituals, traumatized by how Linda is ostracized and mocked by the community, and how she is abused by the men there.

Linda tries to educate John by teaching him to read and telling him about the Other Place, which she pictures as a kind of utopia in contrast to the reservation. The key moment comes when John is twelve. Linda gives John an ancient book her lover found in an old chest. She assumes it is vulgar and "uncivilized," but thinks it might be useful to help John with his reading. It is called *The Complete Works of William Shakespeare*, one of the vast library of books forbidden in the Other Place.

Shakespeare is miraculous. He teaches John about what it is to be human, helps him to understand his emotions, to articulate how he feels, and even to nurture the new in his body and soul.

Several years later, John again is forbidden to be part of a savage ritual. He is pulled out of the ranks by someone who says that "the son of the she-dog" cannot join the ceremony. Others stone him. He runs away, contemplates suicide, and then, the narrator tells us, "He had discovered Time and Death and God." Those are main concepts forbidden in "civilized" society, and John will later find that he is not simply an outsider on the reservation, but he will have great difficulty dealing with life in the Other Place.

After John relates his story to Bernard, he talks about being "alone, always alone." Bernard not only empathizes, he too says that he feels "terribly alone."

As it turns out, John Savage, as he comes to be called, is a cultured person compared to the ciphers produced in the civilized world, the ironic "brave new world" of the title. John has some understanding of both aboriginal myth and the Christian religion, delights in reading, knows his Shakespeare, and is curious and self-reflective. He uses *Hamlet* to deal with his feelings toward his mother and her lovers, and *Romeo and Juliet* helps him to articulate his initial desire for Lenina. The novel thus asks a question that other important, later, speculative fiction works will contemplate. What does it mean to be human?

The people in civilized society in Huxley's work are in Eden, but it is an Eden where no one even contemplates eating the apple or learning from the tree of knowledge. It is a world before the Fall, where there is no consciousness, no choice, no desire for self-determination. No one loves, no one suffers. They exist in an eternal present. They are bodies without souls.

Four characters do have consciousness. They are John Savage, Bernard Marx, Helmholtz Watson, and one of the ten Controllers of the World State whose dominion includes England, Mustapha Mond.

John and Linda are taken out of the reservation to England. John has several encounters that demonstrate to him how odd he must seem to the ordinary members of that society. He desires Lenina and Lenina "wants" him, but those are two very different emotions. Lenina takes soma, goes to John's apartment and offers herself to him in the normal manner of a sexual encounter in the World State. John attempts to tell her of his feelings for her and uses Shakespeare to help him articulate them.

He wants the ritual of love, he wants to perform a task that will show him worthy of his beloved, he wants ceremony. John even talks about living together, monogamy. Linda is befuddled, and simply starts to undress. "Hug me till you drug me, honey … kiss me till I'm in a coma," she says.

John is repelled. "Whore, impudent strumpet," he shouts. "Get out of my sight." Lenina is confused and fearful, John is angry and resentful. There is no opportunity for romance or love in this society.

John then learns that his mother is dying. Linda is in the Park Lane Hospital for the Dying, the only person who looks old, for aging comes quickly in the World State, and then you die. John recalls the Linda of his youth, telling him "stories about the Other Place, outside the Reservation, that beautiful, beautiful Other Place, whose memory, as of a heaven, a paradise of goodness and loveliness, he still kept whole and intact."

Eight-year-old children enter the ward in uniforms, moving everywhere, peering into the faces of the dying, and comment on how strange Linda looks, so fat, with bad teeth. They are being "death-conditioned," John is told. He reacts with anger at this lack of respect and is told he is strange. When Linda dies soon thereafter, John sobs uncontrollably, and is instructed to behave in front of the children.

John rebels. He encounters the work staff of the hospital, all Deltas at the end of their shift, when they are being given their daily ration of soma. He realizes what must be done. "Stop," he yells. "Don't take that horrible stuff. It's poison, it's poison…. Poison to the soul as well as the body."

He asks, "Do you like being slaves?" He opens a window and starts throwing out the boxes of soma. Bernard and Helmholtz enter and attempt to rescue him, though Bernard, filled with insecurity and fearful, tries to deny his association with the savage to the authorities. Soma vapour is then sent into the room, a calm voice starts reciting Anti-Riot Speech Number Two (Medium Strength). Order and normality are quickly restored.

John, Bernard, and Helmholtz are taken by the officials to a room that is the study of the Controller, Mustapha Mond. A Gamma butler informs them, "His fordship will be down in a moment."

What follows are encounters that appear in many dystopian works, especially those that project an authoritarian, conforming society, such as the two works most closely associated and compared to *Brave New World*, the earlier *We* (1921) by Zamiatin and the later *1984* (1949) by Orwell. The philosophical centre of the work is discussed, and in this case debated, by the central ruler with the non-conformists and rebels.

The book that dominates Mond's study is a massive tome, entitled *My Life and Work*, by Our Ford. John Savage browses through it but finds it uninteresting. When Mustapha Mond appears, he addresses John: "So you don't much like civilization?" John shakes his head.

However, the Controller then surprisingly quotes from *Othello*. John asks how he knows it, since he thought no one knew about Shakespeare. Mond notes that since he makes the laws he can also break them, and that he is one of the few with some knowledge of Shakespeare.

John wonders aloud why it is prohibited. "Because it's old.... We haven't any use for old things here," Mond replies. Besides, people in the World State of A.F. 632 will never understand *Othello*, he notes. "The world's stable now. People are happy; they get what they want and they never want what they can't get." They are conditioned perfectly.

As for liberty, he says to John, which you raise when you throw soma out the window, how can you expect people who are ciphers to know what liberty might be? He admits *Othello* is better than the "feelies" that are regularly shown, but stability is more important. "You've got to choose between happiness and what people used to call high art. We've sacrificed the high art. We have the feelies and the scent organ instead."

Yes, he claims, stability is dull, especially compared to struggle or passion. But it is desirable. "Happiness is never grand."

Mond cites two experiments. The first was to establish a society of twenty-two thousand Alphas on the island of Cyprus in A.F. 473. What occurred? "The land wasn't properly worked; there were strikes in all the factories." Chaos reigned and civil war resulted. Nineteen thousand were killed, and the remainder asked the World State to enter and govern.

The second experiment was conducted on another island, Ireland. People were given more leisure, they worked only four hours daily, which could work economically. All that happened was "unrest and a large increase in the consumption of soma." Mond states that people do not want freedom; indeed, they cannot handle it.

He admits that there is a cost, the end of art as it was known, and restrictions on the development of new science. Stability means that clear limits are placed on the introduction of the new.

Then he gets personal. He tells the three men that he, too, was a young person who wanted to experience more than was permitted. He was a scientist who began to work on new knowledge, stretching the limitations of society. He reveals that he was nearly sent to an island, which is, he tells Bernard and Helmholtz, what is going to happen to them. Bernard reacts badly and is escorted from the room. Helmholtz behaves in a dignified and curious manner.

What happens in the World State is that conscious dissenters are ostracized to an island with individuals like themselves, people who Mond notes are interesting and creative. Helmholtz, who has started to write subversive poetry about his own inner life, finds this appealing. But, he asks Mond, "Why aren't you on an island yourself?"

Mond tells them he was given a choice between ostracism and joining the group of people governing, with the possible future position of Controller. He chose the latter.

Huxley doesn't elaborate, but there is an important insight here. Mond's choice is not about ideology or identity, it is about power. We have learned that in those states governed by a single party that claims perfection, whether left or right, the leaders are attracted to power while claiming to be bringing a brave new world into being; they are what Milovan Djilas in 1957 called the new class. This occurs in Fascism, whether in Italy, Spain, or elsewhere, and it occurs in those states that claim to be Communist, whether in Djilas's Yugoslavia, Russia, Cuba, or in modern-day China. Mond is seduced not by wealth or beauty but by power, which he cherishes.

The idea of ostracism is hardly new, for in the classical West, for example, it was offered to Socrates and imposed upon Ovid, among others. Huxley later remarked that this solution regarding intelligent dissent is far more humane than what occurs in other dystopias. He should also have noted that it is also far more benign than what occurred in many authoritarian states. Unfortunately, Huxley does not tell us how life on any island of eccentrics is structured, and whether it is satisfying. It is left to the reader's imagination.

Mond says he has some regret that he did not choose the path of science, but this lament is not at all convincing. Truth, he says, is menacing, and he must carry on his duty. He even claims that he is paying for his choice, but deserves no sympathy.

Then he informs Helmholtz that he has a choice of islands. What climate? What atmosphere? Helmholtz cleverly says he would prefer a terrible climate, for that would be more conducive to writing creatively. How about the Falklands? asks Mond. "Yes, that will do," replies Helmholtz, and he leaves.

Now only Mond and John Savage are left to go further with the discussion. Mond is not The Grand Inquisitor, to whom Huxley referred in a later discussion of his work, but he is the Fordian equivalent.

What about religion? asks John. No need, replies Mond, we no longer have a place for God. "'The religious sentiment will compensate us for all our losses.' But there aren't any losses for us to compensate; religious sentiment is superfluous." After all, no one suffers, no one has doubt, no one needs to transcend the present. Now, the Bible and religious works are in the safe, and Ford is the book on the shelves. In A.F 632, God manifests himself as an absence. Mond sums up, "Christianity without tears—that's what soma is."

John argues for nobility, courage, and passion. Tears, he claims, are a necessary part of a full life, citing Shakespeare. The problem with this civilization is that "nothing costs enough here."

Oh, says Mond, we understand that people need stimulation occasionally. Every citizen has compulsory V.P.S. (Violent Passion Surrogate) treatment, once each month. It floods peoples' bodies with "adrenin." "It's the physiological equivalent of fear and rage. All the tonic effects of murdering Desdemona and being murdered by Othello, without any of the inconveniences."

John insists that he likes those inconveniences. How ridiculous, replies Mond, you want the right to be unhappy. Yes, John states, that's my claim. Well then, says Mond, you will grow old, be ugly, suffer diseases, live in want and filth, fear the future, be in pain.

John ends the discussion: "I claim them all." He claims the right to consciousness and humanity, to have a history, to abandon Eden for the vicissitudes of a life.

In a letter to E.M. Forster written in 1935, Huxley relates that he just had lunch with his friend Bertrand Russell, who argued that those things conditioned by science were progressing, and that this fact was more important than "superficial" matters like ideas, political change, and social manners, even wars. Huxley dissented: "It's nice to think so; but meanwhile there the superficial undulations are, and one lives superficially; and who knows if that superficial trajectory isn't aiming directly for some fantastic denial of humanity."[8]

John is visited by Bernard and Helmholtz before they leave for their island. He reports that he again saw the Controller, this time to ask him to be able to join his friends and go to the island. But "he wouldn't let me...."

He said he wanted to go on with the experiment." John says he refuses to be an experiment. It is time for him to be alone.

He leaves London to live in an abandoned lighthouse. He also revives some of the rituals and elements of life he had while on the Savage Reservation, believing they are more authentic than anything found in "civilization." He purifies himself by making prayers to various deities and imitates Christ on the cross. He then makes a bow and arrows from an ash tree and makes plans to garden and hunt in order to provide himself with food.

Part of the purification is a ceremony in which he beats himself with a whip he has fashioned to the point of drawing blood. John is unaware that his actions are witnessed by three Delta Minuses, and they in turn report the incident.

After this, John is no longer alone. He is photographed and captured on film by a reporter, and he becomes the subject of a popular "feely" called *The Savage of Surrey*. Now he becomes a public freak. Many come and ask that he whip himself in public. The ciphers of "civilization" find pain "a fascinating horror." He is imitated by a mob in a wild bacchanalia, full of frenzy, assisted by soma.

John is horrified by what has happened. He realizes that he belongs nowhere. He cannot return to the Reservation, where he was not permitted to participate in significant community rituals anyway, and the world of the Controller is empty and will never leave him alone. He kills himself.

If Huxley offers any hope, it lies on the islands and the reservations, but these societies seem to have no chance against the power and determination of the World State. It is the world of Ford that will destroy the humanity of Shakespeare.

Huxley remained an important public intellectual for the next three decades, until his death in 1963. He moved in the 1930s to supporting pacifism, then developed a deep interest and wrote many pieces about Eastern mysticism. He lived in the United States from 1937, did some work for Hollywood, and continued to write essays and fiction.

In the 1950s Huxley was introduced to peyote, mescaline, and LSD, and became one of the earliest advocates for the use of experimental drugs to alter consciousness and perception. Hippie culture adopted him. One of his later works was *The Doors of Perception* (1954), in which he described his experiences with mescaline. The title is taken from a quotation in William Blake's *The Marriage of Heaven and Hell* (1790–1793): "If the doors of perception were cleansed everything would appear to man as it is, infinite. For man has closed himself up, till he sees all things through narrow chinks of his cavern."[9] The legendary Jim Morrison—who died at age twenty-seven in 1971, almost certainly from a heroin overdose—and his rock group took their name, The Doors, from the title of Huxley's meditation on drugs.

Huxley's last major work was a kind of utopia, *Island*, published in 1962, a year before he died. Here, he reversed the drugged society of *Brave New World*. Drugs are used on the island to achieve spiritual enlightenment and self-fulfillment. The work is heavily influenced by Huxley's interest in Eastern philosophy and religion and in altering states of consciousness to achieve what was called "oneness." In the end Huxley argued for a merger of East and West, but he clearly abandoned the culture he grew up in. His "enlightenment" was close to the opposite of that defined by Kant.

Huxley was a lover of Shakespeare, but his *Island* is not his version of Shakespeare's *Tempest*. Rather, it is the earlier *Brave New World* that consciously is far closer to the last great play of Shakespeare. The bard's title comes from the moment Miranda sees the party of the King of Naples, the first men she sees other than her father Prospero, including Ferdinand, to whom she will be engaged. She exclaims:

> O, wonder!
> How many goodly creatures are there here!
> How beauteous mankind is! O brave new world,
> That has such people in't![10]

The characters in *Brave New World* have parallels in Shakespeare. John Savage is close to Ferdinand, Bernard Marx has qualities similar to those of Caliban, Lenina is a worldly and debased Miranda, and Mustapha Mond is a Prospero who is of this world, not an island, and who thus makes different choices. Huxley's work is more pessimistic than that of Shakespeare's, reflecting his concern that civilization will defeat goodness and virtue. Shakespeare leaves that ending open, while Huxley does not.[11]

Huxley's work has had enormous influence on thinking about the future in the West. He not only wrote an important dystopia, he also contributed to profoundly shaping the genre. Like Mann, Woolf, Ortega, Brecht, and Freud, we think today as we do in part because of how he taught us to reflect upon the world.

8 FREUD
The Fragility of Civilization

SIGMUND FREUD, ONE of the two most influential and famous intellects of his time, was growing old in 1930. Born in 1856, living in Vienna, Freud had had cancer of the jaw and since 1923 wore a large prosthesis that was always uncomfortable and often painful. There were other complications as well. He wrote in a letter of December 1929:

> The greatest part of my activity has to be devoted to maintaining that amount of health needed to carry on my daily work. A real mosaic of therapeutic measures to compel various organs to serve this purpose. Recently my heart has joined in with extra-systolic arhythmia [*sic*] and attacks of palpitation. My wise physician, Professor Braun, says that all that has no serious significance. He ought to know. Is he already beginning to swindle? One cannot avoid one's fate: perhaps medical deception is also part of that.[1]

Along with Albert Einstein, with whom he would soon carry on an important correspondence about the nature of humanity, Freud was recognized universally in the West as a giant. Many found cause to disagree with some of his ideas, and some of his own pupils challenged him, but he is the person who, moving from neurology to psychology and psychoanalysis, changed the dialogue about human nature forever. His reflections on our complex inner life, our conscious and unconscious, the conflicts and contradictions with which we live, on sanity, insanity, and madness, became central to how humans understood themselves as individuals and social beings. To challenge him was to take on a master, to ignore him was impossible.

Like Mann and many others, Freud was transformed by the Great War, its violence and deaths. Who were we that we could cause so much suffering and meaningless chaos? What have we constructed in that thing we call civilization that might have contributed to the carnage?

It was not until 1947 that W.H. Auden wrote the work *The Age of Anxiety*, which gave its title to the post–Great War era. But the issue and pessimism were apparent throughout the 1920s, given expression by T.S. Eliot, W.B. Yeats, Ernest Hemingway, Paul Valéry, George Grosz, and many others. Freud in the late 1920s reflected on the problems of the time and sat down in the summer of 1929 to write a contemplative essay, *Das Unbehagen in der Kultur*, published at the end of that year, with a publication date of 1930, a book Peter Gay calls "probably his best-known work."[2]

Freud's original title for the short book was *Das Unglück in der Kultur* (*Unhappiness in Civilization*). He changed it to *Das Unbehagen in der Kultur,* *unbehagen* connoting discomfort, unease, or disquiet. He then suggested to the English translator, Joan Riviere, that the English title be *Man's Discomfort in Civilization*. Noting that in the text Freud associates the word *unbehagen* with *unzufriedenheit*, which means dissatisfied or discontented, Riviere correctly decided on *Civilization and Its Discontents*, for while Freud, as always, focused on the individual, the work is about the viability of civilization in general and current Western civilization in particular.[3]

The essay is meditative in tone. Freud interweaves a number of thoughts, suggestions, and conclusions in a way that makes it accessible to readers who were part of the educated public. Here, like Woolf, Ortega, Mann, Brecht, and others, he is taking on the role of the concerned and responsible public intellectual.

Indeed, Freud starts with an issue virtually ignored by many others at the time, the nature and understanding of religion and its role in society. Clearly Freud, who was Jewish in ancestry and identity, though an unbeliever the whole of his life, saw some issues that needed to be taken into account, matters raised by people like Feuerbach, Kierkegaard, Dostoyevsky, and Nietzsche before him. In the modern world there is a great deal of suffering; what meaning might it have? Also, how do we deal with those feelings that we might call spiritual in the modern world where there is a devaluing of spiritual life?

Like those earlier thinkers, Freud implicitly rejects the notion that traditional religious institutional structures can deal meaningfully with these matters. His discussion refers to his earlier work, *The Future of an Illusion* (1927), and what he calls an "oceanic feeling" claimed by some people, including his friend, the well-known and popular novelist Romain Rolland (1866–1944), who won the Nobel Prize in Literature in 1915 with a citation that spoke of "the lofty idealism of his literary production."

Freud accepts that his friend and others might have this feeling, and that it might be something that gives one a sense of a connection with a wider world. It may even be used by organized religions to direct people to their institutions and belief systems.

The ego has needs, and finding meaning is important. Freud likens the oceanic feeling to the emotion of being in love, when "the boundary between ego and object threatens to melt away."[4] But in the end Freud follows the path earlier taken by Feuerbach in concluding it is culture and human needs that create the gods. The oceanic feeling is a reflection of a need, and that need translates itself into a kind of infantile helplessness in the face of the travails of the world and "a longing for the father."

There is consolation in this feeling, but it is one that does not want to deal with the problem raised by Nietzsche, that "God is dead" and we abandoned human beings now need to deal, unaided, with how to find structure and meaning. Religion had answered the question of the purpose of life for the entire culture. Now, purpose is found by the ego, not by a religious system.

Freud's focusing on the ego is something that others had done and will do. It was Kierkegaard who recognized that the thrust of modernity was to make people into objects. Hence, one of the ways the "I" finds meaning, he said, is via the "Thou" of god. The I-It becomes an I-Thou. There is an intimacy that turns object into subject. Later, in existential theology, this relationship will be proposed as the only meaningful one in our dealings with other people as a way of demonstrating and retaining our humanity.

Carrying on with this concept, Freud later in the essay discusses the Biblical cultural norm that exhorts humans to "love thy neighbour as thyself." He regards this as an impossible task, even a harmful one, especially because it inflates our ego, and such a love can only lower the value of love itself. Indeed, he argues that following such a precept puts one in a very difficult situation with regard to others who may not subscribe to this canon. He ironically comments that this cultural norm is taken so seriously by society that the more difficult it is to put in practice, the more value is placed on it.

Freud ends the discussion with a quote from Goethe:

> Wer Wissenschaft und Kunst besitzt, hat auch Religion;
> Wer jene beide nicht besizt, der habe Religion!
>
> (Who has knowledge and art, also has religion;
> Who has neither of the two, let him have religion!)

The common man, Ortega's mass man, may need religion—or as Freud will hypothesize, what he calls a parent and what others will call a belief system outside of himself to compensate for his frustrations and suffering. Others will find their own consolations.

Freud thus acknowledges that life is difficult—"it brings us too many pains, disappointments and impossible tasks." We need to take action to deal with this feeling. He discusses three kinds of behaviour, all associated with the pleasure principle, the idea that we seek pleasure, though it is a goal impossible to fulfill completely in society.

The first pattern of behaviour is that of "powerful deflections, which cause us to make light of our misery." We accept the unhappiness that comes with being human in society and find ways to counter it. The example used by Freud is Voltaire's advice in the famous last sentence of *Candide*, that we should "cultivate our garden." Don't pretend this is the best of all possible worlds; instead, find who you are, take pleasure in shaping the self and in tasks that satisfy.

Another of what Freud calls palliative acts is to imbibe "intoxicating substances," which desensitize us to the cares of our ego. We alter our bodies and its chemistry in order to obtain immediate pleasure, or to shelter us from pain. Yet, Freud noted the danger of this choice as well as the fact that it wastes much human energy "which might have been employed for the improvement of the human lot."

Much attention is given to the third choice, that which Freud calls "substitutive satisfactions," which he believes can go far in helping us to take refuge from pain and obtain much pleasure in civilization. In many earlier works Freud discussed the roles of sublimation and transference in providing us with meaning.

What occurs is that we find acceptable outlets for unacceptable desires. We may want satisfying sexual experiences as often as we like, but we cannot have them in civilization. So we find outlets for these desires that give some consolation. For Freud, one of these is in the production and appreciation of art. For those who engage in its experience, he notes, art gives enormous pleasure—though in the end it is periodic and does not fully substitute for libidinal or other instinctual needs.

Another way we can obtain satisfaction is to join a community working for goals that are beneficial to humanity. Hence, the worthiness of our efforts, and their clear acceptability to others, provide an experience which gives much pleasure.

A source of satisfaction for many is found in the feelings associated with love, of being in love, and being loved by another. Freud asserts that sexual love, which fully if only temporarily satisfies our desire, is among the most profound of human experiences that can provide pleasure.

But love has its limits as well. Romantic love is opposed to civilization and social order, for the loved one now has greater value than anything else. Hence, as we know, the Western idea of romantic love is associated with tragedy and often ends in the death of one or both of the lovers.

Love also can bring great sorrow, as deep as the happiness it can provide. For we are never so vulnerable as when we abandon our ego and unite it with another. We are, as Freud says, no more defenceless against misery and suffering as when we love, for to lose our loved one or the love of our loved one is to encounter profound and unmitigated sorrow.

The enjoyment of beauty is another satisfaction greatly valued by civilization. It even has an effect on us that corresponds to that oceanic feeling and/or what we get from intoxication. It is an enormous compensation for the woes we feel and the suffering we experience. It proves to us that life has something that is worthwhile and, on occasion, transcendent.

Action, too, can be a source of satisfaction. We try out our strength in order to master the external world. That could be in a quest for power in athletic endeavours, or simply engaging in acts that satisfy our id and are acceptable to society. Some of this can be provided by society itself. Clearly, part of the understanding of the growth of fascism is that it can satisfy our need for community and provide an outlet for violence. A true fascist is not someone who does violence to another because he dislikes his ideology or origins. He is someone who does violence because it gives him pleasure, and is grateful to the regime that provides that outlet.

It was Dostoyevsky who first remarked on the paradox that civilization is at once both orderly and progressive and destructive, giving insight into what he claimed about us only a few years after Freud was born. We build, we love power. Dostoyevsky's Underground Man tells his reader:

> Man loves construction and the laying out of roads, that is indisputable. But how is it that he is so passionately disposed to destruction and chaos …? Doesn't his passionate love for destruction and chaos (and nobody can deny that he is sometimes devoted to them; that is a fact) arise from his instinctive fear of attaining his goal and completing the building he is erecting? For all you know, perhaps it is only from a distance that he likes the building and from close to it he doesn't like it at all; perhaps he likes building it, not living in it.[5]

Through building and destroying we obtain some kind of happiness. The goal is everything; attaining it is a time for destruction and for a new dialectic to start.

Power is not only tempting, it is a way civilization develops. But power for an individual can also provide, as Goethe's Faust experiences, as great a pleasure as those things that fulfill our libidinal needs. Power and money are libidinal in the modern world.

We must always remember, Freud tells us, that things are not as they seem. Our acts are often ways in which we fulfill our needs through sublimation and transference. Yes, a cigar might sometimes just be a cigar, an automobile might just be an automobile, and a monument might just be a monument. But mostly they are not.

The great problem with civilization is that its nature is a contradiction. It provides a haven and structure, and it makes us unhappy at the same time. Freud defined civilization in the following manner: "[It] describes the whole sum of the achievements and the regulations which distinguish our lives from those of our animal ancestors and which serve two purposes—namely to protect men against nature and to adjust their mutual relations."[6]

Hence, civilization provides much that we value and that makes our lives pleasant and meaningful. It protects us against nature, gives us shelter and warmth. Invention and application have enabled us, by 1930, to extend our resources, to see with the aid of spectacles, to talk to one another from afar over the telephone, to capture images with photography, to write and communicate, to exploit the resources of nature through cultivation and technology for our benefit.

Freud follows Nietzsche in suggesting that in the modern world we have "almost become a god." That is, if the gods are created by culture as psychological needs and explanations of how things came about, we are now doing what the gods are said to have done. Freud suggests that humans have become "prosthetic gods." Never have we had more power to protect ourselves against nature and build satisfactory lives.

In addition, civilization values beauty, cleanliness, and order, as well as artistic, scientific, and intellectual achievements. Finally, it demands that the individual live within a community, a rule of law rather than one of will and force.

Like Marx, Freud praises the accomplishments of modernity, and has no nostalgia for earlier times. He does not share Rousseau's love of an idealized life before there was community or believe in the notion of the noble savage. Marx praised the bourgeoisie for what they accomplished, and Freud believes in the value of development. But both find modern civilization inadequate because, in different ways, both believe it produces great suffering.

It is said that Marx thought society was sick, and human beings were sane. For Freud it is far more complex—society produces sickness and human beings consequently have anxiety and neuroses.

Freud argues that at one and the same time we need civilization, and we are terribly frustrated by it. What occurs is that the demands of

civilization—of being in a society that peacefully organizes our mutual relations—require all of us to put limits on our desires, in effect to act against our
id by valuing the superego. This conflict is inevitable in any society. What we
want to do—to have sexual experiences to satisfy our libidinal instincts, to
destroy those who oppose us by violent means, to take revenge for whatever
slights we see done against us—cannot be done in an orderly society. It was
Francis Bacon who called revenge "wild justice," and who said that however
just it may sometimes be, it cannot be part of civilized life.

The limits result minimally in frustration, often in a forsaking of happiness. Thus, we need civilization and are at the same time uncomfortable in it,
to the point of severe neuroses in some cases. If the liberty of the individual
as a goal is one of the gifts of modern Western culture, then Freud suggests
that it is limited by law and the need for peace in our relationships.

> The liberty of the individual is no gift of civilization. It was greatest
> before there was any civilization, though then, it is true, it had for the
> most part no value, since the individual was scarcely in a position to
> defend it. The development of civilization imposes restrictions on it,
> and justice demands that no one shall escape those restrictions.

Civilization forces sublimation. It requires us to be something we are not.
We must give up our instinctual needs and desires. It makes life possible and
it makes us unhappy.

Conflict is an important piece of modern thought. It was Hegel who
initiated modern dialectical thinking, and conflicts became both the norm
and the motive force of history. Darwin and Marx both use conflict—Marx's
favourite word was *kampf*, conflict—as substantial parts of their understanding of our development as a species and socially.

For Freud, conflict is part of our normal mental life. The ego is caught
between those two very demanding masters: the id, which instinctually
shapes our desire; and the superego, which tells us not what we should do
but what we ought to do, in following the conventions of civilization. In
society, the conventions win.

The example Freud gives is the place and propriety of our sexual life in
civilization. Western civilization at the time permits these relations only in
marriage, in a relationship between one man and one woman. (Freud did
not here comment on patriarchal society permitting, in some places, sexual activity outside of marriage for men; nor did he comment on a matter
important today, sexual relations between members of the same sex, which
many in 1930 not only saw as perversion, but also labelled the desire as
insane.)

Hence, "the sexual life of civilized man is ... severely impaired." We trade frustration for security. Civilization has built-in psychic discontents.

Indeed, Freud recognizes that the ties that bind us are not simply rational self-interest. He echoes Thomas Mann in noting that our commitment to a community is libidinal and that communities, be they religious or civil, appeal to our unconscious and irrational desires.

The problem is in our nature. If the argument about human nature in the modern world is one of a cross-conversation between Descartes, Hobbes, and Locke, in 1930, after the Great War, for Freud and many others it is Hobbes who wins.

> [M]en are not gentle creatures who want to be loved, and who at the most can defend themselves if they are attacked; they are, on the contrary, creatures among whose instinctual endowments is to be reckoned a powerful share of aggressiveness.

"Homo homini lupus," claims Freud. "Man is wolf to man."

The emphasis on this part of our nature is something Freud develops after 1914. Now, he notes, we no longer can see our neighbour only as someone who might be a friend, but as a person who wants our property, seeks to exploit, has little respect for our person, who might even wish to "cause [us] pain, torture and kill [us]."

If this seems outlandish in 1930, it will appear prescient in 1945. Freud is hardly predicting the gulags, the Bloodlands, and the gas chambers. However, he is on to something that is occurring in Western culture, as neighbours and others will commit unspeakable acts against their fellow human beings and seem to take pleasure in doing so.

This hostility has consequences. The most important is that civilization "is perpetually threatened with disintegration" as a result of our own nature. Hobbes wins: without civilization life would be, as he famously describes, solitary, poor, nasty, brutish, and short.

Culture and civilization, Freud is saying in 1930—and others will echo him only a few years later—is far more fragile than we thought. We must constantly reinforce those things that keep it going: the limitations on our sexual life, the rule of law, the restrictions on our aggressive nature, and the hopeless commandment to love our neighbours, even if we don't like them. If what Auden called the "low, dishonest decade" of the 1930s and then the war of 1939–1945 that followed did not occur, we might accuse Freud of overdoing the pessimism about our relationships. As it is, he simply preceded *1984* and *The Lord of the Flies* in his understanding of what we might do to one another.

Freud critiques Communism in his work and challenges its analysis from the standpoint of his understanding of human nature. In doing so, he finds the weakest part of the Marxist analysis of society and where it ought to go.

He notes that the Communist premise is that we are good, and that the institution of private property and the capitalist system is what has corrupted our nature and relationships. He disagrees with the Marxist notion, as Marx put it in his Economic and Philosophical Manuscripts of 1844, that "private property is ... the product, the result, the necessary consequence, of alienated labour, of the external relation of the worker to nature and to himself."[7]

Rather, claims Freud, our aggressiveness is not created by the institution of property. It reigned almost without limit in primitive times. It even exists in the child in the nursery. We can abolish private property, but we will not thereby abolish our aggressive nature.

Freud's main point about Marxist Communism is that its view of human nature is deeply flawed. It will be impossible to achieve what it hopes to do. After all, the end of history for Marx and Engels was the moment when there was abundance created by bourgeois capitalism and a new social order in which we share the blessings of abundance, something never heretofore possible. At that time, the two claimed, we will be free from having to spend our time fulfilling our "animal needs" of food and shelter, free to shape ourselves and our history.

This is yet another illusion, like religion, says Freud. We will not treat our neighbour well without some compulsion from law and the collective superego. Even if we pretend to have such a system, some people will love power and authority so much that they will become the new lords of the realm. And, indeed, in systems both communist and capitalist after Freud, elites and the wealthy have benefited themselves, even in circumstances where their neighbours suffer.

Civilization is desirable, even necessary, for our survival. It means that we must sacrifice some parts of our dual nature, our sexuality and aggressiveness. This may make us unhappy regularly, but the alternative is far worse.

If Freud could be put on the political spectrum, something he refused to comment upon, he was something of a liberal democrat supporting social measures, like Thomas Mann or José Ortega y Gasset. He tried to find the best balance between the liberty to lead our own lives and our need for authority to regulate, as he called it, "our mutual relations."

Freud rarely commented on his Jewish ancestry or on Jewish matters to 1930. He did not practise the religion, nor did he ever deny his background. He saw himself as a child of the Enlightenment, pursuing his *wissenschaft*, his intellectual inquiries and discipline, wherever it might lead, even if it produced conclusions that shattered some of the assumptions of the Enlightenment.

Still, it is not possible to conclude that Freud, as self-conscious an intellect as ever there was, would forget that his middle name was Schlomo, the original Hebrew for Solomon in English. Moreover, living in Vienna, he was reminded regularly of his Jewishness, for anti-Semitism was openly part of the political and social worlds in that city and its country. As well, psychiatry in its early years was regularly accused of being something of a Jewish discipline.

In *Civilization and Its Discontents,* Freud made two observations about Jewish people that seem to foreshadow the future, just as Ortega was prophetic about Fascism in *The Revolt of the Masses.*

In talking about community as a binding element in society, Freud uses nationalist examples and discusses his idea of "the narcissism of minor differences." He remarks, ironically, that in many countries in the West Jews have rendered a service by giving their hosts an outlet for their aggressive nature. He further notes that "all the massacres of Jews in the Middle Ages did not suffice to make that period more peaceful and secure for their Christian fellows." Anti-Semitic behaviour is easy, but it does no good, for the violence goes on elsewhere as well.

Later, Freud noted that those who believe in a benign, just, and good God have difficulty dealing with the existence of evil. One way of handling this is to have the Devil be the agent of all that is terrible. He likens this to the Jews acting as agents of the Devil in the economic universe of what he calls "the Aryan ideal." Given the purpose of the essay, Freud is clearly sensing something disturbing happening at the time.

To more clearly state his formulation, Freud puts forth the paradox of life as a "struggle between Eros and Death." Some commentators discuss this as a conflict between Eros and Thanatos, but Freud for some reason never used the term Thanatos in writing about this idea, though he did use it in conversation.[8]

Eros exists both to continue the species and to bind us to one another, while the death instinct accounts for our propensity for destruction and aggression and is seen by Freud as the "greatest impediment to civilization." He proposes that what some regard as human history, the development of civilization, now be understood as the playing out of the struggle between our two instinctual needs. Civilization is "the struggle for life of the human species," certainly not guaranteed at all. There is a new dialectic introduced into discussion, a dialectical instinctualism, different from the dialectical idealism of Hegel and the dialectical materialism of Marx.

Freud did not remark on the existence of a realm of thought in the West that includes both Eros and Death as its province. The rise of the Gothic in the late eighteenth century brought with it both a critique of reason and a fascination with the roles of sexual desire and death in our lives. Eros and Death can combine in such matters as revenants, ghosts, and vampires. After all, the fascination with a character such as Dracula (the novel was published in 1897), who is feared by the West as challenging civilization by bringing the irrational to an ordered society, and who unveils and opens the erotic repressed by civilization, is a reflection of how we try to comprehend some of those issues opened for discussion by Freud and his followers.

In his essay, which Freud is offering to a general reading public, Freud by now clearly fears our Death instinct far more than Eros in the future development or the destruction of civilization. How, then, do we cope?

What civilization does is to have its members internalize their aggressiveness into the ego, and monitor and direct it through the superego. In this case, Freud argues that not only do individuals have a superego, cultures also have them in different periods of history. Freud uses military metaphors to discuss how the superego "weakens" and "disarms" our violence, "like a garrison in a conquered city." We are at war internally between life and death, and we are at war with the *lupis* inside of us all.

Guilt is how it is done. Moreover, we impose guilt on individuals to the point where it is so internalized that the thought of doing something regarded as taboo or evil, not even the act but merely the intention, produces fear, anxiety, and a diminishing sense of self. We have a guilty conscience, and we fear the loss of love if we act in unacceptable ways.

Freud notes that this guilt is understood by those who are religious as sin, though he does not discuss the concept of original sin as a way of dealing with our nature in order to protect civilization. He does, however, note that the early Israelites, who experienced the wrath of their God and at the same time were told they were special, a chosen people, turned to their prophets for an explanation of their misfortunes. They were told they had sinned and that they deserved their punishments. As a result, "out of a sense of guilt they created [their] overstrict commandments."

So guilt arises from three fears: that of authority, that of the superego, which we have internalized, and that of the worry that we will lose love or reputation. Further, Freud does not argue that children are innocent, and that they acquire their violent ways fully as a result of socialization. He is no romantic. Children are themselves aggressive, and in the love–hate relationship with their parents—the Oedipus complex is one example—this is demonstrated. The authority of the family matters, and the understanding of what we ought to do is learned.

Civilization moves from uniting with the family to relating to humanity as a whole. It makes great demands on us, some of which we find very difficult, even intolerable.

Freud notes that in his analytic work as a psychiatrist he has found—to his surprise, he states—"that perhaps every neurosis conceals a quota of unconscious sense of guilt." We can punish ourselves, and as a result find ourselves having difficulty in coping with life. The repression of our nature has a profound psychic price.

Near the end of *Civilization and Its Discontents,* Freud makes the claim that he is not opining on the value of civilization. This is disingenuous. Freud values civilization, though he realizes what we give up in order to achieve it. What he seems to be saying, though not clearly, is that he does not value every ordered society that claims to be civilized. He has, in this book and elsewhere, come down on the side of what he calls a "humanitarian ideal," though not systematically in the manner of a philosopher such as Mill or Ortega. He realizes, as did Mann and others, that civilization can throw up a society that loves the libidinal desire for aggression and death.

Freud claims not to be a prophet, but he is Cassandra-like in his concerns, along with many at the time, though he is more far-sighted than most. He sees his own time, 1930, as an important moment. In his last paragraph Freud tells the reader that the "the fateful question" of the time is whether Western culture can rise to the task of "mastering the disturbance of [its] communal life by the human instinct of aggression and self-destruction." He suggests that now we have both mastered nature and possess the capacity to destroy human life—this even before the notion of nuclear power's possibilities. The book ends with the question of whether Eros can conquer Death, just as in the ancient myth Venus subdued Mars.

The essay, written for the public, was a success, and the first edition sold out by 1931, when a second printing was done. In between there was the German parliamentary election in September 1930, yielding a result that startled many and caused some real fear. The Socialist Party remained the most popular group, gaining 24.5 percent of the vote and 147 seats (of a total of 577) in the Reichstag. However, in second place came the Nazi Party, which increased its support dramatically from 2.6 percent and 12 seats in the election of 1928 to 18.3 percent and 107 seats in 1930. To celebrate, Nazi supporters destroyed shops, department stores, and restaurants associated with Jews.

For the second edition of the book, Freud decided to add one sentence at the end of his last paragraph: "But who can foresee with what success and with what result?" The question is clear, but even today, the answer is still murky.

Freud's musings on survival, instinct, and human nature did not end. Shortly after the publication of the book, he entered into an exchange with Albert Einstein, someone whom he admired, on the issues he raised.

Einstein was active in public life as a leader in peace movements, and soon as a Zionist who favoured the establishment of a Jewish state. He initiated the correspondence with a letter to Freud in 1931.

Einstein made clear that he had read and thought about Freud's concerns, and that he greatly admired his work and the clarity of his thinking. Einstein indicated he hoped that the West's intellectual leaders might have a greater influence on public affairs. He had little respect for the political leaders of his time. "Political leaders or governments owe their power either to the use of force or to their election by the masses. They cannot be regarded as representative of the superior moral or intellectual elements of a nation."[9]

Hence, Einstein asks whether it would be useful for a number of public intellectuals to gather together in a group to discourse about the main moral issues of the time and to try to influence public affairs. "Do you not share the feeling that a change could be brought about by a free association of men whose previous work and achievements offer a guarantee of their ability and integrity?"

Einstein acknowledges the problems that might arise by trying to bring together such as group; after all, he takes account in writing to Freud of what he terms "the imperfections of human nature." Still, it is worth the effort in a difficult time. He believes that many good people feel powerless and are "paralyzed by an attitude of painful resignation." Einstein was not one of those lamented by Yeats who lack conviction.

The purpose of such an association would be to fight against war, which Einstein believes is in the air. It would work with like-minded people in the League of Nations.

Einstein was a participant in an organization called the International Committee on Intellectual Co-operation, associated with the League of Nations. Its first chair was the noted philosopher Henri Bergson, and its members included Thomas Mann, Béla Bartók, Marie Curie, and Paul Valéry. The group asked Einstein to initiate a correspondence with a person of his choosing on the issue of war and peace.

Einstein chose Freud. The two men were already what could best be called colleagues who had great respect, even warm feelings, for one another. Einstein wrote to Freud formally on July 30, 1932, accompanying the letter addressed to "Mr. Freud" with a personal note wishing Freud warm regards and thanking him for the "many a pleasant hour which I had in reading your works."

The issue he asked Freud to discuss was, "Is there a way of delivering mankind from the menace of war?" Einstein does not mention any of Freud's works in his letter, but its language and concerns make it highly probable he had read and thought about *Das Unbehagen in der Kultur*.

Einstein asks Freud to give him some insight into this matter from the viewpoint of someone who has deep knowledge of the inner life of humanity. Einstein, with both modesty and personal understanding, calls himself an amateur in these matters.

Still, Einstein sees both a problem and proposes a solution. The problem is nationalism and its force in the lives of those belonging to nations. The solution is to establish an international body, with both legislative and judicial powers, to deal with those conflicts that arise between nation-states.

Einstein is not naive. He realizes that nations are jealous of their sovereignty, and that human beings are flawed. However, he would like the experiment to occur, something not remotely possible in the current diplomatic and political reality.

Though he is writing to Freud, Einstein posits a psychological factor at work: humans love power, and the governing groups of each nation will resist any limitations. Indeed, though Einstein probably did not consider it, he too, like Freud, is following Hobbes, for the latter claimed not only that power is desirable by humans, but that it is not at all a stable matter, and to keep the power one has, it is necessary to continually attempt to increase it.

As well, Einstein notes that there are economic matters at play. Powerful economic interests see war as an opportunity to increase their wealth and authority. Moreover—sounding in one paragraph like Marx—Einstein suggests that the ruling class has control of the main elements of information and authority, including the schools, the press, and religious institutions, thus—and now he echoes Ortega—giving them great power to influence the emotions and actions of the masses.

He agrees with Freud on the fundamental issue about human nature: "man has within him a lust for hatred and destruction" to the point where it occurs in the collective as well. Einstein does not exempt the intellectual class from all of this. They, too, can succumb to and feed the collective madness.

The role of the intelligentsia was an important issue at the time, because Julien Benda's important work, *Le Trahison des Clercs* (*The Betrayal of the Intellectuals*) was published in 1927 and frequently discussed after. Benda claimed that French and German intellectuals in the nineteenth and early twentieth centuries contributed to the beliefs and atmosphere that caused the growth of a nationalism that glorified violence, was irrational and even racist, and they in turn contributed mightily to the outbreak of the Great

War. They not only betrayed their role, they were intellectually dishonest. Certainly, our public intellectuals of 1930 were not going to follow that road.

How, then, asks Einstein, might we make all armed conflicts impossible to occur? Like Freud, he fears we will destroy ourselves as a species. Freud signalled he would reply, and he did so in a long letter in September.

He includes many of the ideas he discussed in *Civilization and Its Discontents*, though he deals with the question of human nature from a different angle and adds some thoughts. Freud first suggests that Einstein's dichotomy of might versus right should be revised. For might he would substitute a harder word, violence. "Conflicts between man and man are resolved, in principle, by the recourse to violence." This occurs from the time of early societies and, indeed, this violence does satisfy our instinctual, aggressive nature.

Violence as ordinary ends with the rule of law, something Freud believes cannot happen unless the majority of a community is united and stable. So— it is impossible to know whether Freud is following Hobbes, consciously or unconsciously—we give power to a system that gives us security. There is still a tension, because instability is ever present, coming from a ruling group that seeks to extend its power, and attempts by the ruled to extend their freedom and even to institute some kind of equality. Freud is modern—nothing ever remains the same, all is in flux.

Human history is a series of conflicts. The dilemma today is that this is exacerbated because of our enormous capacity for killing and destruction. After all, until recently in human history people were killed in wars one at a time, and the civilian population was at times excepted from this violence.

He agrees with Einstein. The only way to end war is to have a body with judicial and executive power, a "central control." Clearly, the League of Nations, which he regards as progressive and a worthwhile experiment, does not qualify.

Moreover, there is no unifying principle. Indeed, the most influential institution in the West, Christendom, has hardly been a force for peace. Christian nations war with each other at least as often as they war with others. Nationalism—which had been a source of hope for many, from Mazzini to Wilson—fosters violence. And Bolshevism arms itself and is filled with hate for others.

In the political realm and on the matter of war, Freud sees our instinctual needs as complicated. Here, the antimony is discussed as love and hate, and Freud states that they are blended in human affairs, not separated. Hence, of course war satisfies our "lust for aggression and destruction." It is also made possible by appeals to our ideals and erotic desires. In fact, words are not reality—our idealism often masks and legitimizes our aggressive and erotic desires.

What is to be done? First, we can redirect our instincts toward positive ends. We can also attempt to use Eros to rein in our violence. Eros, he notes, can be directed to something beloved, even without any sexual intentions. Second, we can bind ourselves together in community and identify with something larger than our own ego.

Perhaps it is too early in September 1932, but Freud does not consider that the manipulation of Eros and the legitimization of violence toward others not in the community might produce the opposite of what he wishes to happen. After all, it is Freud who gives us a way of understanding the appeal of Nazism and other fundamentalist authoritarian systems and how they manipulate and direct human desire to their horrific ends.

Freud ends his discussion with an appeal to values. Why, he asks, do we not just accept the fact of war as ordinary in the affairs of humanity?

> Because every man has a right over his own life and war destroys lives that were full of promise; it forces the individual into situations that shame his manhood, obliging him to murder fellow men, against his will; it ravages material amenities, the fruits of human toil, and much besides.

He joins Einstein: "Pacifists we are," he states. It must be noted that Einstein (and presumably Freud) did not carry his pacifism so far that he argued we should counter all violence and evil by turning the other cheek. Einstein regretted that he had to support some violent response to some evil, even if it meant abandoning fundamentalist pacifism. What he did not do was to make this response heroic. He understood, as Freud notes, that we diminish our humanity when we harm or kill others for whatever reason.

Freud appeals to our intellect in regarding what he calls "the cultural development of mankind" as something that has progressed. Culture, which values thought and reflection, helps us to master our instincts. As well, it helps us to redirect our violence in a manner that is "an introversion of the aggressive impulse," for positive ends. War and culture, Freud tells his friend, are opposed to one another. He hopes, no more than that, that culture and the fear of the enormous destruction that will be the result of future wars, might "put an end to war in the near future."

Freud did not, at the time, reflect that in some places what he regarded as the community of culture would be either destroyed, confined to prisons, or exiled. As his friend Thomas Mann noted, by 1936 German culture, as he understood it, no longer resided in Germany. To push it further, Russian culture was more present in the gulags and underground than in St. Petersburg or Moscow; much of Italian culture was coming to be exiled as well; Spanish culture was dying on the battlefields of the civil war and, except for those who went into exile, would be inhibited for decades under Franco; in a decade French culture would be underground; and others. Europe itself was in a crisis of culture that could not restrain violence and evil.

However, the crisis of culture was not between those who claimed to represent it and those who did not. There was culture in Germany and elsewhere in the 1930s, though it was neither liberal nor democratic, and it was found revolting by Freud, Einstein, Mann, and many others. Its German form was clearly defined by Jeffrey Herf in 1984 as what he termed reactionary modernism.

This culture in Germany came out of its romantic past. It made a distinction between *Kultur* and *Zivilisation*, fusing technology (*Technik*) with the former rather than the latter. *Kultur* did not come out of the Enlightenment, and unlike *Zivilisation* it was not associated with intellect, rationalism, materialism, individualism, and analysis. Rather, *Kultur* for the German fascists was about blood, soul, feeling, sacrifice, and community. Germany was to be a *Kulturnation*, not a *civilization* in the French cosmopolitan model. They created a new synthesis of technology and culture, as they defined it, as the spirit (*Geist*) of the new Germany.[10]

Mann came to understand this in the years following his remark. In an address given in late May 1945 at the Library of Congress in Washington, just after the end of the Second World War in Europe, Mann became one of the first to point to the idea of reactionary modernism. He now said that there were not two Germanys, as he had claimed a decade earlier, but only one. The empire created in the last half of the nineteenth century by Bismarck "was purely a power structure aiming toward the hegemony of Europe, and notwithstanding its modernity [it] clung to memories of medieval glory." It prefigured National Socialism in "its characteristic and menacing factor: the mixture of robust timeliness, efficient modernness on the one hand and dreams of the past on the other—in a word, highly technological Romanticism."[11] Mann, from *Mario and the Magician* forward, came to fear the influence of romanticism in politics and society.

Einstein graciously replied to Freud in December 1932, thanking him, and going further: "You have earned my gratitude and the gratitude of all men for having devoted all your strength to the search for truth and for having shown the rarest courage in professing your convictions all your life."[12]

That December turned out to have great importance in Einstein's life. He travelled to the California Institute of Technology in Pasadena for research that month, planning to return to Germany in March. The Nazis earlier had been active in trying to discredit him and his work. They called relativity

"Jewish science," and enlisted several scientists who disagreed with relativity to pronounce it publicly as a fraud. There were threats to his person.

After Hitler came to power on January 30, 1933, Einstein changed his plans. He announced he would not return to Germany in March and withdrew his membership in the Prussian Academy of Sciences. In late March he renounced his German citizenship. Later that year he formally immigrated to the United States and took up residence in Princeton, New Jersey, where he joined the new Institute of Advanced Study at Princeton University. He never set foot in Germany again.

Einstein was active politically from this time on, when he thought it appropriate. Among other matters, he wrote to President Roosevelt about atomic power, was engaged in the efforts to extend civil rights in the United States, and contributed to the founding of Israel as a state. When the first President of Israel, Chaim Weizmann, died in 1952, Einstein was asked by Prime Minister David Ben-Gurion to succeed him. He declined, stating he was not the right choice, though he was profoundly committed to his Jewish identity and to the state.

Freud wrote a bit of a confession in a letter of 1931: "In some place in my soul, in a very hidden corner, I am a fanatical Jew. I am very much astonished to discover myself as such in spite of all efforts to be unprejudiced and impartial. What can I do against it at my age?"[13] This brings to mind the Yiddish saying "You should not worry if you forget that you are a Jew, because the world will regularly remind you of it."

Freud, too, had to face the hard reality of the times. In May 1933 the Nazis had one of their public book burnings, which included Freud's works. He wrote to his friend Ernest Jones, "What progress we are making. In the Middle Ages they would have burnt me; nowadays they are content with burning my books." As we know, they were not content at all.

Freud hoped that he would be secure in Vienna, and for a time seemed convinced that what was happening in Germany would not fully spill over to Austria. As well, despite the fact that many friends and some family counselled him to leave his beloved apartment, in which he had lived and worked for over four decades, Freud was stubborn. He did not want to be driven out of his home by these people.

He continued to write and work, as much as he could in his declining physical state. He corresponded with Thomas Mann, whose works he admired and whom he regarded as a friend, and others. On Freud's eightieth birthday, May 6, 1936, Thomas Mann personally delivered a congratulatory statement in praise of his work signed by Mann, Romain Rolland, Jules Romains, H.G. Wells, Virginia Woolf, Stefan Zweig, and 191 others. In part, it read,

The eightieth birthday of Sigmund Freud gives us a welcome opportunity to convey to the pioneer of new and deeper knowledge of man
our congratulation and our veneration. In every important sphere of
his activity … this courageous seer … has for two generations been a
guide to hitherto undreamed-of regions of the human soul…. [A]nd
we feel sure, if any deed of our race remains unforgotten it will be his
deed of penetrating into the depths of the human mind….

   We, the undersigned … cannot imagine our mental world without
Freud's bold lifework.

In his honour, Mann wrote an essay, "Freud and the Future," which he delivered publicly on May 8 and read to Freud that July.

It was the *Anschluss* that sealed Freud's fate and ended his life in Vienna.
The Nazis entered Austria on March 12, 1938. Some historians call it an
invasion, but it was hardly that at all, as Hitler and his troops were welcomed
and greeted with joy and cheers by most Austrians. Freud and his family were
openly threatened. Finally, though reluctantly, he decided to leave.

Friends in international diplomacy made arrangements to protect Freud.
The British government cooperated by granting him and his family special
permits to enter and live there. He entered Britain in June and settled permanently in a house in Hampstead, London, in September. His furniture had
arrived, and his study was organized as it had been in Vienna, including the
famous couch used by his patients.

Many visited, including family, H.G. Wells, Arthur Koestler, Marie
Bonaparte (a long-time supporter who helped him to leave Vienna), his
good friend the novelist Stefan Zweig, Chaim Weizmann, and representatives
of the British Royal Society and of the Yiddish Scientific Institute, whom he
welcomed.

On July 19, 1938, Zweig brought Salvador Dalí to visit Freud, something
Dalí was anxious to do, for his admiration for Freud and his intellectual debt
to him was profound. Dalí did a portrait of Freud, a sketch. Zweig did not
show it to Freud, for he feared that the gloomy mood of the image would
disturb him. Freud wrote the next day to Zweig,

   I really owe you thanks for bringing yesterday's visitor. For until now
   I have been inclined to regard the surrealists, who apparently have
   adopted me as their patron saint, as complete fools (let us say 95%, as
   with alcohol). That young Spaniard, with his candid fanatical eyes and
   his undeniable technical mastery, has changed my estimate.[14]

Leonard and Virginia Woolf visited in January 1939. Freud was having
a hard day, was clearly not well, and the encounter was somewhat awkward.

Leonard noted, "There was something about him as of a half-extinct volcano, something sombre, repressed, reserved.... He gave me the feeling ... of great gentleness, but behind that, great strength."[15]

Freud died on September 23, 1939. His death spared him the knowledge—and the suffering that would have accompanied it—that four of his five sisters died several years later in concentration camps, in places now notorious: Treblinka, Auschwitz, and Theresienstadt. *Homo homini lupis.*

Freud's influence in his time was unmatched in the *Geisteswissenschaften*, the humanities, as was Einstein's in the *Naturwissenschaften*, the physical sciences. His insights were used in all areas—from literature, art, and the study of religion and philosophy, to politics and history. He opened for discussion matters that had been sealed, and he changed the way we think about ourselves and our nature. He tried to be a healer in a difficult time, no small task. And he tried to remind us that even if life could sometimes be difficult, it could also be noble. Above all, he changed the discourse about humans and society forever.

Freud, like many other original thinkers, has been re-evaluated and criticized by many after his death. They rightly note that his work was the product of a white, heterosexual bourgeois class in Vienna at the beginning of the twentieth century. He was, in making universal claims, too Eurocentric and Western. In particular, Freud has been seen to have placed too much emphasis on the early years of one's life and on infantile sexuality in his ideas about personality development. He has rightly been criticized for having a misogynist slant to his thinking. Some critics challenge his model of the human mind. Even the value of the "talking cure," the basis of Freud's work with patients, has been brought into question in a new era of drug therapies.

Today, some in psychology and elsewhere will tell you that he is no longer as relevant as he was, or that his work is flawed. Perhaps. Perhaps not. But like Darwin and other groundbreakers, even his critics are still standing on his shoulders. Auden summed him up:

> He wasn't clever at all; he merely told
> the unhappy Present to recite the Past
> like a poetry lesson....
> if often he was wrong and at times absurd,
> to us he is no more a person
> now but a whole climate of opinion[16]
> (*In Memory of Sigmund Freud*)

9 YESTERDAY AND TODAY

IT WAS FRIEDRICH NIETZSCHE and Benedetto Croce—an unlikely pair—who in the Modernist era changed the way history was understood. They paved the way for the death of the dominant, positivist history, the notion that history was somehow objective, that the past could be reconstructed, as the father of the discipline, Leopold Ranke, stated, *wie es eigentlich gewesen* ("as it actually happened"). Nietzsche in 1874 called for a "critical" method in studying the past, one that was to be "in the service of the living." Croce's dictum in 1916 was "all history is contemporary history."

Time present, time past, and even time future are woven together, as T.S. Eliot and others of the interwar period constantly remind us.

Hence, we study the important ideas of 1930 not simply because they might be interesting in their context, but because they have meaning in ours. These writers and artists have much to teach us today, for the issues they addressed and the conundrums they faced have hardly gone away. They remain central to our lives today, and thus Mann, Woolf, and the others have much to tell us about how we understand who we are and how to deal with issues in modernity.

The 1930 intellectuals found themselves in what they believed to be a new time. Their time is still with us. They provide two important considerations at once: they help us to understand what is happening today, and they give us some distance from our maelstrom in order to provide perspective and quiet reflection. Today and yesterday are intertwined.

Today, Europe is possessed by matters that centre on the European Union. Since the financial slump of 2008, Europe has faced a series of crises that, more than any time previously, have pragmatically called into question the future of the union.

The euro as a currency is being questioned. Greece faced default, Germany led a response stressing austerity, and there is a sense that those countries that refused to enter the eurozone (Bulgaria, Croatia, the Czech Republic, Denmark, Hungary, Poland, Romania, Sweden, and the United Kingdom) were wise to retain fiscal flexibility and sovereignty. German austerity has been countered by French attempts to stimulate the economies of the continent. There is no agreement on a single policy, just great unhappiness at being stuck in an economy that seems to be resisting growth.

Then, in the summer of 2015 there began a large movement from Middle Eastern and North African nations of refugees and migrants seeking to make their future in Europe. The response to this humanitarian crisis was ad hoc and incoherent for a time. Germany welcomed immigrants; Britain was keen to contain the number; countries such as Denmark and Hungary built legal and real walls. Others—Italy and Greece among them—tried to do something but found themselves overwhelmed.

The ad hoc response to the wave of immigrants again raised the question of the sovereignty of states versus the complex regulations of the union and being told how to behave by bureaucrats from Brussels. It further led to racist responses from some groups, who argued that people from Islamic cultures do not belong in Europe and should not be welcomed. The governments of some countries made that argument, such as Hungary and Poland. Even in states such as the UK, Germany, and France, the support for right-wing nationalist parties grew dangerously. The very flawed response to immigration seriously weakened support for the union.

And recently, the United Kingdom had a referendum on remaining in the EU. Roughly 52 percent voted to leave, a decision some commentators are likening in importance to the fall of the Berlin Wall in 1989.

The Brexit decision has produced a double crisis. First, there is the fact that the second-largest member of the EU will leave, possibly triggering other states to reconsider their membership. Europe and the West are facing populist revolts against globalization and xenophobic responses from many who believe they are not benefiting from open borders and free trade.

As well, there is a rise of nationalist fervour against the cosmopolitan assumptions of an integrated Europe and a more connected world. The divide is not only between rich and poor, or between those who fear immigration and those who encourage it. Young people support the union and the choices it gives them. The elderly tend to find the EU dislocating and troublesome.

The second crisis is one that is internal to the United Kingdom, a union of England, Wales, and Scotland (since 1707), and Northern Ireland (since 1922). Scotland and Northern Ireland support membership in the EU. England is divided between the cosmopolitan centre around London, which supports it, and the rest of the nation, which voted to leave, as did Wales. The

Scots are pondering how to remain in the EU, even it means the breakup of the United Kingdom. All is in flux.

Looked at from the perspective of the twentieth century, the European Union has been extremely successful. It solved the problem of Germany and the balance of power that helped to create the two most devastating wars in history. It has institutionalized rights and democracy, though these get challenged regularly. It has created a very large free trade zone in the world, and one that is prosperous. It has a set of elaborate checks and balances, perhaps too elaborate, but ones that protect its citizens. It has its troubles—these days immigration, the protection of poor states from the rich, and virulent racism and nationalism—but it can still look forward.

Whither Europe?

Some answers to this question can be found by looking at the Europe of today in relationship to the central issues discussed by our public intellectuals of the 1930s.

- **The viability of a secular Europe with Enlightenment values**
  Europe today, the Europe of the European community and the euro, is more profoundly secular than ever. Religion and religious institutions continue to play a less prominent role as time moves forward, a trend going back possibly to the seventeenth century, certainly in force from 1789. None of the major 1930 figures saw religion as having a role in ameliorating the conditions of the day.

  The most influential of the religions, Roman Catholicism, is struggling to make the papacy and its ideology relevant, but the history of the Church from 1930 leaves little to support this.

  The Roman Catholic Church chose wrong in too many matters. It made pacts with Hitler and Mussolini and helped to legitimize Fascism everywhere. Many of its clergy and members were complicit in the Holocaust and other ethnic cleansings. The role of women in modernity has hardly been addressed. The Church has been besmirched by the pedophile acts of a number of its priests and the cover-ups of its rulers. The Vatican Bank and the finances of the Church resembled a mafia institution. A number of its leaders have made Vatican II into a minor event.

  There have been some positive developments. On the ground, many nuns and priests continue to work to help the poor, the sick, and those in need. The church played an important role in supporting Solidarity and in moving Poland toward democracy. Vatican II remains a watershed for many, and like the revolutions of 1848, may be an event that wins historically, if not in its own time. The papacy is finally no longer held in a stranglehold by Italian Cardinals. Pope Francis has given many hope that the church can modernize.

Other religious institutions are also less meaningful in public life than ever before. The Church of England gets smaller by the decade and closes churches regularly. Scandinavia, long a bastion of Lutheranism, is relentlessly secular in its public institutions. Sweden disestablished its church in 2000, Norway in 2012. Other sects face similar issues as religion grows in Africa and Latin America and fades in Europe.

Religious institutions in the West have little power, though they do retain much influence, most notably in the United States. In Europe, religious institutions still are central to many in dealing with life-cycle issues: birth, rites of passage, marriage, death. As well, religious tradition still organizes the calendar—there is nothing like the new calendar introduced in France during the revolutionary era. People still celebrate Christmas as a family event, even if it feels like a capitalist acquisition holiday; Easter is the spring festival; local areas still hold festivals recognizing their patron saints. Socially, religion matters. Politically, it is negligible. Yet, in the many discussions surrounding the issue of whether Turkey should belong to the European Union, there are those who argued against it because they believed that Europe is "Christian" in its nature.

The growing Muslim population in Europe is posing a new challenge. Many European Muslims retain their Islamic faith and find it meaningful in their everyday lives. Islamic culture itself has not experienced the historical developments that have contributed to the secularization of modern Europe.

The Enlightenment still matters. Many in Europe see Enlightenment values as the keystone to the goals of the continent. In the European Union they are embodied in the values of liberalism, democracy, and human rights. There is also the notion that civic life is what binds us. Religion, though it has its institutions, is seen as a private matter, in the tradition articulated by John Stuart Mill in *On Liberty*: you are free to practise peacefully whatever belief you like; but the state functions as a secular civic body.

The battle with the Enlightenment occurs in two areas: with the continuity of nationalism as an ideology, and with beliefs associated with what has come to be called postmodern thought.

None of the 1930 intellectuals viewed nationalism as an answer to the dilemmas they faced and articulated. Mann despised German nationalism and the new fascism that fed off of it. Ortega worried that the masses would be moved by the ideology to the point of glorifying violence. Freud and Einstein saw a need to supersede national interest through international bodies that would transcend national sovereignty. It was a menace.

However, it can be argued that of all the modern ideologies born in the nineteenth century—among them, socialism, positivism, communism, anarchism, Darwinism, liberalism, conservatism—the one that has had the most influence is that of nationalism. The idea that identity is in the nation, that we are joined by language, heritage, and culture, that blood matters, remains powerful. In places in Europe it has become central, replacing traditional religion, often something like a religion to believers. We no longer burn people who are religious heretics, but we do engage, on occasion, in the contemporary practice of ethnic cleansing.

One of the several points where Marx (and many others) erred was in predicting the end of nationalism as history unfolded. In spite of many attempts to transcend it, Europe—and much of the rest of the world—organizes itself along national boundaries, and people still identify with their nation.

To those in 1930 who hoped to see it die, the evidence of the power of the nationalist ideology was displayed in August 1914. Many on the left, socialists of many varieties, and those who were active in peace movements, had hoped that war could be avoided by a general strike, echoing Marx and Engel's plea, "Workers of the world unite." Nothing happened, as the workers of, say, Britain and Germany, eagerly took up war against one another and supported the national state.

Nationalism persists today, even as the theory has changed. Now, following Benedict Anderson and others, we see nations as "imagined communities," a created identity, not part of our nature. No matter in practice—the appeal to the nation, whether to Mother Russia in the Crimea, or to a separate Scotland or Catalonia—is a powerful social statement.

It is not widely understood how modern is the idea that motivated the peacemakers in Paris in 1919, as they redrew maps and sovereignties on their understanding of the ontology of the nation. Before the nineteenth century, loyalties were religious, dynastic, familial, and local. Many states in Europe were empires containing people who spoke many different languages. For example, the Hapsburgs ruled over Germans, Hungarians, Romanians, Italians, Czechs, Slovaks, and others. Many in Europe hardly travelled more than ten kilometres from their home. National languages are a recent creation with the introduction of the central authority of the state, national military service, and universal education.

The worship of the nation meant "the invention of tradition," as Hobsbawm called it, the establishment of national holidays, monuments, and celebrations of modernity. After all, the national day of the French, with a long history, goes only as far back as an event in 1789, first officially celebrated in 1889. Others do the same.

The European Union grew in part as an attempt to transcend the violence associated with Europe organized only on national lines. A big issue after the Second World War was the question of how to prevent yet another war. Some saw this issue arising from the change in the European and world balance of power that resulted from the Franco-Prussian War of 1870–1871, a need to integrate a united Germany into a system that would ensure peace.

Judged by the difference between the years 1870 to 1945 and 1945 to the twenty-first century, the EU has been successful. Europe is so integrated that a war emanating out of its centre is virtually impossible.

The problem of Germany has been solved, on one level. First, Germany was occupied and divided into four zones; then it was two states, East and West, corresponding with the postwar Cold War. In 1989 it was united, to the joy of some and the chagrin of others, one of whom joked that he loved Germany so much he would like to see several of them exist.

A united Germany is now the most powerful player on the European continent, though its past limits its international power and authority. Will this last? Will Britain withdraw from Europe as it leaves the EU? Can France again become a partner and counterweight to Germany? Will Russian irredentism destabilize the continent? Still, European integration, even with countries outside the EU such as Russia, has mitigated the threat of severe violence.

Nationalism persists and appears to be growing in Europe in a more frightening manner, in the rise of racist neo-fascist and quasi-fascist parties in many countries. What was once thought impossible after the defeat of Hitlerian Germany is now coming into being. There is now a group of political parties openly racist and authoritarian, notably Jobbik in Hungary and Golden Dawn in Greece. There are others on the margin, appealing in code to national identity and opposed to immigration, including the National Front in France, the Party for Freedom in the Netherlands, The Alternative for Germany in Germany, the Northern League (now call the Lega) in Italy, the True Finns in Finland, and the Danish People's Party in Denmark. There are parties on the right claiming that the EU is an anathema, including the United Kingdom

Independence Party in Britain. It is now possible in Europe to look for votes and secure power through appeals to nationalism, resentment, and hatred.

There are, as well, nationalisms that have no relation to the EU or to democracy and the institutionalization of human rights, the most important being present in the new Russia, after the end of the Soviet Union in 1991. The first change in the map of Europe by invasion since 1945 occurred in 2014, with the annexation of the Crimea by Russia from the Ukraine. Russia remains something of an outlier for Europe, claiming as it has for centuries that it has a special history and destiny different from others sharing the continent.

The Enlightenment tradition is cosmopolitan in the end. Its values are universal, not national. The battle between the Enlightenment view represented by such people as Voltaire and the particularist tradition of Romanticism, begun by Herder, continues.

A second major challenge to the Enlightenment tradition comes from postmodern thought, an outlook that became current in the 1980s. Postmodernism is a broad cultural term for an intellectual outlook that rejects some of the most cherished traditions of modern Europe: for example, a belief in the rationality of the human personality, the idea of progress, and the value of originality in creative work. Postmodern philosophers, in their analyses, try to "deconstruct" traditional ideas and beliefs in an effort to point out that what is considered true is simply the belief system of a dominant social/political structure and/or a set of assumptions based on cultural norms.

Postmodern thinkers argue that there are no universal truths. Rather, there are truth-systems in each culture or society, none of which is intrinsically better than any other. The emphasis now is on differences instead of universal norms, and postmodernists challenge our ability to derive values that are applicable to everyone. Hence, they stress plurality, fragmentation, and multiplicity, a celebration of many voices and attitudes rather than one.

Postmodernism clearly resembles relativism. Fixed meanings are not acceptable to postmodern thinkers, who claim that we construct meaning through our actions, values, and language, rather than finding it in an objective or coherent world. They talk about life as ambiguous, contingent, even chaotic. Many do not find this problematic, but open and creative, a kind of liberation from the constraints of tradition. Postmodernists are willing to consider many ideas outside the rational tradition, including fantasy, the strange, the exotic, and the marginal, as a way of constructing reality.

There can be no such thing as a single postmodernism. True to its posture, the very grounds of its concerns are contested territory between extreme and moderate positions. Postmodernism is thus more an attitude of mind than a philosophical system. It can be regarded as in the Western philosophical tradition of Skepticism, a challenge to the legitimacy of accepted beliefs. By its nature, it is negative about current cultural assumptions and open to fresh ideas. Some thinkers maintain that this is a normal feature of the evolution of thought, and that this cycle of certainty and uncertainty has been occurring in Europe since the Renaissance.

This skepticism expresses itself in the desire to cross traditional boundaries between intellectual disciplines and traditions. The postmodern thinker Michel Foucault (1926–1984) worked in an area that includes history, philosophy, and sociology. In his *The History of Madness*, one of his most influential works, Foucault is concerned with madness and identity as a social construct rather than as a rational category.

Because postmodernists seriously challenge notions of progress, groups such as the Green movement can be viewed as postmodern phenomena. The attack on major industrial powers on behalf of the poor is supported by postmodern ideas. Feminists and others who are marginal find themselves comfortable in the postmodern camp. Many movements in the last several decades that challenge the power structure and the military-industrial complex have had the support of postmodernists.

Postmodernism, in its skepticism, thus denies the existence of universal norms. It claims there are no certain criteria to help us determine truth from falsehood. Existence has no ultimate meaning; the autonomous, rational individual is a myth. Some postmodernists seem to build complex, elaborate systems to tell us that there is no system.

Critics of postmodernism claim that its posture is so relative, it offers no criteria of judgment. Anything goes. They accuse the postmodernists of being part of the "me generation," concerned only with the satisfaction of self, to the detriment of reason, tradition, and the family. If there are no criteria of progress, they say, how and why do you deal with oppression, starvation, and disease? What standards are there for reforming society?

The defenders of the Humanistic and Enlightenment traditions are wary of postmodernism, though some acknowledge its openness, tolerance, and contributions to thought. They continue to value reason, the autonomous individual, and most importantly, the idea of a fixed set of universal human rights. Many religious thinkers are disturbed by the lack of fixed values and the denial of any reality outside of the self. The skeptical postmodernists suggest that the Humanist, Enlightenment, and religious traditions favour one set of people—wealthy white male heterosexuals, whether in the West or in other industrial societies—over others. The tension between these positions continues, and is expressed in a vigorous, creative debate.

Those who argue on behalf of a set of universal values and a shared humanity cite an inherent contradiction in both some existential and postmodern thought in support of their position. While existentialists will suggest that we create ourselves, their main figures were hardly neutral in asserting the importance of humanist values. Camus, for example, strongly supported concepts of justice and the dignity of all human beings in his works, and de Beauvoir borrowed from people like Mary Wollstonecraft in forwarding the rights of women.

Similarly, postmodern thinkers such as Foucault, Derrida, and Barthes might assert, along with Marx, that all ideology is a justification for the domination of a ruling class, but they call attention to such matters as the violation of human rights, modern genocide, the plight of the poor, and environmental degradation in asking for political action.

If any tradition from the Enlightenment has more or less ended, it is belief in the idea of progress. The vision of Condorcet and others of the unfolding of history as a story of progressive development no longer can be sustained after the first half of the twentieth century. Progress is now normative—we get more sophisticated technologically, let us say, not in a valuative way—but the world is no longer seen as automatically better as time moves on.

Indeed, "progress," as Northrop Frye pointed out in his *The Modern Century* (1967), can be so distorted as to assume that figuring out how to kill more people faster is called by its name. Frye suggests that what we call progress can result in the alienation of true progress, the feeling that we cannot, or ought not, keep up with some developments. He cites the medieval legend of the Wild Hunt, in which those who cannot keep up with the march to nowhere fall behind and turn to dust. When modernity began, it was Frankenstein and Faust who came to the fore as prevailing myths; now it is Sisyphus and the Wild Hunt.

Still, if there are any shared values in Europe—and there are—they are those associated with the Enlightenment and articulated in such documents as the Universal Declaration of Human Rights and the European constitution. The International Court of Justice, with its concern about crimes against humanity, is one attempt to put those values into effect.

- **Coming to terms with a new, darker view of human nature**
  The 1930 intellectuals—especially Freud, Ortega, and Mann—must be given their due on the issue of our nature. They wrote at the beginning of a terrible fifteen years and, sadly, their concerns were vindicated. They played Cassandra, and they lived through the fulfillment of their warnings.

  Today we live with the echo of their concerns. We fear the unrestrained power of those of our species. Freud's "homo homini lupis" is part of our assumptions about the need to restrain unbridled power. It is demonstrated daily in cruel and thoughtless acts throughout the world. Moreover, as Mann correctly saw, the power of charisma and the true believer can overturn civilization. And mass man keeps making his claims as if he has been parachuted into the world.

  From another perspective, the critique of human nature—the understanding of our capacity for violence, even sometimes the pleasure we take in it, and our willingness to be led—has at its core a very harsh judgment of the politics of the far left.

  The greatest failure of Marxism and some varieties of socialism is not in their analysis of what is or what might come to be. It rather lies in their failure to recognize that human nature may not be suited to creating a society that asks of us to give what we can and take only what we need. As well, they never acknowledged that human misery is not simply created by the structure of society, that we human beings, as Dostoyevsky saw, not only like to build but also to destroy.

  The goal of Marxism, as stated by Engels, was to transcend necessity, to reach a point where we will be free of our "animal needs" and able to shape our own lives and history. The assumption, unstated, was that we would create the good society because, at this point, our goodness would be able to be reified. Necessity created an unfair world. Freedom would solve that. It hardly needs to be said that every Communist society, in Europe and elsewhere, is far more unfair and corrupt than the social democracies they scorn.

  Hence the Liberal tradition still has its followers and has proven more resilient than anyone expected it to be in 1930. Liberalism has its optimism, and for a time it was on the side of the now-abandoned idea of progress. However, Liberal theory also had its doubters, including Tocqueville and Mill, who believed in democracy and feared it at the same time.

  Liberalism has provided two great gifts to the West, both of which have come to be part of what defines Europe today. The first is the idea of universal human rights, often breached in the nineteenth and twentieth centuries even in those places that espoused it, sometimes breached today, a commitment that gives both dignity to others and the ability to try to shape our lives, peacefully, in a manner we see appropriate.

Some argue that *universal* human rights did not become something accepted by the liberal West until after the Second World War. Either way, today it is an idea that resonates as part of Western ideology.

The second gift is the constitutional tradition bequeathed by Liberal thought, a combination of British pragmatism, French cosmopolitanism and rights, and American practice. The latter two traditions introduced on the cusp of the beginnings of what we call modernity, the 1780s, a unique notion—the idea that we can *re*constitute the state. The result created a new human possibility. Old regimes now were in terror, for their hold on law and sovereignty could be challenged. Now state-making could be a creative process. The result over the last two centuries has been transforming, and the fact that Europe itself has a constitution is part of this development.

Further, the Liberal constitutional tradition is one that mediates between freedom and authority. Power in the state is necessary. Power in a person or a single institution is to be feared. Hence, Liberalism has power restrained, limited, and dispersed. We are, as the primary French document reminds us, both individuals and citizens. As well, the constitution in the Liberal tradition is defended by an independent judiciary, an absolute necessity if a state wishes to call itself democratic.

A most important moment for the Liberal tradition was its union with a form of socialism at the turn of the twentieth century. The work that most incorporated and spread this idea was that of a German moderate socialist living in England, Eduard Bernstein, in his *Evolutionary Socialism* (1899).

Bernstein argued that the facts of economic and social development since 1848 do not bear out Marx's predictions, a statement that made him a reviled "revisionist," a heretic in the eyes of orthodox Marxists. The result, Bernstein believed, was a need to rethink socialism and its relationship to the developing democracy. He claimed, "democracy is a condition of socialism to a much greater degree than is usually assumed, i.e., it is not only the means but also the substance."[1]

Bernstein's ideas had great influence in Western Europe, and helped to foster the development of what has come to be called social democracy. If the EU today is to be called by any ideological term it is a social democracy, as are many of its members. This fear of the 1930 intellectuals did not finally come to pass, though it took a world war to decide it—Europe as a whole is more socially democratic than anything else, though there certainly are exceptions.

Conservatism also remains important in Europe's political life. At the time of writing, there are many European governments that are centre-right in their politics, including the important states of Germany and the United Kingdom.

Most conservatives in Europe are "red" rather than "blue." Moderate conservatives accept the welfare system instituted by other parties and defend national public health care and pension schemes. Not even Margaret Thatcher challenged these. The American version of conservatism today, which seeks to dismantle the New Deal, opposes public health and welfare schemes, and supports tax breaks for the rich and corporations, is rejected by virtually every main conservative party in Europe. They are centre-right, though of course there are right-wing conservatives in most places.

Conservatism has made its own contribution to European affairs. One of its main insights is in recognizing the importance of social institutions and tradition. Conservatives, from Edmund Burke in the late eighteenth century to today, are wary of quick political solutions to deep and complex matters. Society matters—and political solutions and haste can destroy the fabric of social life.

As well, conservatives have always viewed human nature as flawed, and therefore there needs to be restraints imposed on it by tradition and religion. One result is that conservatives are willing to tolerate inequalities in conditions far more than do those left of the centre on the political spectrum.

The two main political ideologies of the twentieth century, Bolshevism and Fascism, are both elitist in practice, whatever their rhetoric. Bolshevism is filled with contradictions between what it says it is and what it actually does. It claims to foster equality, but creates a new, rigid elite; it quotes Marx on the need to be free, and yet eliminates or jails people on the claim of necessity; it terrorizes its own people.

Fascism, though these days attracting a number of Europeans who are turning to "blue" conservatism, is racist, elitist, and cynical. It appeals to Ortega's "mass man" and, like Bolshevism, destroys what Freud would regard as a civilized life.

The new view of human nature—flawed, given to irrational decisions, angry at others, wanting one's "appetites," as Plato called them, attended to—raised the question of whether humans really want to be free. Too much has transpired since 1930 for anyone to suggest that all we want is to have choice. Many have commented on how humans seem to desire to "escape from freedom" and be nurtured by one or another belief system that is authoritarian. Perhaps Europeans have become social democrats in spite of themselves, flawed as it sometimes can be, recognizing that the alternatives are far worse.

Today, in Europe and the West, reflections on the distribution of wealth arise out of a consideration of human nature and its relationship to politics and society. Thomas Piketty's *Capital in the Twenty-First Century* (2013) has focused the issue.

Piketty persuasively argues that what is inherent in capitalist economics is a development dangerous to democracy and the kind of society premised by the establishment of the EU and its constitution. Historically, the rate of return on capital in liberal social democratic states has been much higher than the rate of growth. Hence,

> when the rate of return on capital exceeds the rate of growth of output and income, as it did in the nineteenth century and seems quite likely to do again in the twenty-first, capitalism automatically generates arbitrary and unsustainable inequalities that radically undermine the meritocratic values on which democratic societies are based.[2]

Piketty's work does not directly discuss the matter of human nature, but it has as its assumption the idea that humans will constantly seek to increase their wealth, something far closer to Adam Smith than to Marx.

However, the followers of Smith and Hayek, and there are many today in the leading capitalist countries, argue that this competition for more, whatever the more is, is good for the community as a whole. They are wrong, claims Piketty, because what he calls "the forces of divergence" in the political economy result in high levels of inequality. The outcome is the creation of a favoured class made up of those with inherited wealth, which results in far less social mobility and economic opportunity than is healthy for a democratic society.

In short, the political economy of Europe and the West is antagonistic to its stated social democratic goals. This is, as Marx would have said, a contradiction of capitalism, though it is not the contradiction identified in Marx's analysis. Indeed, in the first part of the twenty-first century, the gap between the rich and poor has grown larger, with the top few percent gaining materially, and the rest worse off than before.

This phenomenon has been exacerbated since the recession of 2008, the worst economic crisis since 1929. Those responsible for the debacle, the bankers, hedge fund managers, and other leaders in finance, have been rescued by states, using the very taxes paid by those they are exploiting. Few of these masters of the financial universe have suffered or been punished for their misdeeds, though many in the middle class who bought into the bubble have lost homes and/or had their lives seriously diminished through unemployment or the chipping away of the welfare state in the name of "austerity."

Piketty's study is an old-fashioned one, as he admits. It is a work in the tradition of political economy, recognizing that economics and politics are intertwined in a world where values are promulgated through such things as laws, regulations, and taxes. Being a work of political economy, it is also a study in another traditional kind of knowledge, called moral philosophy, as was Smith's *Wealth of Nations*, Malthus's *Essay on Population*, Ricardo's *Principles of Political Economy and Taxation*, and Marx's *Capital*.

Moral philosophy deals with, among other things, human nature and values, and it is here that Piketty's work can help in the understanding of the new, darker view of human nature.

The unspoken assumption of *Capital in the Twenty-First Century* is that human beings have no restraints when it comes to their desire to accumulate value, be it money, land, or even art. Hence, while we can possibly agree with Freud that we have libido and a reservoir of violence inside of us that needs to be restrained, we need to add one other dimension to human nature in our time.

We have greed. We want. We have no sense that there is something called "enough." Many in power who pay homage to "enough" in public have great wealth, some of it hidden. We will simply accumulate because that gives us both satisfaction and a sense of our own worth. Commodification has become something of a monster that threatens the meritocracy and social and political equality that underscores social democracy. Europe (and especially the United States) is tending, in actuality, to a kind of aristocracy of wealth, an oligarchy of power, some states more than others—Germany and Britain more than Sweden and Denmark.

This, of course, is not limited to the Europe of the EU. Other wealthy states, not democratic, are witnessing this development—from the new princes of China to the oligarchs of Russia.

When Thomas More wrote his *Utopia* in 1516, he too realized that the society he was living in was inherently unjust. Indeed, the first part of the two-part work is devoted to a discussion of the problems of England. More wrote, "hideous poverty ... exists side by side with wanton luxury."

More then wrote about the imaginary island of Utopia, where life was highly regulated, property was dispensed with, and life was just. At the end of his reflections, More asked why it was that the world did not emulate his Utopia. He put the blame on we humans—the world would have "(adopted) Utopian laws, if it were not for one single monster, the prime plague and begetter of all others—I mean Pride.... Pride is too deeply fixed in the hearts of men to be easily plucked out."[3]

More blamed, above all, one of the Seven Deadly Sins, that of Pride. Piketty's findings speak to another of those seven, that of Greed. (The others traditionally are Lust, Gluttony, Anger, Sloth, and Envy.) The result is that, if left alone, the political economy of capitalism will destroy social democracy in practice. Shakespeare, who well knew the power of money, has Gloucester speak in *King Lear*, as he acknowledges his own past greed while helping a homeless person (who is actually his disguised son):

> Let the superfluous and lust-dieted man
> That slaves your ordinance, that will not see
> Because he does not feel, feel your pow'r quickly;
> So distribution should undo excess
> And each man have enough.[4]

Piketty suggests some solutions, including a tax on capital, but these will not be elaborated upon in this discussion of human nature.

The issues raised by the 1930s intellectuals have been mitigated, but they demand constant attention. Europe still has to be wary of authoritarian political movements, all of which challenge most of the humanitarian purposes of the EU. It needs to pay attention to racism in the context of nationalist ideologies and practices. It needs to attend to the distribution of wealth. The EU has given Europe the stability of peace. Europeans must remain vigilant to guarantee social democracy and human rights, which can be undermined by oligarchic practices.

- **The rise of the politics of irrationality**
Europe since 1945 has been living, and living peacefully and well, with a wonderful contradiction. Its politics and social goals are based on the articulation and implementation of Enlightenment values—human rights, egalitarianism, and the liberty of the individual, all derived from an era trusting of "reason" and viewing humans as rational beings. At the same time, there is an acknowledgement that we are not rational at all in many of our choices, that we do not even regularly choose from

alternatives based on self-interest, but instead on identity, desire, and the unconscious.

We pretend to be rational, knowing we are pretending, because giving in to the other side of human nature would only realize the fears articulated by Freud and Ortega.

Europe has chosen to institutionalize both private choice and public democracy and decency. Countries that wish to join the EU have to pass democracy tests, and there are pressures exerted when a member country seems to be crossing the line into authoritarianism.

However, the area of personal liberty is growing ever smaller in Europe and the West. In theory, there is still a protection for what Liberalism calls "self-regarding acts," those matters that affect only the individual actor—for example, what books we read, what we choose to eat, whether we decide to work out, take a walk, or simply be sedentary.

In practice, the area of personal freedom is narrowing with great speed in an era shaped by the fear of terrorism and sophisticated technology. Privacy is disappearing. Our emails are scanned. There are security cameras recording our every move in public, no more so than in the mother of democracies, Great Britain. Governments can easily know what we buy, who we converse with, where we go to pray, what books we read, and what language and ideas we use with friends and others to talk about politics, society, and personal matters.

We accept Big Brother as part of our lives. Many welcome him. Indeed, those who try to stop Big Brother and ask us to consider what is happening are deemed by many states to be violating the rights of government to unilaterally make decisions regarding privacy. People like Edward Snowden are labelled criminals, even though it can easily be argued that they are telling us that governments are violating their constitutions and committing illegal acts. Never in social democracies has Machiavelli's observation that the state can do many things denied to individuals been more evident and less considered.

This erosion of privacy and the intrusions of corporations and governments into our lives seem to be accepted by the populations of Europe and the West. Governments have power, but so do large multinational corporations, especially those like Apple and Google, which control how we obtain information and our communications. Indeed, these corporations can even resist attempts by governments to make them reveal information related to apparent criminal activity. The shift in our time from manufacturing economies to service economies with information at the centre has realigned corporate power.

Many have commented on the close association between government and large corporate organizations. Corporations lobby hard for deregulation from government supervision, and for laws that benefit them and increase their profits while lowering their taxes. They talk laissez-faire, but they practise corporate welfare. As well, in the West, the players who run large corporations are sometimes those who are recruited to run political parties and governments. Politicians easily move into the corporate world when they leave parliaments. The interchange between this new power elite in business, government, and powerful law firms is ever-present.

The politics of irrationality raises some large issues. These days, there are political parties operating in many European countries whose stated goals include the destruction of much that is democratic. How do we deal with democracies choosing anti-democratic political parties? Nazi parties are prohibited in some countries. What about parties that do not call themselves Nazi or Fascist, but appeal to racism and the cult of authority? What are the limits?

Ortega was correct in his fear that mass man would demand immediate satisfaction of his desires. The result in social democracies has been an inability and/or unwillingness of mainstream political parties to deal with long-term issues, and a fear of alienating popular opinion. After all, politics runs on four- or five-year cycles, even if states are supposed to last forever. How do we deal with matters such as the environment? How do we raise enough funds to implement policies of social democracy when raising taxes means not getting re-elected? How does the modern state deal with its responsibility for the next generations in an atmosphere where only the present matters?

Mann's fear of charisma and magic trumping liberty and reason was real in 1930, and still resonates today. Politics resembles both propaganda and entertainment, not a good portent. In times of crisis, there is a clear desire for magical and authoritarian solutions to deep social problems. How does the West make politics more dignified, more about choices than about desire?

Woolf and Nardal warned that political equality did not mean social equality. A veneer of political egalitarianism does not automatically provide opportunity for those on the margin—the several Others, the poor, the eccentric. How do we conduct public policy to create more social equality? How do we distribute wealth to create opportunity? How do we foster a meritocratic political and social environment?

In Europe, in the distribution of wealth and the institutions of power, there is a tendency in many states to become, in reality, oligarchies with a veneer of democracy. The same group holds wealth, political power, and social status. They rotate themselves between industrial and financial corporations, state power, and control of the legal system. Here, Brecht and Weill's condemnation of capitalism and its values becomes prescient. When does a democracy in practice turn into "soft Fascism"? Here, the trend is led by the United States, but Europe is becoming more elitist and wealth is being more concentrated in the hands of that elite as the years go by.

- **Mass culture and its dangers**
  If anything, the concern of Ortega about the nature of the new mass man was a lesson learned on the political level of Europe. The appeal to totalitarianism, to true believers, is very limited in the Europe of the EU, though present in other parts of the world, notably the Middle East.

  However, there are at least two ways that Ortega must be revised at the beginning of the twenty-first century. First, there is the matter of his formulation of mass man giving up his personality to join a crowd, feeling more comfortable as part of a mass.

  Ortega was working out of a context that accepted many of the ideas of Gustave Le Bon, including the notion that joining a crowd effaces our individuality. This formulation has been successfully challenged in the last several decades.

  A number of earlier assumptions about crowds have been rejected by scholars either because empirical evidence has overturned them or because they don't make sense logically. Among these is the idea that people lose their ability to think clearly and rationally when in a crowd because of the influence of the mass. However, crowds are sometimes very rational and orderly when pursuing a goal, though the goal may be seen as irrational by the powerful institutions and groups at the time. Moreover, the older thesis had crowds behaving emotionally at all times, whereas it has been demonstrated that behaving emotionally does not necessarily mean one cannot behave rationally and with a clear goal in mind. In Europe, the crowds that helped the success of Solidarity in Poland, among others, were both rational and emotional.

  The idea that crowds make for anonymity and that therefore people in crowds might do things other than what they would otherwise do because they are unaccountable has also been revised. It has been shown clearly that people in crowds usually are part of a smaller group that includes friends, family members, or associates. As well, crowds are hardly unanimous, and members of crowds are not necessarily blind followers.[5]

The most radical scholarly change has been the understanding of crowds as possibly contributing to democracy rather than always having an authoritarian subtext. Elias Canetti has argued that crowds give individuals the opportunity to act in a free manner.[6] As Christian Borch recently wrote, "the bodily compression of crowds in fact liberates individuals and creates a democratic transformation."[7]

Certainly, crowds in Europe in the last several years have been various, many of them forwarding democratic ideas. Mass man is not as robotic or thoughtless as Ortega made him out to be in 1930.

A second revision of Ortega has to do with culture. Ortega's work has in it the inherent traditional assumption that there is a distinction between "high" and "popular" culture, his noble man contributing the former and the masses being suppressed by the latter. High culture is thought to include those cultural products given the status of having high aesthetic value, produced by an elite, which transcend class and have permanent value. It is contrasted often with low or popular culture, which is thought to be ephemeral and not as profound.

This distinction may have had some validity in 1930, but it is certainly not true today. The availability of dissent in digital form has totally changed its sociology and nature. Resistance and political change can be and are encoded in popular texts, be they traditional ones like books, or new forms like online groups and tweets. Indeed, the Nobel committee in Norway awarded the Nobel Prize in Literature for 2016 to Bob Dylan, signalling that in our postmodern world what we regard as literature is very different from the modernist 1930s.

Music and politics have often had a close association in the modern West. Much music, from religious hymns to national anthems, is supportive of the power structure. And there is racist music, white power music, and misogynist music.

However, in the last fifty years in Europe and the West, popular music has often challenged existing authority and pointed to change. Dylan's songs attacked racism and the Vietnam War. The Beatles, especially John Lennon's "Imagine" and "Give Peace a Chance," were subversive enough to have their music banned in eastern Europe for a time.

Three female members of Pussy Riot, the Russian punk-rock anti-Putin band, were put on trial for "hooliganism" in 2012 for performing a song with the title "Virgin Mary, Drive Putin Away," in the largest Russian Orthodox cathedral in Moscow. Another of their songs was "Holy Shit," which, they explained, relates to the close association between the Orthodox patriarchy and the Putin government and "is our evaluation of the situation in the country." They called their sometimes very short public appearances guerrilla performances. One of the band members, Nadezhda Tolokonnikova, stated, "Pussy Riot's performances can either be called dissident art or political action that engages art forms. Either way, our performances are a kind of civic activity amidst the repressions of a corporate political system that directs its power against basic human rights and civil and political liberties."[8] Tolokonnikova also made a video for a new song, titled "Make America Great Again," attacking the then candidacy of US President Donald Trump.

Folk music often was used to appeal to national values in the face of oppression and occupation. During the late twentieth century, folk music was crucial in such countries as Hungary and multi-ethnic Yugoslavia, as it provided ethnic groups with the opportunity to express their national identity in a time of troubles and in a changing Europe.

Popular films also can provide opportunities for ideology and dissent to be codified and disseminated. The documentary has become a powerful tool in revealing what is often suppressed or disregarded. Two recent documentaries that do this are *Fire at Sea* and *My Friend Boris Nemtsov*.

The documentary *Fire at Sea* (2016) by Gianfranco Rosi is widely regarded as one of the most important statements about the refugee crisis in contemporary Europe. Rosi filmed on the tiny island of Lampedusa, just eight square miles, an island belonging to Italy but closer to North Africa than to Italy itself. It now exists as both a small place whose inhabitants gain their living from the sea and a landing point for over four hundred thousand refugees over the last few decades from Africa and elsewhere escaping very hard times.

Rosi shows us the lives of the islanders and the despair and troubles of the refugees who land there, letting the viewer make the moral and political connections. Above all, he shows ordinary human beings dealing with an extraordinary crisis of humanity. The local doctor, Pietro Bartolo, treats the illnesses and aches of the people of Lampedusa and is drawn into looking after many refugees. He does so with patience and compassion, as he calls these people who are desperate his brothers and sisters. In the film, while treating a rescued woman who is pregnant he says, "there was no end to them—no end." Then he looks at the camera and asserts: "It is the duty of every human being to help these people."[9]

In a later interview Bartolo states,

For me, nothing has changed, perhaps nobody realizes it. But I will always be the Lampedusa doctor taking care of Lampedusa, and our brothers who come from the sea. As I always say, everything comes from the sea. I welcome everyone, especially those who need help....

I've seen so many terrible things, so many dead children, so many dead women, so many raped women. These things leave you with a great big empty hole in your stomach. These are nightmares that haunt me very often.[10]

But Bartolo does what he can, with quiet dignity, testifying to our common humanity in a manner akin to that of Camus's fictional Doctor Rieux in *The Plague*.

The Russian documentary *My Friend Boris Nemstov* (2015)[11] by Sofia Rodkevich is a tribute to the popular Russian politician and fierce critic of Vladimir Putin who was assassinated in February 2015 on a bridge near the Kremlin in Moscow. Many believe that the assassination was ordered by Putin, though in the fog that is Russian authoritarianism this is impossible to prove. Indeed, Nemstov had been publishing reports on corruption in Russia and its government and had organized public marches of dissent. He even predicted his own assassination.

Another part of popular culture in Europe connected with dissent is the satirical journal. Such magazines, some only online, poke fun at authority and in some cases conduct important investigative journalism. In Europe, they exist all over—from *Aszdzienik* in Poland, *Academia Catavencu* in Romania, *Frigidaire* in Italy, *El Jueves* in Spain, *The Phoenix* in Ireland, to *Private Eye* in The United Kingdom.

Recently, it is two journals in France that have made a big difference in the political discourse. The office of the journal *Charlie Hebdo* was firebombed in 2011 after it renamed an edition *Chiara Hebdo*, attacking the prominence of sharia law in Libya and elsewhere. The issue focused on the oppression of women, gays, and those who challenge existing fundamentalist Islamic regimes.

In January 2015, two militant Islamist gunmen entered the offices of *Charlie Hebdo* and killed twelve people, shouting "Allahu akbar" (God is great) and "the Prophet is avenged." This attack was in response to the magazine's publication of cartoons that criticized Islam and used the figure of Mohammed in a manner some thought to be insulting and blasphemous. The magazine continued to publish and the French president described the act as one of uncivilized terror. The next issue had a print run of five million copies and the whole of the Western world came out in support of freedom of the press. The phrase *Je suis Charlie* was adopted by many journalists and millions of others supporting freedom of expression.

Another French journal, *Le Canard Enchaîné*, revealed in early 2017 that François Fillon, the conservative candidate of the Republican Party for the coming April presidential election, had "hired" his wife and children, and paid them roughly a million euros over the years to do little or no work. Fillon's candidacy was seriously wounded and he did not survive to contest the second round of the presidential election.

Open fundamentalism is not a danger in Europe, though racism still exists among some of its populace and is used in a coded manner by some politicians to appeal for support and votes. Hence, fundamentalism, hidden behind angry rhetoric, can still be a danger from within. As well, some nationalist parties and groups flirt with authoritarianism, attacking democratic processes by blaming them for permitting a loss of tradition and coherence.

However, mass culture remains an important social and political matter. Television is still sometimes banal and superficial, though some of the series made by independent producers do contain serious critiques of capitalism's requirements on human beings, and on matters of race, gender, and class. Journalism, with some notable exceptions, is on occasion more akin to mass entertainment and/or propaganda than it is to news.

Europe and the West have also continued the trend toward the commodification of culture, which contributes to elitism. Art, theatre, and opera are not only expensive to produce, they are expensive to attend. Hence, the wealthy and the haute bourgeoisie have access to them, while the petite bourgeoisie and the lower classes are left out.

"High" art is also supported by the wealthy because they benefit from it. Works of art are not simply aesthetic experiences, they are investments. The Western cult of the original—fairly recent since it began roughly in the late seventeenth century—has made Monets and other works of art not only pieces that we worship in a museum, but very, very valuable objects that increase in value on an open market where owning one of them is a matter of prestige as well as taste.

Not only has art been commodified, taste too has come to be part of this. Museums mount shows and advertise them in the manner Gucci and others advertise their products. And things such as clothes, automobiles, and perfumes are valued because they are thought to display the special qualities of those who consume them.

Governments have contributed to this development. It is now expected that even those parts of culture that are part of the state— museums, zoos and aquaria, science centres, and the like—will charge admission to their exhibitions. This is caused not by the greed of the institutions but by the fact that these bodies are underfunded by governments and need the additional revenue to survive. The result is that it is very expensive for the poor to go to a museum; in effect they are excluded. The last refuge of egalitarianism in cultural institutions is the public library.

Mass culture is most dangerous in times of trouble, because it can be used by extreme political groups that offer simple solutions to complex issues, appeal to the desire to blame someone else for one's own deficiencies, and act to puff up one's own identity.

Ortega, however, was correct in his critique of higher education, and his work on that subject still resonates. Education is still focused on specialization and professionalization and is becoming more so as higher education is increasingly viewed as job training more than anything else. Elites have their own schools, especially in Britain and France, and this provides for the continuity of the domination of a small upper class.

Still, education remains the best opportunity for social mobility. Even the elite schools cannot ignore those from the lower classes who have fine intellects. The most important meritocracy remains that of the mind.

- **Identity and the Other in the midst of Western civilization**
For the Other in Europe, it was hoped that 1945 would be a watershed to a new era. The horrors of the Holocaust and the victory of the allies seemed to be the trauma that would put an end to anti-Semitism. Women played an important role in the war and now had the vote in France and elsewhere. Blacks served in armies and would gain respect and recognition. The promise did not come into being in most cases.

The period since 1945 raises a hard question. Is European culture and society (and that of the West in general) deeply anti-Semitic, anti-feminist, and racist?

Western civilization has tended to think of itself as open, liberal, tolerant, and egalitarian. Is that so only for those who conform to the norm—who are white, indigenous to whatever place they live, nominally or deeply Christian, and identifying strongly with the nation? Are outsiders still always to be outsiders, no matter what they do or how far they assimilate? Can even those who appear to adopt the local norm, at least in their public lives, but who remain multiple in their identities, ever be seen to belong? Tragically, is there something built into European culture as it is taught and practised that automatically marginalizes women, Blacks, Jews, Roma, and Muslims?

There are no easy answers to the above questions. The fact that they still must be asked means that Europe has not yet become the model of social democracy and tolerance that it would like to be.

Of these outsider groups, women have made the most gains, especially white middle-class heterosexual women in western Europe. The women's movement moved from Virginia Woolf and the Nardal sisters to implement some of their goals. Women are now part of the workforce, earn their own money, and can have rooms of their own. They are becoming a stronger force in the worlds of business and the professions—women are now lawyers, doctors, and professors; they sit on the boards of corporations and have responsible positions; they are members of parliamentary bodies and have even been heads of governments.

There are still barriers to women, more social than political, more based on the networks of power that had been in the hands of males for centuries than on institutional structures, but these are receding by the decade. Men still rule in many places, but women are doing much better.

The Nazis had one victory in their sadistic and violent time in power. Europe is not quite *Judenrein*, empty of Jews. However, it will never again be a centre of Jewish life or culture, as it had been from the early modern period to the first half of the twentieth century. This has moved elsewhere—to Israel and North America, where roughly 90 percent of the Jews in the world (now nearly 14 million) live.

To note some stark changes: In Poland in 1933 there were about 3 million Jews (9.5 percent of the population); today there are about 3,200 (0.01 percent); in European Russia in 1933, there were 2.5 million, today in Russia there are 190,000 (0.13 percent); in Hungary 445,000 (5.1 percent), today 48,000 (0.49 percent); in the Netherlands 156,000 (1.8 percent), now 29,900 (0.18 percent); in Germany itself there were 500,000 in 1933 (0.75 percent), now 119,000 (0.15 percent). The largest Jewish population today in Europe is in France, with 478,000 (0.75 percent); second is the United Kingdom with 290,000 (0.46 percent).[12]

Anti-Semitism is still a force, even where there are few Jews. It appears regularly in France, Poland, Austria, and eastern Europe in general, though opposed by their states and governments. More Jews are emigrating out of Europe—today the annual rate of Jews who move from France to Israel is over 5,000. The main reasons given are fear of being assaulted in France and the lack of a decent future.

Germany itself is especially sensitive to any manifestation of anti-Semitism. It has undergone an internal reflection called *Vergangenheitsbewältigung* ("Coming to Terms with the Past") since 1945, and has clearly accounted for its past behaviour. Germany has paid reparations to many who suffered from 1939 to 1945, and has memorialized its sad history, including making certain that it is part of the educational curriculum. It has become a friend of Israel.

Other countries have been less forthcoming, and less accountable. Austria regularly blames Germany for all that was evil, claiming itself to be a victim even though it welcomed the Anschluss and was responsible for crimes against humanity. On occasion it tells some truths. Poland also stresses its victimhood in the Second World War, sometimes ignoring the atrocities committed by some of its citizens. Polish lawmakers recently passed a bill that will enable fines and/or jail sentences for people who blame Poland or the Polish people for Nazi atrocities, including the deaths of hundreds of thousands of Jews at Auschwitz. The use of the term "Polish death camps" has been outlawed. Russia blames the West. When East Germany existed, it claimed to have no knowledge of any racial crimes against others.

There are still open acts of anti-Semitism in Europe: Jews are killed simply because they are Jews in Toulouse, Belgium, and elsewhere; synagogues and cemeteries are desecrated; there is discrimination, sometimes open, sometimes subtle. What does continue to exist in most places is something that could be called casual anti-Semitism, a posture that makes it acceptable to regard Jews as somewhat different and dangerous to the public good.

With regard to Israel, Europe is often ambivalent. They supported its creation but are unhappy about some of its government's behaviour with regard to Gaza and Palestine. Indeed, occasionally we witness the irony of the grandchildren of those who committed terrible crimes against Jews and others, descendants of those who gained from colonialism and imperialism, lecturing Israel about the morality of its acts.

Jews remain an Other in most of Europe. There are museums that deal with the history of Jews in various places—Amsterdam and Venice, for example—but there are few places where Jews have power, and virtually none (Britain may be the exception) where there is an accepted assimilation. It is as if many Europeans are happy to memorialize the Jews who lived in their midst in the early modern period, but are unwilling to deal with why a Jewish presence hardly exists in Europe today.

As a result of the economic crisis that began in 2008, several political parties in Europe—in Hungary, Greece, and the Netherlands openly, in France more subtly—are anti-Semitic in their policy and discourse. Even in Germany, in the city of Dortmond, a neo-Nazi was elected to the City Council. That this is acceptable does not speak well for Europe.

The *mission civilisatrice* of colonialism, in which Blacks were to become Frenchmen and Europeans, never became realized. Blacks remain outsiders in Europe, in part because they realized they would never be fully accepted, in part because Europe never fully accepted them.

There are few Blacks in Europe in significant political positions. There are few Blacks on the boards of corporations or banks. Black culture is part of European culture only when Europeans adopt some its modes of representation.

When a Black person does get into power, as is the case in France with the appointment of Christiane Taubira as Minister of Justice of France in 2012, there are many instances of openly racist remarks and incidents. In 2013, she was compared to a monkey three times within a few weeks. At a rally opposing same-sex marriage, a twelve-year-old child taunted her with a banana. Italy's first Black minister, Cécile Kyenge, has experienced open racist hostility, not only in the streets but from other parliamentarians.

The one area where Blacks are accepted is that of sports. Black tennis players, and especially Black football players, play and star in European leagues and for national teams. Yet even there, there are racist slurs from fans and others.

The insights of the Nardal sisters and other 1930 Blacks hold. For all of the rhetoric of equality and assimilation, Blacks in Europe remain outsiders. They were correct in insisting that they needed a deeper identity than that of being French or European.

Another Other, one also persecuted during the horrors of 1939–1945, are the Roma. Those who live in countries other than Romania are subject to beatings and discrimination. Several authorities in cities and rural areas have attempted to deport Roma and destroy their settlements.

Lesbian and gay culture is slowly becoming acknowledged in western Europe. Same-sex marriage is making headway, even in such a traditionally conservative society as Spain, which legalized it in 2005; social services for spouses and partners are being institutionalized. In Iceland, Prime Minister Johanna Siguroardóttir in 2009 became the first openly gay person to head a government.

Eastern Europe has been less accepting of gay culture, and in Russia the government is openly antagonistic to homosexuals. This posture is often supported by religious authorities. The Roman Catholic Church and the various Orthodox Catholic churches still view homosexuality as an aberration and homosexual acts as sins.

Islam is the new Other in Europe. Indeed, whereas Jews had been the main Other in the 1930s, now Muslims, ironically, have become the main Other in the twenty-first century. There are now very large Muslim populations in several countries. According to the Pew Research Center, the total number of Muslims in Europe in 2010 was about 44 million (6 percent), excluding Turkey. France had 4,700,000 (7.5 percent of total population); the United Kingdom, 2,870,000 (4.6 percent); Germany, 4,119,000 (5 percent); Italy, 1,580,000 (2.6 percent); the Netherlands, 914,000 (5.5 percent); and Sweden, 451,000 (4.9 percent).

Muslims in Europe range from those who fully integrate into the local culture and those who integrate but still keep their Muslim identity, to fundamentalists who view the local culture as dangerous and heretical.

The age of terror has magnified the issues surrounding Muslim culture in the West. It has proven impossible, so far, to integrate adherents to fundamentalist Islam into European society, even accepting the idea of multiple identities, which many do not. There is fear that some parts of Muslim society are so antagonistic to the West that they are training terrorists from within. Another fear is that some idealist youths who are going to the Middle East to fight in support of their beliefs will return to their homes in Europe and act as local terrorists there. Nearly 1,000 French citizens have fought in Syria, the number increasing as the war continues. In late 2013 Manuel Valls, the interior minister of France at the time, and then prime minister, said that jihadism is "the greatest danger [France] will have to face in the next few years."[13]

A more complicated matter involving Islam in Europe is that this Other is opposed to some other Others. Some Muslims are openly anti-Semitic; some are openly opposed to gays and lesbians; and women do not fare well in fundamentalist Muslim culture, though this is a culturally based practice rather than one taken from the Qur'an.

A matter of concern for Europe is the insistence on the part of fundamentalist Muslims that they be permitted to practise sharia law in their communities, sometimes even invoking the Western ideal of religious freedom. No state has bent on this matter—we belong to a civic community, they argue, and its rules trump all other arrangements. When you are a citizen, you take on those rights and obligations. You are free to practise whatever you like privately; you are not free to discriminate or abuse others in the name of religious freedom or your religious beliefs. This question was decided in 1789 in France, later elsewhere. It is settled.

However, some European states have legislated against certain forms of dress in public in the name of civic equality, an incursion into the self-regarding acts favoured by Liberal ideas. How, or whether, to integrate into mainstream society is something that is being debated among Muslims in Europe, as it was among Jews in the nineteenth century.

Two matters are not settled. Can the countries of Europe be truly multicultural, creating an atmosphere where different groups live in harmony? Is Europe still white, male, heterosexual, and Christian in identity, if not in practice? Europe will have to answer these two matters more clearly as time moves forward.

- **Finding ways to represent the postwar world**
Europe has a very rich cultural history. Two periods stand out as both extraordinarily innovative and wonderfully creative, so much so that they not only changed cultural discourse, they also provided the base for what followed. They are the Renaissance (ca. 1450–1520) and Modernism (ca. 1880–1920).

The latter became the basis for the critique of European culture and changed forever modes of representation and the way we write, read, and make art: names such as Proust, Joyce, Woolf, Picasso, Matisse, Braque, Freud, Einstein, and Planck remain part of our lives.

Today, even with the claims of postmodernists that we have entered something new, we live in a culture that uses both the individualism and realism of the Renaissance and the inner world and abstractions of Modernism. Both still matter.

Hence, not much has changed in some of the arts. In music the eight-tone row is sometimes abandoned, and we are accustomed to chords introduced by Modernism. Yet "classical" music in public forums is mainly in its nineteenth-century guise. Orchestras and conductors sponsor contemporary music, but they get their audiences via Bach, Mozart, Beethoven, and Brahms. Opera is much the same, although now there are surtitles. Ballet is the most ossified of the arts—it has hardly developed since the Modernist period.

What is surprising is that even in popular music, not much has been done that goes beyond the work of Weill and Brecht. Broadway has its musicals, and some—*Guys and Dolls, My Fair Lady*—are brilliant, yet they are not changing or experimenting with how we use art to gain insight into who we are and what is going on around us.

It can be argued that the world of popular music is very innovative, and no one will deny the brilliance of the Beatles or other musicians of the 1960s. Moreover, the protests of the sixties were led and fuelled by rock and folk music. And the influence and creativity of jazz is one of the great musical innovations of the twentieth century. Youth still finds some of its voice in contemporary and world music.

In the visual world there has been a major change in how the discourse is conducted with the introduction of film, television, and, now, the digital world. What has certainly occurred is the diminution of the visual arts—painting, sculpture, and so on. The innovations of the Modernist period and their offshoots—people like Picasso, Dalí, Chagall, and Kandinsky—first served to change the visual arts forever, with the abandonment of the illusion of realism, the introduction of abstract modes of representation, the openness to experimentation, and the quest to integrate psychology with art.

However, the visual arts lost its monopoly on visual culture with technologies developed after the Great War. It can also be argued that with that loss came a crisis of identity. What, actually, are they doing? In the world of art as a critique of culture, little was left. Film both recorded and critiqued. Television made the first serious charges of inhumanity during the Vietnam War. Photography does what Goya did in his 1808 paintings and his *Disasters of War*.

The visual arts continue to thrive in some places. After all, abstract expressionism had its admirers, and Op and Pop Art mesmerized New York for a time. Contemporary art is part of most major museums, central to places like the Guggenheims and MOMA. But the period of its great creativity and centrality to Western culture is over. If we have had Michelangelos and Picassos after 1945, they may more readily be found in film and photography.

Interestingly, the most admired and popular artists today are the Impressionists (Monet, Manet, Degas, Renoir, etc.) and the Post-Impressionists (Van Gogh, Gauguin, and Cézanne). Shows of their works are attended faithfully by the bourgeoisie of several continents and have made the Musée d'Orsay, the Orangerie, the Metropolitan Museum, the Van Gogh Museum, and others citadels of worship. In contrast, many local churches in Europe are empty, some holding masses perhaps once a month. Museums of late-nineteenth and early-twentieth-century art are the places now attended by the bourgeoisie and wealthy celebrating an aesthetic that speaks to their lives.

The continuing popularity of the Impressionists and Post-Impressionists, and the extraordinary valuation of their works in the marketplace, speaks to a modern posture. The world we inhabit culturally, on its edge, is that of Einstein, Freud, Woolf, and others, a world also scarred by two great wars and many smaller ones. It is a world of relativity, multiple perceptions, the unconscious, chaos, and a view of human nature that makes us all suspect. However, Europeans find this world very uncomfortable and thus retreat to a more comfortable and safe one—that of the Impressionists, the order of classical music, the closed drama of Puccini—a theatre of realism.

We live in Einstein's world, but we behave often as if we were still in the universe of Newton. There is a longing for order, coherence, predictability, and that means we may admire Modernism but on a daily basis we do not want to live with its assumptions. Bach is safe, but Bartók is annoying; Wordsworth is charming, but Dada is disturbing; Dickens tells a fine story with a beginning and an end, but Woolf is troubling. We know we live in an incoherent and relativist world, but we prefer laws of nature. Modernism may be admired, but it is also resisted.

It was hoped at one time, around our year of 1930, that film would become a medium of experimentation and innovation, providing great insights into our world and our ways of seeing and knowing. Film seemed to be moving in very original directions.

Salvador Dalí combined with Luis Buñuel to make two films at the time. The first, in 1929, clearly designated a surrealist film, was *Un Chien Andalou.* The title itself, *An Andalusian Dog,* had little to do with what transpired on the screen. The plot, if one could call it that, is disjointed, as scenes succeed one another as if in a dream. Though very short (about twenty minutes in length), it proved popular and ran for eight months.

Buñuel stated that he and Dalí adopted a rule: "No idea or image that might lend itself to a rational explanation of any kind would be accepted." He also stated, "Nothing, in the film, symbolizes anything. The only method of investigation of the symbols would be, perhaps, psychoanalysis."[14] The most famous image, opening the film, was that of a man slitting a woman's eyeball with a razor.

The film's premiere was attended by Picasso, Le Corbusier, and many of those in Breton's group of surrealists. Buñuel and Dalí were relieved, surprised, and simultaneously disappointed that their attack on the bourgeois world and its perceptions of reality was successful.

In 1930, Buñuel directed, and he and Dalí wrote the screenplay for a second collaboration, a film with sound, *L'Age d'or* (The Golden Age). The title in this case is ironic, for the film is an open attack on capitalist values, the sexual repression of contemporary bourgeois society, and the Catholic Church. A couple's attempts at romance and sexual pleasure are continually thwarted by social mores. As a result, there are images of a woman masturbating, a male waiter getting pleasure from rubbing a wine bottle, the woman giving fellatio to the toe of a religious statue, and the couple making love in a muddy field during a religious ceremony, among others. References to images associated with the Marquis de Sade abound; a crucifix is used as a symbol of sadism.

The film opened in Paris in November 1930. In this case, the filmmakers got their desired response. Riots ensued several days later, led by those who were offended at its open displays of desire and the attacks on bourgeois culture and the Church. Indeed, some of the protesters claimed that Buñuel and those who made the film must have been Jewish. On December 10 the Prefect of Police of Paris arranged to have the film banned.

Today, filmmakers in Europe are neither as experimental nor as controversial. There are serious and fine films that examine social and political issues, from *The Bicycle Thief* (1948) to *Ida* (2013). However, many films shown in Europe emanate from Hollywood, and it continues to dominate the industry as a whole. These productions are as tame as can be, driven only by the need to entertain and make money. One longs for the day when art could, on occasion, cause riots.

Theatre is a much older art form than is film, and there is much continuity. Two new developments since 1930 have influenced contemporary theatre. The first is sometimes referred to as the Theatre of the Absurd, represented best by Samuel Beckett and Harold Pinter.

Beckett's *Waiting for Godot* (1953) is arguably the most important play of his generation. Beckett is sometimes bracketed with existentialist philosophers because his work deals with what has come to be called the void. Life is seen to have no intrinsic meaning; we are sad creatures longing for certainty in a world that is incoherent; life is a struggle.

Beckett's plays reflect this new universe, one influenced deeply by the events of the 1930s and the Second World War. Yet *Godot* (the titular character who never appears) is a play with some redemptive ideas. The two main characters take some pleasure in their relationship and friendship—they are not alone. As well, when there is a moment of crisis, when someone cries for help, Beckett has one of his anti-heroes deliver something of a discourse, unusual in itself because the dialogue in the play is terse.

> Let us not waste our time in idle discourse! (*Pause. Vehemently.*) Let us do something while we have the chance! It is not every day that we are needed. Others would meet the case equally well, if not better. To all mankind they were addressed, those cries for help still ringing in our ears! But at this place, at this moment of time, all mankind is us whether we like it or not. Let us represent worthily for once this foul brood to which a cruel fate consigned us ...! What are we doing here, *that* is the question. And we are blessed in this, that we happen to know the answer. Yes, in this immense confusion one thing alone is clear. We are waiting for Godot to come.[15]

Like Camus, Beckett argues that we shape who we are through our actions, and that we need to universalize our decisions in order to lift them up from the personal to the moral. Meaning may not be out there, but we can create it, even while we wait for a revelation, perhaps a messiah.

Pinter's works, like those of Beckett, change the discourse. His plays, usually set in ordinary places with ordinary people, use silences masterfully to create a sense of menace and to try to get at how words both mask reality and shape it. Pinter has been likened to Kafka. Indeed, just as there are experiences that are "Kafkaesque," there are situations that are "Pinteresque," strange and sinister without quite revealing what is happening. As well, Pinter, like Kafka, rarely gives the audience much information about his characters. We know only what it is that the character is experiencing at the time. He stated,

> A character on stage who can present no convincing argument or information as to his past experience, his present behaviour or his aspirations, nor give a comprehensive analysis of his motives, is as legitimate and as worthy of attention as one who, alarmingly, can do all these things.[16]

We wonder what it is that Beckett and Pinter are saying, yet we recognize that they often tell us about modern life far more profoundly than traditional realist dramas.

A second main development in the theatre is one Brecht might have liked. It is a theatre of confrontation, in which the traditional, safe division between the audience and the stage is effaced. A fine example is Peter Weiss's *The Persecution and assassination of Marat as performed by the Inmates of Charenton under the direction of the Marquis de Sade* (1964), known as *Marat/Sade*.

The play takes place in the madhouse of Charenton, as the inmates, including the Marquis de Sade, are engaged in acting in a play as "therapy." They are watched by the keeper of the asylum, representing "reason," and by the audience. Slowly, the play turns both political and into a debate on human nature. The keeper, Coulmier, likened to Marat and Napoleon, claims that the proponents of the French Revolution began it because of the high and noble ideals and goals of the age of reason; de Sade argues that it is about power, libido, and desire, masking themselves as progress.

As the inversion occurs, those in the madhouse seem more sane than their keepers. The audience is confronted and the division between the paying patrons looking for entertainment and those deemed "mad" is no longer clear. (Just as in the time of the play, members of the bourgeoisie would go to the madhouse to be entertained by observing the fantasies and behaviour of the inmates; see Goya's paintings on this matter.)

Coulmier, the voice of "reason" says,

> But today we live in far different times
> We have no oppressors no violent crimes
> We are well on our way to achieving our goal
> There's bread in plenty and there's also coal
> And although we're at war anyone can see
> It can only end in victory.

The chorus of the "mad" replies ironically,

> And if most have a little and few have a lot
> You can see how much nearer our goal we have got
> We can say what we like without favour or fear
>   and what we can't say we can breathe in your ear
> And though we're locked up we're no longer enslaved
> And the honour of France is eternally saved
> The useless debate the political brawl are over
> There's one man to speak for us all....[17]

There is a long history in European thought, going at least as far back as Shakespeare and Cervantes, of having the "mad" be far more insightful than those ordinary mortals who are "sane." "Much Madness," wrote Emily Dickinson, "is divinest Sense." Weiss uses madness and confrontation to make us question our most fundamental assumptions and, in the Brechtian mode, to challenge our complacency. All three playwrights disturb.

In literature, the works of our 1930 intellectuals still resonate. The experiments of Virginia Woolf in the form and presentation of the novel are still guiding many writers. The attempt of Thomas Mann to understand the irrational in our lives is part of many works. The dystopia of Huxley has been followed by a growing number of works in that genre.

The most important development in the European novel is one begun and popularized outside Europe, by the Colombian Gabriel García Márquez, known as magic realism. García Márquez discussed how he came to write as he did in his Nobel Prize Address of 1982, entitled "The Solitude of Latin America." He noted that the geography, the experience, and the reality of Latin Americans was very different from that of Europeans. Still, outsiders, Europeans and North Americans, used their own categories of analysis and different experiences to try to understand Latin America. Moreover, not only were those categories imposed on Latin America, but Latin Americans themselves often privileged European models. The result was that, for his continent, "our crucial problem has been a lack of conventional means to render our lives believable. This ... is the crux of our solitude." For "the interpretation of our reality through patterns not our own serves only to make us ever more unknown, ever less free, ever more solitary."[18]

García Márquez and others in Latin America experimented with literary form and developed what has become known as magic realism, most notably in García Márquez' great masterpiece, *One Hundred Years of Solitude* (1967).

"Magic realism," said García Márquez, "expands the categories of the real so to encompass myth, magic, and other extraordinary phenomena in nature or experience which European realism excluded."

In this case, many Western writers adopted some of the techniques and narrative discourse of magic realism. Among them: time bends—time can be psychological, mythic dreamlike, discontinuous; cause and effect is sometimes now replaced by the unexpected or the disruptive; normal perceptions are not always how the world is seen—disruptions, inversions, and reversals are ordinary; the rational is replaced by the incredible, the marvellous, the uncanny, the disquieting; and closed stories are rare—now tales are open-ended. Narratives are sometimes discontinuous, sometimes what has been styled a narrative collage.

The critique of the traditional mode of perception and the way stories are told has, at its core, a critique of normal society. Magic realism dovetailed with some of what had been going on in Europe, most notably the narrative techniques of Kafka, Beckett, and Pinter. What the new Latin American novel did do was to heavily influence the West, which in time has adopted its mode of discourse. It has had as revolutionary an influence as did the Russian novel of the last half of the nineteenth century. It certainly legitimized a much broader and deeper perception of how humans live their lives.

A second development has been the influence of such writers as Joyce, Kafka, and Woolf on literature in the West in general, which is in accord with the perceptions of magic realism. The universe is no longer presented as rational and coherent. There is a struggle to find ways to use words to get at inner reality. Social realism is trumped by psychological realism, a literary equivalent of the idea of relativity. The reader is no longer comfortable, as she is asked to be far more active than in traditional tales. The world is depicted as full of ambiguity, contradiction, and paradox. The story ceases, but there is no ending. Chaos is normal; order is what we pretend to have.

The result has been a European literature that is diverse. There are different kinds of tales—from Camus's *The Plague* (1947) and Mann's *Dr. Faustus* (1947), to Günter Grass's *The Tin Drum* (1959) and John Fowles's *The Magus* (1966), from Italo Calvino's *Invisible Cities* (1972), and Salman Rushdie's *Midnight's Children* (1981), to Angela Carter's *Nights at the Circus* (1984). Literature is far more open than it was before.

Creativity in our postmodern world has a broader range of expression than in the modernist culture of 1930. Novels are still written, political philosophy is articulated and refined, musical theatre is vibrant, and dystopias are by now ordinary.

Creativity has new forms, not simply new content. World fusion music is enormously open and experimental. The group Ultra-red attempts to pursue "a fragile but dynamic exchange between art and political organizing." They use electronic music and what is called "sound art" to work with artists and organizers in such areas as migration experience and policy, community development, and the politics surrounding HIV/ AIDS. Their work includes installations as well as conventional radio broadcasts and performances.[19]

Christo and Jeanne-Claude have pioneered the creation of massive public installations in the process of redefining sculpture and art and bringing artistic consciousness out of the traditional museum. In 1962 they closed a street in Paris with a wall constructed out of eighty-nine oil barrels, a statement about the Berlin Wall built a year earlier. They have wrapped trees, walls, bridges, and monuments as conceptual artists.

Street art and graffiti, some sponsored by governments, some simply created by individuals and groups, have become global and some have contributed to the political and aesthetic global culture. *Bandes dessinées* (drawn strips), or comics, are now taken seriously. Along with graphic novels, they often make serious statements about culture and society and are now viewed as an art form. France has led the way on the European continent, and the works of Jacques Tardi and Enki Bilal are important contributions. Many video games are texts that deal with power and authority.

Architecture in Europe is now open to new forms. The Guggenheim Museum in Bilbao, created by the Canadian-American architect Frank Gehry and opened in 1997, is one of the great works of architecture in the modern West. It curves, moves visually, is in harmony with its surroundings, brilliantly fulfills its purpose, and finally, is beautiful. Indeed, it is so stunning that it eclipses the contemporary works of art that are shown inside.

A different structure full of historical and political meaning is the Jewish Museum in Berlin designed by Daniel Libeskind, which opened in 2001. Libeskind combined a traditional baroque entrance with modern design and space to emphasize the centrality of Jewish presence and history in the identity and past of the city. He also created an open space visitors must traverse that is a Void, reached by bridges, signifying absence and the difficulty of even articulating the events of the Holocaust.

There is, as well, a piece of European architecture still in the making that celebrates modernism, the *Sagrada Familia* Cathedral in Barcelona, designed by Antoni Gaudí (1852–1926). Begun in 1822, its work sometimes suspended by events—including the Spanish Civil War—it is now at the stage where one can say that when it is finished, likely in 2026, it will be the most interesting cathedral built in Europe since the Renaissance.

The expressive world of the early twenty-first century is very different in its possibilities and forms than that of 1930. There is no question that the 1930 public intellectuals still have much to offer. Their works are among those that we must return to every so often to learn how we came to be who we are and to find instruction.

However, while the 1930 artists and writers provide guidance, especially in their questions and concerns, we now must think about the categories of thought and kinds of analyses that are appropriate to our own times. The intellectuals discussed in this work are part of the Modernist movement that contributed much to the interwar years and beyond. Now, in the postmodern world, whose culture exists in ways very different from 1930, we need to develop a critical consciousness of a different sort. Without question, we can borrow from the past. Not to do so leaves a vacuum unfilled. But the worlds of Plato, Cicero, Aquinas, Michelangelo, Newton, and others, including Mann, Woolf, Ortega, and Freud, are no longer what Europe happens to be. 1930 offers great insight into our times, but it cannot supply the template of understanding. That is our task.

- **The epistemological dilemma**

It was Yeats who in 1919 said, "The best lack all conviction, while the worst / Are full of passionate intensity."

Half of that insight is still true—the worst do have passionate intensity, feeling secure in their beliefs, willing to trample on others. The worst also display those characteristics outlined by Ortega: they feel free to make their personal and ideological demands universal; they ask for instant satisfaction; they do not know what a struggle it has been to develop a decent civilization and to institutionalize human rights. They have no problem of knowledge—their beliefs and desires are enough to give them certainty, be they fundamentalist religious types, nationalists willing to do the dirty job of ethnic cleansing, or true believers in one dogmatic political stance or another.

However, the best no longer lack all conviction. The atmosphere of the interwar period among many decent people, the pessimism bordering on nihilism, has diminished in light of events from 1930. Now, there is a willingness to defend some universals, even if, paradoxically, there is a resistance to settled truths. Europe, in the EU, is socially democratic. It has made human rights universal. It has put into place institutions that protect due process and the dignity of the individual. It will resist authoritarianism in its many forms.

The problem of knowledge is still with us. The world is no longer as coherent and orderly as it was thought to be until Modernism. Europe has learned to live with uncertainty and to create a better political structure and political economy. If religion is on the wane and nationalism persists, Europe has learned to avoid the worst excesses of the latter. There is now a distrust of passionate intensity, and resistance to it in most of its forms.

We do agree that science offers certain answers. Medicine continues to advance; we know much more about the solar system than did Galileo; chemistry offers some sense of a coherent organization of cells. We have a method and we try to replicate data so as to have some confidence in the results.

The issues raised by scientific knowledge are very thorny ones, but they fall into the realm of moral philosophy. Do we continue life under any circumstances? Do we support abortion and/or designer babies? How do we respond to the evidence that we are irrevocably changing the climate and living conditions on the planet?

Social science pretends to be scientific, though its value for public policy is not as clear as many would like to think it is. The fact that the study of politics is now called political science does not increase the value of the truths claimed by its practitioners or philosophers.

For certainty, scientists and social scientists have substituted probability, which helps to understand matters and people en masse, but does little to accommodate the individual. If you visit a medical specialist and are told that you have a disease that kills only 50 percent of those who contract it, that is hardly consoling. In truth, if you are told that 10 percent will die, it does not make you more immune to the fatal consequences. Similarly, if you are a woman, a Jew, or a Roma, and are given data that suggests that only 20 percent of you will experience violence in any given period, that does not help you as an individual.

However, if Europeans lack certainty, a clear *Weltanschauung*, if fewer people are willing to sign on to something like the Ten Commandments, there is still a broad agreement morally on what is called a frame of reference. We do make judgments based on an ethical code.

Is civilization fragile, in part because of our epistemological uncertainty? Yes. Freud and Ortega were correct in 1930. Our social and political structures are not as confident as they sometimes seem. Our very nature, sometimes, is too destructive. Ortega's mass man is still with us and makes his intolerant claims. But we now know more about that fragility than Europeans did in 1930, and that gives us occasion to pause.

Italo Calvino's novel *Invisible Cities* (1972), which includes a dialogue about perception and reality between power (Kublai Khan) and experience (Marco Polo) is in part about empires, their transitory nature, and the impossibility of fixing reality in the face of a world that is always in flux. It is about our time, using past, present, and future to illuminate how we live.

At the end of the book the emperor reflects on utopias and dystopias, trying to understand his own atlas and authority. He says to Marco Polo, sadly, alluding to both Dante and the existential present, "it is all useless, if the last landing place can only be the infernal city, and it is there that, in ever-narrowing circles, the current is drawing us." Marco Polo answers,

> The inferno of the living is not something that will be; if there is one, it is what is already here, the inferno where we live every day, that we form by being together. There are two ways to escape suffering it. The first is easy for many: accept the inferno and become such a part of it that you can no longer see it. The second is risky and demands constant vigilance and apprehension: seek and learn to recognize who and what, in the midst of the inferno, are not inferno, then make them endure, give them space.[20]

Europe in the 1930s can be said to have chosen the first way. It has learned that it must try to take the second path, chosen by all the 1930 public intellectuals in this book.

- **Fascism: norm or aberration?**

Fascism is still with us, though it can be recorded that Bolshevism is dead. Even so-called Communist states—Russia, Belarus, China, and Cuba outside Europe—are, in content and practice, fascist enterprises. Still, one of the great epithets of European political life is that of "Fascist." Putin calls his Ukrainian opponents fascists. Greek democrats call members of the Golden Dawn fascists. Some Americans are called fascists by left-wing Europeans. Even Fascists will spit out the word "fascist" to insult and try to marginalize their opponents, as Erdoğan has done in Turkey.

Fascism retains many of the characteristics of the models of the 1930s and later, especially those of Mussolini's Italy and Franco's Spain. It supports a single-party state, with the party running the state. The party itself is a kind of loyal elite, organized in a military style. The party demands full commitment to the group or the cause. It is corporate, not individualist.

Fascism also appropriates nationalism, most especially ethnic rather than civic nationalism. It claims identity is derived from belonging to the nation, and almost always it has a racist undertone. Values are monist, not pluralist. Stress is placed on the importance of the collective, of sacrificing one's self for the higher cause espoused by the party/nation.

Most Fascist states at their beginning, or soon thereafter, stress the importance of the leader as the embodiment of the group. Hence, the leader sometimes is seen as having a spiritual or mystical quality, in addition to being powerful. Violence is valued in Fascist parties. It is seen as a test, as a positive, as a show of superiority.

Socially, Fascism is elitist, the elite sometimes being the new men of the Fascist Party, many of whom enrich themselves through the state. It is highly masculine in its orientation, stressing the family and traditional gender roles as well as force and virility. When it is useful, Fascists will also try to tame and/or appropriate the power of the church in their state on behalf of its cause.

In the aftermath of the Great War, several European states turned to Fascism, including Spain, Portugal, Italy, Germany, and Hungary. Spain and Portugal continued to be Fascist into the 1970s.

In eastern Europe, after the Second World War, the states to the east of the Iron Curtain became, so they said, Communist. But in practice, they more closely resembled the Fascist model—East Germany, Poland, Romania, Stalinist Russia, Bulgaria, Albania, Yugoslavia, and others.

Fascism is still present in Europe in two ways. Fascist parties exist and compete for seats in parliaments of states and in the European parliament. After the crisis following the economic recession of 2008, Fascist parties have grown more popular. They are authoritarian, anti-immigration, usually anti-Semitic, anti-Muslim and anti-Roma, often blame "outsiders" for domestic troubles, and highly ethnically nationalist. They are racist, either openly or in coded terms. In the end, they have little commitment to democratic values and practice.

It is not at all clear what would happen if a Fascist party won an election in an EU state. Would the EU tolerate a move to authoritarian politics? This is unlikely, but it has not been fully tested.

There is one European country that is turning Fascist, Turkey, but it is not a member of the EU. Erdoğan's Turkey is moving from a quasi-democratic state to a Fascist one, as Erdoğan appropriates power and makes his party into one that absorbs state power. Certainly, Turkey's entry into the EU is moot in this situation.

One favourite ploy of Fascist states is to continue some of the institutions of democracy while undermining them at the same time. This is most clearly demonstrated in Europe by what is happening in Russia. There are courts, but the judiciary is no longer independent. Trials are held, court processes exist, but they have no relationship to democratic justice systems. There are elections that are manipulated in many ways, most notably by limiting who might be the opponents and by full control of the media. Democratic claims are made in the midst of a Fascist reality.

In Europe (and the West, most especially in the United States) there is a trend toward the appropriation of wealth in the hands of fewer people. The gap between rich and poor is getting wider, while the middle class is shrinking. The result, in practice, is that somewhere along the way, slowly, insidiously, democracies start turning into oligarchies. Power is in the hands of fewer people, in spite of elections and due process. Thus, and this is far more apparent in the United States than in Europe, the monolithic quality of Fascism becomes reality in the face of a polity that is theoretically pluralist.

When does all this transform democracy into soft Fascism? No one has conducted a clear study of the matter. However, there are columnists in some newspapers and blogs who note that Europeans now seem more willing to accept authoritarian politics than before the 2008 economic downturn. The rise of openly Fascist parties has made some centre parties move further to the right.

In the first masterful study of the Hitlerian period in English, Allan Bullock's *Hitler: A Study in Tyranny* (1952), Bullock asked near the end of the work whether the Hitler phenomenon was a German issue or a

Western one. He concluded it was the latter, that wherever you are in the West, something like it could happen there. Fascism pokes its nose up every so often. Democrats in Europe must remain on their guard.

- **The dystopian trend of thought**
Utopian writing is no longer done. It ended with the Great War and with the new view of human nature discussed by our 1930 intellectuals. It coincided with the death of the idea of progress, and is unlikely to be revived soon. Now, dystopias are what we do.

The classic post–Second World War dystopia is Orwell's *1984*, which has taken a place in the pantheon that includes Zamiatin's *We*, which heavily influenced Orwell, and Huxley's *Brave New World*.

The genre of dystopia seems to be one that is mainly used in the English-writing world, less so on the European continent. Major French contributions include Jean-Luc Godard's film *Alphaville* (1965) and Beckett's novel *Le Dépeupleur* (*The Lost Ones*, 1970). Russian writers lately are following Zamiatin. Olga Slavnikova's *2017* (2006) predicts political unrest taking the form of street protests and laments exploitation of several kinds, including that of the misuse of natural resources.

Themes of major dystopias, including those of Anthony Burgess (*A Clockwork Orange*, 1962), Margaret Atwood (who has written several, including *The Handmaid's Tale*, 1985, and *Oryx and Crake*, 2003), and P.D. James (*Children of Men*, 1992), are all cautionary tales and predictions of where we might be heading. They reflect a consciousness of the loss of innocence and fears that regress has replaced progress. Eden and the Golden Age are long behind us.

The themes of many dystopias during the Cold War dealt with the possibility of nuclear disaster and the end of civilization. Today, they deal with the loss of individuality and the power of the state, the environmental disaster that seems almost inevitable and its consequences for society and humanity, and the possibility of genetic transformation, including the end of humanity.

Some dystopias also fit the genre of science fiction, including the film *Blade Runner* (1982), which was based on Philip K. Dick's science fiction novel *Do Androids Dream of Electric Sheep?* (1968). They often discuss technological matters and the introduction of robotic beings that are very much like humans. Indeed, some have robots that act more "humanely" than do biological humans.

Writers of dystopias use literature in the service of politics and morality. They continue a tradition in Europe where the novel came to be one of the main places where social and political matters were discussed.

After all, the first novel—and a model for so many others—Cervantes's *Don Quixote* (1605, 1615) can be viewed as protest literature, attacking the coarseness of existence and the violence and inhumanity of its own time. Subsequent writers, Goethe, Balzac, Turgenev, and others, used the novel to comment on the most important issues of the day. We still need stories and myths. Speculative fiction remains a valuable tool of reflection about who we are and where we are going.

Europe today is facing its most important set of decisions since the fall of the Berlin Wall and the collapse of the Soviet Union. Heretofore, the EU expanded and brought new states under its constitution. However, several of these new members, most notably Poland and Hungary, are systematically destroying their democratic constitutions and arrangements. What will Europe do in the face of this trend?

Moreover, in some of the core EU states there are movements to challenge either membership in the EU and/or membership in the euro bloc. The United Kingdom will be leaving the EU in 2019, though no one can predict with confidence what the new relationship will be. There are serious challenges to continued membership in the EU by organized political parties in France, Germany, Italy, the Netherlands, Belgium, Greece, and others. And what will the EU do if several states vote to leave and/or abandon the euro?

The European experiment has turned out to be more fragile than it was believed before the social and economic events of 2008, just as American democracy is brittle today. The present crisis is hardly simply financial and/or economic. It is also one of both liberal democracy and the continuity of peace on the European continent. The new wave is given the name of populism, but it more nearly reflects a combination of ethnic nationalism, anti-immigrant rage, anger at liberal leaders and elites who are seen to be serving their own interests, and a willingness to accept a quasi-fascist state if it is seen to be able deliver the goods.

From 1945 to the fall of the Berlin Wall in 1989 there was a Europe that was integrating, expanding, and putting together a new diplomatic and political infrastructure. And, above all, it kept the peace.

In 1989, the year the Berlin Wall was torn down, the historian-philosopher Francis Fukuyama published an essay titled "The End of History," which had wide distribution and influence. It dealt with the rise and decline of major ideologies in modern history, such as democracy, communism, and fascism. He hypothesized that Western liberal democracy had won that battle, as most states in the West that had been Communist or Fascist were moving toward liberalism.

In brief, his thesis was, "What we may be witnessing is not just the end of the Cold War, or the passing of a particular period of postwar history, but the end of history as such: that is, the end point of mankind's ideological evolution and the universalization of Western liberal democracy as the final form of human government."[21]

From 1989 to 2008 the European Union expanded into eastern Europe, embraced much of the continent, introduced the euro, and provided freedom of movement for member-state citizens via the Schengen Agreement, incorporated into the mainstream of European Union law by the Amsterdam Treaty in 1997, which came into effect in 1999.

Fukuyama, like many before him who thought they had the secret to historical development, was profoundly wrong. We have, in the last decade, been witnessing the end of the end of history. Liberal democracy is being challenged virtually everywhere it had a foothold.

There are only two leading countries, one outside Europe, that have democracy embedded in their history and or constitution that do not have important right-wing xenophobic, anti-immigrant, ethnic, misogynist, nationalist political parties vying for power: Canada and Spain.

Where are we now, a decade after the 2008 crisis? Europe needs to clearly define itself again. What is happening is a retreat into nationalism in the United Kingdom, Italy, Poland, Hungary, and elsewhere. Inside national states there are smaller movements that are themselves a form of nationalism—in Scotland, Northern Ireland, Catalonia, northern Italy, and Belgium, among others. There is also the trend of skepticism about the euro, as countries like Spain and Greece falter and have no clear way to fix their problems in a system where they cannot adjust their currency.

Europe needs to attend to these matters. It must, as the European Parliament and the President of the European Council, Donald Tusk, are trying to do, insist on certain universal rights and a democratic polity. It must attend to the problems created in economic hard times by the euro. It is not enough to say, as many do, that keeping the euro is a better choice than abandoning it. It has to find a way to make those countries that now use the euro—but would not choose to do so if they had to start all over again—believe that the unified currency is not helping to defeat democracy and a decent standard of living.

There are other divisions arising out of the geopolitical circumstances in Europe that are not discussed as much as they should be. One is north–south tensions. The problem states economically after the 2008 recession were Portugal, Italy, Ireland, Greece, and Spain, given the nasty acronym PIIGS. The south is teetering and the northern states, especially the economic powerhouse of the EU, Germany, made great demands on their economic policies and behaviour. Ireland is recovering. Spain is also moving forward, though its unemployment rate is now 17 percent, having been over 25 percent. Portugal and Italy are stable, but still a worry. Greece is a disaster, beholden to regular bailouts from the wealthier north.

The north–south differences are not a new way of looking at Europe. Thomas Mann made much of the divide in many of his works, including *Mario and the Magician*. The north is stereotyped as austere, dark, disciplined, frugal, and above all, mainly Protestant. The south is said to be sunny, light, sensual, self-indulgent, and Catholic. The stereotypes sometimes are distorted, but they are used regularly.

And there are north–south divides in many countries. In the nineteenth century the Englishman Disraeli, later to become Prime Minister of Britain, famously wrote in his novel *Sybil* (1845) about "the two nations" that was the reality in Great Britain, divided between north and south:

> Two nations; between whom there is no intercourse and no sympathy; who are as ignorant of each other's habits, thoughts, and feelings, as if they were dwellers in different zones, or inhabitants of different planets; who are formed by a different breeding, are fed by a different food, are ordered by different manners, and are not governed by the same laws.... *the rich and the poor.* [22]

It remains so. The wealth of today's United Kingdom is mainly located in the Greater London area. The north of England and Scotland and Wales are far poorer than the capital area. The political divide is now so great as a result of the Brexit vote that Scotland may well leave the union in the next decade.

Italy and Germany also have north–south differences that are important in their economy and politics. In Italy, the *mezzogiorno*, the south, has always been the poor cousin of the united country. Most immigrants from Italy to North America come from that area. There is today a Northern League Party, officially known as the Lega, whose program supports transforming Italy into a federal state with strong local autonomy in both the political and economic realms. In some areas there are Northern League politicians who support the secession of the North from Italy and sovereignty for a new state to be called Padania.

The south of Germany, especially Bavaria, is Catholic. The north is Protestant. Bavaria sometimes behaves as an entity of its own, and its political leaders enter coalitions with their own interests in mind. Often part of the coalition government in power, Bavarian politicians work to retain strong local powers.

Then there is the more profound east–west divide that is still part of the European reality, regardless of which states have joined the EU. Western Europeans share a common cultural history, in that they experienced the Renaissance the Reformation, the Scientific Revolution and the Enlightenment before entering modernity around the events of the French and Industrial Revolutions. Not so for the East, including contemporary Poland, the Balkans, Russia, and Turkey.

Moreover, the events from 1945 to 1991 and the fall of the Soviet Union divided Europe, as imaged by Churchill's metaphor of an "iron curtain." The commitment to liberal values is far more deeply institutionalized in the west of Europe than in the east, and this has brought about some serious divisions as the EU has expanded.

Today, in Poland and Hungary, what the Prime Minister of Hungary, Victor Orbán, called "illiberal democracy" in 2014, is turning those states into quasi-authoritarian regimes. Both are on the border of what is accepted in the European arrangements that they signed when they joined the EU after it enlarged to the east in 2004.

Then there are Russia and Turkey. Putin's Russia is virtually a dictatorship as well as being a kleptocracy. Its leader regards the fall of the Soviet Union as a calamitous event that needs to be rectified. He views the EU and NATO with anger and scorn, and Russia is determined to do all it can to weaken both arrangements.

Turkey is turning into a dictatorship as well, after decades of both westernization and the attempt to develop a stable, constitutional state. Under Recep Erdoğan, human rights are being violated daily, journalists are in jail, and free speech, especially criticism of Erdoğan, is limited. After an attempted coup in 2016, the Erdoğan government incarcerated over 70,000 people and purged over 45,000 people from the military, the judiciary, the civil service, the police, and educational institutions, including every university dean in the country, all in the name of protecting the state.

Erdoğan and the Justice and Development Party (AKP) that he co-founded arranged for a referendum in April 2017 on eighteen changes to the constitution that, if approved, would cripple parliament and give the president (Erdoğan himself) dictatorial powers. It barely passed. Moreover, the opposition challenged the result, claiming that many ballots were illegal.

Results carried by the state-run Anadolu news agency showed the "yes" vote had about 51.3 percent for those agreeing to the changes, compared to 48.7 percent for the "no" vote. Istanbul, Ankara, and Izmir, Turkey's three largest cities, voted against the changes, as did the vast majority of Kurdish voters and many of the coastal cities, indicating a general decline in AKP support. However, nothing stopped Erdoğan from immediately putting the changes into effect. Many commentators regard this as the most significant political event in Turkey since it became a republic in 1923.

Hence, some eastern European states are questioning the liberal democratic foundation of the EU. Two large and powerful eastern European states that are in both Europe and Asia, Russia and Turkey, are now openly hostile to the rest of Europe. A decade ago, Turkey was negotiating to gain entrance to the EU. Now this is a moot point. The east–west divide, long a part of European history, seemed to be fading a few decades ago. Now it is clearer than at any time since 1989.

In the midst of all these matters that seem to be pulling the EU apart, on March 25, 2017, the leaders of twenty-seven states of the union gathered in Rome on the sixtieth anniversary of the signing of the Treaty of Rome by six countries. They agreed that "Europe is our common future," even while knowing that four days later the United Kingdom, the twenty-eighth member, which did not attend, would invoke Article 50 of the treaty, the clause that will take the UK out of the union in two years' time.

The politicians were aware of the difficulties, which they defined as "regional conflicts, terrorism, growing migratory pressures, protectionism and social and economic inequalities." Nonetheless, they all asserted that "Europe is our common future." For most, it was not a platitude. For Germany, France, Italy and many smaller countries, the EU is now central to their lives. It remains the biggest trading area on the planet. Together, the countries of the EU contribute more funds to humanitarian projects than any other political unit. It has made Europe open to travel and to labour.[23] Above all, Europe is at peace and is a force for peace in the world, this after the bloody years from 1914 to 1945, which our Modernist public intellectuals of 1930 were warning against.

Populism and nationalism, racism even, threaten the EU itself, as groups in many countries blame the union for their woes, as though they might be better off without it. They have seemingly won in the United Kingdom and threaten elsewhere. This tension is not new to Europe. Globalization, cosmopolitanism, and the idea of universal human rights has vied with nationalism and authoritarianism for two centuries.

Three elections in 2017 testify to the divisions in Europe as a whole. In March, elections in the Netherlands resulted in the pro-European party then in power, the People's Party for Freedom and Democracy, led by Prime Minister Mark Rutte, receiving the highest number of votes (21.3 percent) and seats (33), a loss of eight seats in the 150-member parliament. They entered into a coalition with several smaller parties in order to form a new government.

There was relief in many quarters after the Netherlands result because the country did not follow the United States in choosing a populist, nationalist government, and it also seemed to reject the anti-European sentiment behind the UK's support for Brexit. Optimists were happy. However, pessimists pointed to the increased support for the right-wing Party for Freedom (PVV), which came in second with 13.1 percent of the vote and twenty seats in parliament, a gain of five seats. The PVV is anti-immigrant, highly nationalist, racist, openly anti-Islam, and skeptical about the value of Netherlands belonging in the EU.

France had a presidential election in April and May 2017. The traditional leading parties did not survive the first round in a system where, if no candidate obtains a majority, the two leading vote-getters run in a second election. The centre-right Republican Party, led by François Fillon, who was involved in a financial scandal, received 20.01 percent of the vote. The Socialist Party, which held the presidency under the unpopular François Hollande, put up a new candidate, but fell to only 6.36 percent.

Three outliers did well in France. Emmanuel Macron, who founded a new centrist pro-European party, *En Marche*, led all candidates with 24.01 percent. Marine Le Pen, leader of the National Front, a party long associated with right-wing anti-European sentiment, protectionism, nationalism, and anti-immigration, came second with 21.3 percent. Fourth, nearly third with 19.58 percent of the vote was Jean-Luc Mélenchon, who founded the movement *La France Insoumise*, Unbowed France, in 2016. Mélenchon and his party were to the left of the Socialists. They advocated a new constitution that would end the presidential system of France's fifth Republic, enact new labour laws favouring workers, and a change in the treaties of the EU related to monetary policy, agriculture, and the environment. Failing to transform the EU would result in France's exit from the association if the party held power.

The second round pitted Macron against Le Pen. Most of the defeated parties asked their members to support Macron, Le Pen being considered unacceptable because of the nationalist and racist history of her party. However, Mélenchon did not support Macron, thinking him too tied to business and the policies of the right. Even so, Macron won overwhelmingly, 66.1 to 33.9 percent. EU supporters breathed easily again, but it is worth noting that the two anti-European candidates, Le Pen and Mélenchon, received a combined 40.88 percent of the vote in the first round.

It was Germany's turn in September 2017. Angela Merkel, Europe and the West's most prestigious leader, led her Christian Democratic Union (CDU) and its Bavarian fraternal party, the Christian Social Union (CSU), into an election for the fourth time. She prevailed, again much to the satisfaction of EU supporters. However, the Social Democratic Party (SPD) and the CDU/CSU, the centre of German democracy and EU support, both fared worse than in the previous election in 2013. Merkel's party went from 41.5 percent of the vote, which translated into 311 seats in parliament in 2013, to 32.9 percent and 246 seats. The SPD had won 25.7 percent of the vote and 193 seats in 2013. Now they received 20.5 percent and 153 seats.

As a result of the 2017 election, Germany has a new third party, the Alternative for Germany (AfD), founded in 2013. That year they received 4.7 percent of the vote in the federal election, not quite reaching the 5 percent required to obtain representation in parliament. In 2017 they jumped to 12.6 percent of the vote, thus gaining 94 seats in the legislature.

As in the Netherlands and France, the bad news in Germany tempered, perhaps even outweighed, the good. The AfD is a nationalist party that campaigned on an opposition to the EU and the need to reclaim Germany's sovereignty. However, its nationalism is racist and alludes to supporting elements of Germany's Nazi past. They argue that Germany should repudiate the culture of shame with reference to its past and take pride in its history and identity. Language that had been part of Nazi propaganda has been revived, including the use of the heavily loaded word "Volk" to describe the German people. Seemingly innocent, the term was and is used by the right to refer to white people who are "racially" German. Of course, while it includes many people, it also excludes all Others, among them the large Muslim and refugee groups who have come to Germany and were welcomed by the CDU and the SPD.

As well, the AfD wishes to ban same-sex marriage and advocates traditional roles for women in the family. They support re-armament and conscription. The memory of events in Germany from 1918 to 1945 is long in Europe and the West, and a good number of people from the centre, left, and moderate right shivered when the election results were announced.

A fourth election to consider is that of the United Kingdom in June 2017. The Brexit referendum was called in 2016 by the then Conservative Prime Minister, David Cameron for all the wrong reasons, mainly hoping to end Conservative Party squabbles. Cameron and others assumed that the "Yes" side would win, and he immediately resigned after the vote, to be replaced by Theresa May.

May made a calculation in 2017 as deadly as that of Cameron the year before. With the polls showing the Conservatives doing very well, she called a snap election in May, expecting to obtain a large majority and badly defeat the opposition Labour Party. That did not happen. The Conservatives obtained 317 seats to Labour's 262 in a parliament of 650. They needed to obtain the support of the right-wing Democratic Unionist Party based in Northern Ireland, which won ten seats, to make a majority and form a weak government with a wounded prime minister.

As a result of the miscalculation of the Conservatives and the divisions inside their party, the United Kingdom is narrowing its world at a time when others are doing the opposite. They are negotiating to leave the EU, and so far they have not put forth a coherent plan for how they will handle their place in the world after. They claim to have a "special relationship" with the United States, but in the time of Trump that is irrelevant. The rest of the EU members, known as the EU27, have united against the UK, stating that they will not permit the UK to have the benefits of being a member of EU when they have chosen to leave it.

While the Netherlands, France, Germany, and others seem to have rejected the populist, protectionist, and isolationist trends in the US and the UK, they cannot be sanguine about the latest election results. The March 2018 election in Italy, in which two populist right-wing nationalist, anti-immigrant parties gained the most votes, is a warning. Europe's centre-left, its liberal and democratic supporter, is very weak. The odour of fascism is in the air, and it is getting stronger. In Turkey, Hungary, and Poland it is being institutionalized. The EU is more fragile today than it has been in some time.

Ironically, it is Germany that is now, again, at the centre of the issues and the debate. Today it is a Germany very different from that of 1914 or 1939. Germany has become a defender of stability in economics, democracy in politics, the acceptance of the Other in society, and the recognition that the EU is essential in keeping the peace.

There is a sense that most Germans still have *Vergangenheitsbewältigung* (coming to terms with the past) in their consciousness, though they have dealt with the years 1933–1945 more comprehensively and honestly than any other European country that engaged in Holocaust activities. They know what evil is, and they know that it can come from them. Hence, over the course of the last six decades, they have become staunch defenders of human rights and bilateral cooperation. Europe is essential to their healing.

Angela Merkel has great stature, deservedly, but she, like all of us, will pass from the scene. It remains important that her successors, wherever they stand on the political spectrum, continue to lead Europe well.

The crisis is real, but it should not be magnified. Europe's role in the world since 1957 has been more positive than at any comparable period of time in the last several centuries. These are tough times in a world turning to nationalism and authoritarianism. But the course chosen by most Europeans since 1957 is likely to survive and make an important contribution to peace, prosperity, and human dignity. It is a different world from that of 1930, but the leaders of Europe use a language not all that different from that of people like Mann, Ortega, and others in this study.

With the election of Trump, the role of the United States in world affairs is changing very quickly. The US is no longer a reliable ally, no longer looked to for leadership, no longer to be counted upon, and if anything, is feared. The American Century (1917–2017) is over. There is now a void in the West. The EU, for all of its problems, can fill it. There is still a great mission to be undertaken.

The public intellectuals of 1930 were, each in his or her own way, similar to dystopians. They feared where humanity was headed, in some cases they feared what they discovered about human nature. They wrote and created art. They did so in order to both help us to know about ourselves and offer some redemption from a hard time. They did so because, in spite of their fears, and in spite of their pessimism, they had hope that our better nature would triumph. Their works are relevant today, as they were in 1930.

Epilogue
EUROPEANS TODAY

OUR COUPLE LIVING in Europe in 1930 was rightly uneasy, though no one could have accurately predicted the next fifteen tragic years, certainly the most violent and problematic in Europe's long history. They struggled, not only economically but morally and personally, as they managed to get to 1945.

The moral quandaries they faced had to do with the treatment given to some of their neighbours, possibly with occupation, possibly witnessing people they knew being rounded up and taken to concentration camps that often became extermination centres. They tried to do the right thing, they resisted being cruel and indifferent, though to the very end of their lives they felt they could have done more.

Their personal lives were deeply changed. They lost their son, who died in battle in 1943, and they experienced a deep, profound suffering they did not even know was possible. Some of their extended family, though they were civilians, also died. They found that they lost some friends, because their political and civil decency did not go well with those who decided that they were superior because they belonged to a special nation, race, or class.

Yet they survived, and they went on to make a decent life for themselves, their daughter, and their daughter's family in the far more peaceful postwar years. The Cold War was ever-present, but on whichever side of the curtain they dwelled, they felt more optimistic about the future.

They lived to see their two grandchildren, born in 1952 and 1954, and to get to know them, a special pleasure at the end of lives that had endured recession, Depression, and two great wars, the actualization of Freud's troubled "homo homini lupis."

Their great granddaughter was born in 1982. She attended university and has a degree in languages, specializing in English and German. She

213

soon took up a position as a translator for a major commercial firm, and on occasion, finding that she had oral as well as written talent, would provide simultaneous translations at business and academic conferences.

She married later than did her ancestors, in 2012 in a small civic ceremony at the age of thirty, and is now pregnant with her first child. Her husband works in the real estate section of one of the major banks of the country. She intends to continue working, though both she and her husband will have considerable parental leave when the baby is born. They expect to use the excellent daycare services provided by the state and private care in the home for the child. Instead of purchasing a house in a suburb, they will continue to live in their major city, close to their work and the various cultural and sporting activities they enjoy.

The couple read less than their great-grandparents, though they watch a lot more—television, YouTube, visuals on their various computers, tablets, and smartphones. They no longer buy physical books; rather they read on their tablets and can buy and download anything they want in a matter of seconds. They don't own a dictionary or an encyclopaedia—that sort of information is available at the touch of a key. They like films and some television series; about once a month they will spend a whole day in bed on the weekend watching several films or a number of episodes in a series.

The lives and times of their great-grandparents fascinate the couple and many of their friends. From their grandparents they have heard about the Depression years, the anxious times, bloody in some cases, leading to the Second World War and the war itself. They wonder what their ancestors did at the time, not only how they survived but the choices they faced and made. They watch documentaries about the time, fictional series based on fact about the war years, and they read histories and novels about the period. What several historians have called "the Years of Catastrophe" still resonate in the minds of many Europeans, from Britain to Russia, from Norway to Italy.

The couple inform themselves about the world by subscribing to a newspaper online, perhaps the *New York Times*, the *Telegraph*, *Le Monde*, the *Corriere della sera*, *Die Welt*, or *El País*. They also read several online political reports and blogs. He spends much time with financial reporting via his tablet. Hence, their home is not paperless, but it is more technological than anything their ancestors might have imagined. Both use smartphones everywhere. If they lose electricity and/or wireless connectivity for any length of time, they feel they have lost some of their capacity to cope.

Our couple is engaged in their local community. They belong to a gym, volunteer on occasion at community events, always vote during elections. They prefer to be social rather than political and have little reverence for the political leaders of their country, relating much more to their region and city. They support the local football team and take in the World Cup and European championship religiously.

If there was one word to describe how our couple felt about their lives and the future today, it would be ambivalent. They are alternately hopeful and pessimistic.

Their Europe is not in crisis as it was in 1930. The EU and organizations like NATO have given Europeans a sense of stability in their political and diplomatic relations. A war emanating out of the centre of the continent, or a war between two major powers seems highly unlikely, given the way integration has occurred since 1945.

Yes, the Balkans sometimes flare up, and crises in countries like the Ukraine cause concern. But Russia's economy and that of western Europe are so interdependent, despite Russia's antagonism to much of what has happened diplomatically after the fall of the Soviet Union, it is agreed that anything resembling the two major wars will not occur out of Europe.

Hence, peace is taken for granted. Our couple did not serve in the military and, in thinking about the future of their unborn child, they envision a life separate from the threat of war. In this European world, there is no conscription, no presence of wounded veterans, no bombed neighbourhoods waiting to be rebuilt.

The assumption of peace is no small achievement, given Europe's history. Our couple and their friends, and their children, live their lives as if they will have a normal life expectancy.

The pessimism lies in the economic sphere. Our couple know they are fortunate to have reasonably secure jobs. Some of their friends and the younger siblings of their crowd are in the position of having excellent credentials, a fine work ethic, a desire to be economically independent and build lives, but no job.

Unemployment in the euro area is finally declining, though it is now in the region of below 9 percent. France is at 8.8 percent, Italy at 11 percent, and Turkey at 10.6 percent. Ireland has moved far down to 6.2 percent, as has Portugal at 7.8 percent. Spain has moved down from 25 percent to 16.1 percent. Greece, at a difficult 20.8 percent, is doing better. Youth unemployment is far worse, though it too is moving down: 17.3 percent in the EU area; over 30 percent in Greece, Spain, and Italy; about 21.5 percent in France and Portugal; 16.4 percent in Sweden; and even 11.5 percent in the United Kingdom.

There is deep concern and much reflection on what all this will mean in the next few decades. What has occurred is that in Europe (and elsewhere in the West) the tacit social contract with the next generation is fraying, perhaps even ending. It was believed that if a youth obtained a decent education and good credentials, worked hard, and more or less obeyed the rules of citizenship, there would be something stable at the end—a job and a career, perhaps not a perfect one, but one that led to an entry into the bourgeoisie, a stable life, and a decent future.

No longer. Our couple have siblings and friends with university degrees, some with more than one degree, who still live with their parents because they cannot find work in their field. Many a waiter and waitress and clerks in retail shops are more educated than the people they serve. They desperately want to build a life, to be part of the system, to settle and have a family. They do not know if they will ever be able to do so. Even our couple worry about his job. What will happen if the bank he works for consolidates with another, or if there is another recession?

The Brexit vote in the United Kingdom reflected great divisions in that state. Not only did London want to remain in the EU and the rest of England vote to leave; not only did Scotland and Northern Ireland vote to stay, and England and Wales chose to leave. There was a great division between old and young, and youth in the UK are now far more limited in their choices than they were before the vote.

Hence, there is pessimism about the economy that hits home for many families. Even the decision to create the euro is under question, though it is generally agreed that the consequences of abandoning it would be far worse than the status quo. Still, what if Spain had retained its own currency and could devalue it to deal with economic stagnation? What if Greece still had the drachma, and did not have to be periodically bailed out of its follies by other euro countries? There is a clear sense that the system is not doing what it was designed to do.

Moreover, how to deal with the economic malaise is itself creating some rancour among countries. Austerity was the initial response, Germany the leader, wanting other countries to be little Germanys in their economic models. What was forgotten, claimed France and others, is that the crisis of 2008 meant that demand was deeply dampened. Hence, they suggested a Keynesian solution—this is the time to pump more money into the economy, mainly to build infrastructure and create jobs—and to increase the demand for goods and services through government action. The argument continues. The economy remains fragile in some places. The recovery is weaker and slower than others in the past.

The result for the next generation is that they have little confidence in their political leaders. They don't know the way out of their personal dilemma, and they don't believe that the political leaders and structures of their countries are doing a very good job in moving forward. Politics, for them, makes little difference. We do know that cynicism about public service is not good for social democracy.

With a few exceptions, the youth of Europe have not taken to the streets about this matter. They do rage against the 1 percent and 10 percent, and feel that the system is weighted in favour of the wealthy and against them, but no uprising is occurring.

What is happening is emigration. For example, many youths in Portugal go to Britain in search of jobs, though the Brexit decision may stop this; Spanish youths move to Latin America; Irish youths—after a short pause starting in the 1990s—continue the sad emigration to Britain, the continent, and, mainly, North America. Our couple now have one of their siblings and several friends living abroad.

What does push some of those in our couple's generation to political action are movements based on national identity, especially integral movements, those smaller groups asking for autonomy from a larger political entity. The fall of the Soviet Union was welcomed by many of the smaller national entities in the Russian federation: Georgia, the Ukraine, and Kazakhstan, for example. The Baltic members of the federation, Latvia, Lithuania, and Estonia, were ecstatic. All became sovereign states.

In western Europe there are autonomy movements in Catalonia, from Spain, and Scotland, from the United Kingdom. In Italy there is a group devoted to establishing a north Italian state. Belgium is constantly threatened with a breakup into two states, Flanders and Wallonia. Basques in northeastern Spain and southwest France argue for a small national entity and are reviving their language.

With the exception of the Basques in Spain, there have been demonstrations and speeches, but these movements are not violent in the streets. It is clear that there are many who question the growth and centralization of the nation-state since the French Revolution. Their identity is local, and they have revived their ancient languages and celebrate a separate history. Many national governments have accorded more autonomy to these local groups as a way of dealing with their claims and demands.

European leaders and public intellectuals, in the main, are prepared to do whatever is necessary to defend social democracy and human rights. They will not idly accept street violence or groups who think they can abuse others in the name of whatever ideology they claim to support. Some lessons of history have been learned. They pay attention to Santayana's dictum that those who forget the past are doomed to repeat it.

Nonetheless, our couple and those in their social circle sometimes feel that their lives lack meaning. Perhaps their continued interest in the years

1930–1945 lies in the clarity of the moral landscape at that time, as seen in retrospect from the present, though of course those living today can suggest how they might have behaved but cannot really be certain about what they would have done living then. They feel they lack the intellectual tools to critique and reform the postmodern world in which they find themselves.

Our couple want stability, prosperity, and the good life promised by peace and prosperity. Yet, they are ambivalent. There are no great causes.

The one issue that moves our couple and their friends deeply is that of the destruction of the environment. They read the articles in the science journals about global warming and its consequences, and they agree that this is already happening. They are tempted to support the Green party in their country, though they wish it had greater influence. They want their government to take steps, even if unilateral, because most governments in Europe (and elsewhere) simply ignore meaningful action on this long-range matter, deciding that votes and popularity will be lost if they took measures that affected taxes and lifestyles today. This is the one social and political movement that would attract them and their friends if it could gain momentum. They are looking for leaders with the courage to take it on.

They would like to have the certainty of the nineteenth century, but cannot go back. Their consumer society and the goal of being wealthy is not enough. They feel they are drifting along in a tide that sometimes seems without purpose. Meaning is obtained in relationships, work, and commitment to community.

Thucydides, the father of European historical study, stated over two millennia ago that he wrote about the Peloponnesian War because it was an important moment, and there were lessons to be learned about war, how it occurs, and what happens when it becomes a total reality. Greeks, he was saying, pay attention to this momentous moment, because it can inform your lives forever.

Today Europeans need no fictional dystopias. They have an abundance of dystopian events and examples in their history from 1914, including the warnings of our 1930 public intellectuals and the years they lived through seeing their sad prophecies become realized even more horrifically than they imagined. We can echo Thucydides. Europeans, pay attention, because the works of 1930 and those years from 1930 to 1945 can inform your lives forever. Your history is your own cautionary tale.

It was Camus who said,

Man's unbroken testimony as to his suffering and nobility cannot be suspended; the act of breathing cannot be suspended. There is no culture without legacy, and we cannot and must not reject anything of ours, the legacy of the West.[1]

Aleksandr Solzhenitsyn, in challenging his state, which manipulated history and truth for its own ends, claimed that there is no possibility of a reasonable future without first facing the truth about the past. He quoted a Russian proverb that has two parts. "Don't dig up the past! Dwell on the past and you'll lose an eye," says the first part. But the proverb continues, "Forget the past and you'll lose both eyes."[2]

ACKNOWLEDGEMENTS

THIS BOOK HAD its origins in my teaching, as I came to realize the confluence of interests of so many public intellectuals in the year 1930. Conversations with students, friends, and colleagues clarified many of the ideas in this work, and I am grateful to all those who listened and reflected along with me.

My four readers read the chapters as they were written and contributed to them in important ways. They were patient with my revisions and were very fine critics. They are Jan Rehner, Fran Cohen, Martin Sable, and Adrian Shubert. As always, Jan was a fabulous listener as well as a reader. Tim Blackmore also made insightful and useful remarks and suggestions as a reviewer for WLU Press. Siobhan McMenemy, my editor, pushed me gracefully to make this a better book than the first manuscript happened to be.

My two teachers to whom this book is dedicated, Joan Kelly Gadol, who taught me at City College, and A. William Salomone, who guided me in graduate school at New York University, remain, scores of years later, profoundly present. Without them, this book could never have happened.

NOTES

INTRODUCTION

1 José Ortega y Gasset, *The Revolt of the Masses* (New York: W.W. Norton and Company, 1932), p. 18.
2 W.H. Auden, *September 1, 1939*, Poets.org, https://www.poets.org/poetsorg/poem/September-1-1939

PROLOGUE

1 Paul Valéry, *The Outlook for Intelligence*, translated by Denise Folliot and Jackson Mathews (New York: Harper and Row, 1962), p. 26.
2 Valéry, "On the European Mind," Modern History Sourcebook, August 1997, https://sourcebooks.fordham.edu/mod/valery.asp.
3 Valéry, *History and Politics*, translated by Denise Folliot and Jackson Mathews (New York: Bollingen Foundation, 1962), p. 308. Emphasis in original.
4 Arthur Haberman, *The Making of the Modern Age* (Toronto: Gage, 1987), p. 235.
5 Haberman, p. 237.
6 Haberman, p. 251.
7 Haberman, p. 250.

CHAPTER 1

1 Thomas Mann, *Briefe an Otto Grautoff und Ida Boy-Ed* (Frankfurt: S. Fischer, 1975), pp. 236–237.
2 Letter of June 12, 1930 to Otto Hoerth, in *Letters of Thomas Mann, 1889–1955*, selected and translated by Richard and Clara Winston (New York: Alfred A. Knopf, 1971), p. 177.
3 Goethe, *Faust*, translated by Walter Kaufmann (New York: Doubleday, 1961), pp. 161, 177.
4 Pankaj Mishra, "Welcome to the Age of Anger," *The Guardian*, December 8, 2016.
5 Robert Musil, *The Man Without Qualities*, vol. 1, translated by E. Wilkens and E. Kaiser (London: Secker and Warburg, 1953), pp. 40–41.
6 Musil, "Helpless Europe," in *Precision and Soul*, edited and translated by Burton Pike and David S. Luft (Chicago: University of Chicago Press, 1990), p. 131.
7 William L. Shirer, *Berlin Diary* (New York: Alfred A. Knopf, 1941), pp. 16–19, 21.
8 Thomas Mann, *The Coming Victory of Democracy* (London: Secker and Warburg, 1938), p. 80.
9 Mann, p. 80.
10 Nigel Hamilton, *The Brothers Mann* (New Haven, CT: Yale University Press, 1979), p. 298.

11   Mann, "An Appeal to Reason," in *The Weimar Republic Sourcebook*, edited by Anton Kaes, Martin Jay and Edward Dimendberg (Berkeley, CA: University of California Press, 1994), p. 154. https://books.google.ca/books?isbn=0520909607.

12   Mann, *The Coming Victory*, p. 86.

13   Mann, pp. 94–99.

14   Mann, pp. 94–99.

15   Fyodor Dostoyevsky, *Notes from Underground* and *The Double*, translated by Jessie Coulson (Harmondsworth: Penguin Books, 1972), p. 31.

16   Yevgeny Zamiatin, *We*, translated by Clarence Brown (Harmondsworth: Penguin Books, 1993), p. 203.

CHAPTER 2

1   Jenny Hartley, *The Selected Letters of Charles Dickens* (Oxford: Oxford University Press, 2012), pp. 331–332.

2   Laura L. Doan and Jay Prosser, eds., *Palatable Poison: Critical Perspectives on the Well of Loneliness* (New York: Columbia University Press, 2001). https://books.google.ca/books?isbn=0231118759.

3   Virginia Woolf, *Three Guineas* (New York: Harcourt Brace, 1938), p. 217.

4   Jane Goldman, *The Cambridge Introduction to Virginia Woolf* (Cambridge: Cambridge University Press, 2006), p. 69.

5   Virginia Woolf, *The Diary of Virginia Woolf*, vol. 3, edited by Anne Oliver Bell (New York: Harcourt Brace Jovanovich, 1980), p. 312.

6   Virginia Woolf, *A Writer's Diary*, edited by Leonard Woolf (New York: Harcourt Brace, 1953), p. 159.

7   Woolf, *Diary of Woolf*, vol. 3, p. 209.

CHAPTER 3

1   Robert C. Tucker, *The Marx–Engels Reader*, 2nd ed. (New York: W.W. Norton, 1978), p. 595.

2   John Stuart Mill, *On Liberty* (Indianapolis, IN: Bobbs-Merrill, 1956), p. 7.

3   W.B. Yeats, "The Second Coming," in *The Collected Poems of W. B. Yeats* (New York: Macmillan, 1950), pp. 184–185.

4   George Orwell, *The Collected Essays, Journalism and Letters of George Orwell*, vol. 1 (New York: Harcourt, Brace and World, 1968), p. 512.

5   League of professional groups for Foster and Ford, "Culture and the Crisis: An open letter to the writers, artists, teachers, physicians, engineers, scientists, and other professional workers of America," New York, October 1932, Internet Archive, https://archive.org/stream/CultureAndTheCrisisAnOpenLetterToTheWritersArtistsTeachers/CC_djvu.txt.

6   Trevor Curnow, "José Ortega y Gasset and the Practice of Philosophy," *Practical Philosophy*, vol. 7, no. 2 (2005), p. 35, http://www.society-for-philosophy-in-practice.org/journal/pdf/7-2%2035%20Curnow%20-%20Gasset.pdf.

7   José Ortega y Gasset, *Mission of the University*, translated by Howard Lee Nostrand (Princeton, NJ: Princeton University Press, 1944), pp. 1–99.

CHAPTER 4

1   Bertolt Brecht, *The Rise and Fall of the City of Mahagonny*, Introduction by A. R. Braunmuller, translated by W.H. Auden and Chester Kallman (Boston: David R. Godine, 1976), p. 12.

2   Introduction to *Mahagonny*, p. 12.

3   Introduction to *Mahagonny*, p. 12.

4   Ronald Taylor, *Kurt Weill: Composer in a Divided World* (London: Simon and Schuster, 1991), p. 115.

5   John Willett, *Brecht on Theatre* (London: Methuen, 1974), p. 22.

6   Willett, *Brecht on Theatre*, p. 23.

7   Taylor, *Kurt Weill*, p. 115.

8   Taylor, p. 115.

9   Ronald Sanders, *The Days Grow Short: The Life and Music of Kurt Weill* (Los Angeles, CA: Silman-James Press, 1980), p. 92.

10 Taylor, *Kurt Weill*, pp. 115–116.

11 Bertolt Brecht, *The Threepenny Opera*, translated by Ralph Mannheim and John Willett; with commentary and notes by Non and Nick Worrall (London: Methuen, 2005), pp. xlvii–xlix.

12 Frederic Ewen, *Bertolt Brecht: His life, His Art, and His Times* (New York: Citadel Press, 1967), p. 178.

13 Lotte Lenya, Foreword to *Threepenny Opera* by Bertolt Brecht, English book by Desmond Vesey, English lyrics by Eric Bentley (New York: Grove Press, 1964), p. v.

14 Lenya, Foreword to *Threepenny Opera*, p. xi.

15 Bertolt Brecht, *Collected Plays*, vol. II, edited by John Willett and Ralph Mannheim (London: Methuen, 1979), pp. 318–319.

16 Bertolt Brecht, *The Threepenny Opera*, edited by John Willett and Ralph Mannheim (London: Methuen, 2015), p. lxxvi.

17 Willett, *Brecht on Theatre*, pp. 33–39.

18 Sanders, *The Days Grow Short*, pp. 157–158.

19 Willett, *Brecht on Theatre*, p. 36.

20 Robert C. Tucker, *The Marx–Engels Reader*, 2nd ed. (New York: W.W. Norton, 1978), p. 105.

21 Taylor, *Kurt Weill*, p. 165.

CHAPTER 5

1   Ean Wood, *The Josephine Baker Story* (London: Sanctuary, 2000), p. 168.

2   Bennetta Jules-Rosette, *Josephine Baker in Art and Life: The Icon and the Image* (Urbana, IL: University of Illinois Press, 2007), p. 144.

3   Lynn Haney, *Naked at the Feast* (London: Robson, 2002), pp. 164–165.

4   J.L. Hymans, *Léopold Sédar Senghor: An Intellectual Biography* (Edinburgh: Edinburgh University Press, 1971), p. 42.

5   T. Denean Sharpley-Whiting, *Negritude Women* (Minneapolis, MN: University of Minnesota Press, 2002), p. 17.

6   All Achille citations in this section are from his preface to the complete collection of *La Revue du Monde Noir* (Paris: Jean Michel Place, 1992), pp. vii–xvii, p. 55.

7   T. Denean Sharply-Whiting, "Femme negritude, Jan Nardal, La Dépêche africaine, and the Francophone New Negro," *Souls*, vol. 2, no. 4 (Fall 2000), pp. 10–11, www.columbia.edu/cu/ccbh/souls/vol2no4/vol2num4arti.pdf.

8   Jennifer Anne Boittin, *Colonial Metropolis* (Lincoln, NB: University of Nebraska Press, 2010), p. 143.

9   Hymans, *Léopold Sédar Senghor*, p. 42.

10 This quote and others from "Pantins exotiques" are from the story in T. Denean Sharpley-Whiting, *Negritude Women*, translated by T. Denean Sharpley-Whiting and Georges Van Den Abbeele (Minneapolis, MN: University of Minnesota Press, 2002).

11 All quotations for this story come from "En Exil," in *La Dépêche africaine*, vol. 2, no. 19 (December 1929), p. 6 (my translation).

12 Sharpley-Whiting, *Negritude Women*, p. 55.

13 Sharpley-Whiting, p. 55.

14 *La Revue du Monde Noir*, Collection complete (Paris: Jean-Michel Place, 1992), p. 4.

15 *La Revue*, p. 6.

16 *La Revue*, p. 185.

17 *La Revue*, pp. 301–302.

18 *La Revue*, p. 302.

19 *La Revue*, p. 58.

20 *La Revue*, p. 98.

21 *La Revue*, p. 352.

22 *La Revue*, p. 166.

23 *La Revue*, pp. 343–349.

24 *La Revue*, p. 349.

25 *La Revue*, p. 349.

26 *La Revue*, p. 347.

27 *La Revue*, pp. 118–120.

28 Boittin, *Colonial Metropolis*, p. 154.

29 Hymans, *Léopold Sédar Senghor*, pp. 43, 34.

30 Hymans, *Léopold Sédar Senghor*, p. 36.

31 Patricia A. Morton, *Hybrid Modernities, Architecture and Representation at the 1931 Colonial Exposition, Paris* (Cambridge, MA: MIT Press, 2000), p. 3.

32 Morton, *Hybrid Modernities*, p. 313.

33 Morton, *Hybrid Modernities*, pp. 97–98.

34 Frantz Fanon, *The Wretched of the Earth* (New York: Grove Press, 1984), pp. 100–103.

35 Fanon, *The Wretched of the Earth*, pp. 13–14.

CHAPTER 6

1 Arthur Ellridge, *Gauguin and the Nabi: Prophets of Modernism* (Paris: Terrail, 1995), p. 50.

2 "Maurice Denis," Musée d'Orsay, Exhibitions, October 2006, http://www.musee-orsay .fr/en/events/exhibitions/archives/exhibitions-archives/browse/4/article/maurice-denis -6780.html?print=1&.

3 André Breton, *Manifestos of Surrealism* (Ann Arbor, MI: University of Michigan Press, 1969), p. 26.

4 Breton, *Manifestos*, p. 160.

5 Art Encyclopedia, "Louis Vauxcelles (1870–1943)," accessed February 2018, http://www .visual-arts-cork.com/critics/louis-vauxcelles.htm.

6 Thomas Mann, "Tonio Kröger," in *Death in Venice and Seven Other Stories* (New York: Vintage, 1954), p. 131.

7 "Art: Carnegie Show," *Time Magazine*, October 20, 1930, http://www.time.com/time/ magazine/article/0,9171,740596,00.html.

8 Richard Cavendish, "The Fauves at the Salon d'Automne," *History Today*, vol. 55, no. 10 (2005), https://www.historytoday.com/richard-cavendish/fauves-salon-d%e2%80 %99automne).

9 "Paul Cézanne's Impact on Henri Matisse," 2011, https://www.henrimatisse.org/matisse -and-cezanne.jsp.

10 W.H. Auden, *September 1, 1939*, Poets.org, https://www.poets.org/poetsorg/poem/ September-1-1939.

11 "George Grosz," Geni, November 4, 2015, https://www.geni.com/people/George-Grosz/ 6000000037620464207.

CHAPTER 7

1   Aldous Huxley, *Letters of Aldous Huxley*, ed. Grover Smith (New York: Harper and Row, 1969), p. 343.

2   Huxley, *Letters*, p. 345.

3   Aldous Huxley, *Complete Essays,* ed. Robert S. Baker and James Sexton (Chicago: Ivan R. Dee), 2001, pp. 276–280.

4   Huxley, *Complete Essays*, p. 281.

5   Huxley, *Letters*, p. 351.

6   John Stuart Mill, 190 Parl. Deb. H.C. (3d ser.) (March 12, 1868), cc1459-549, http://hansard.millbanksystems.com/commons/1868/mar/12/adjourned-debate #S3V0190P0_18680312_HOC_54.

7   Frances Galton, "Definition of Eugenics," DNA Learning Center, https://www.dnalc.org/view/10901-francis-galton-s-definition-of-eugenics.html.

8   Huxley, *Letters*, p. 391.

9   William Blake, *The Marriage of Heaven and Hell* (Boston: John W. Luce and Company, 1906), Internet Archive, https://archive.org/stream/marriageofheaven00blak/marriageof heaven00blak_djvu.txt.

10 William Shakespeare, *The Tempest* in *The Riverside Shakespeare* (Boston: Houghton Mifflin, 1974), 5.1.182–184, p. 1634.

11 Ira Grushow, "Brave New World and The Tempest," *College English*, vol. 24, no. 1 (October 1962), pp. 42–45, http://www.jstor.org/action/showPublication?journal Code=collegeenglish.

CHAPTER 8

1   Ernest Jones, *Sigmund Freud: Life and Work* (London: Hogarth Press, 1953–1957), vol. 3, p. 148.

2   Peter Gay, introduction, in Freud, *Civilization and Its Discontents* (New York: Norton, 1961), p. xxiii.

3   Jones, *Sigmund Freud,* vol. 3, p. 148; Freud, *Civilization and Its Discontents*, translated by David McLintock, foreword by Leo Bersani (Harmondsworth: Penguin, 2002), p. xxiv.

4   Sigmund Freud, *Civilization and Its Discontents*, translated by James Strachey (New York: W.W. Norton and Company, 1961), p. 13. All subsequent quotations from this book in this chapter are taken from this edition.

5   Fyodor Dostoyevsky, *Notes from Underground* and *The Double* (Harmondsworth: Penguin, 2009), pp. 39–40.

6   Freud, *Civilization and Its Discontents,* p. 42.

7   Robert C. Tucker, *The Marx–Engels Reader*, 2nd ed. (New York: W.W. Norton), 1978, p. 79.

8   Jones, *Sigmund Freud*, vol. 3, p. 273.

9   All the quoted correspondence between Einstein and Freud is from The Einstein–Freud Correspondence (1931–1932), Arizona State University, http://www.public.asu.edu/~jmlynch/273/documents/FreudEinstein.pdf.

10 Jeffrey Herf, *Reactionary Modernism: Technology, Culture, and Politics in Weimar and the Third Reich* (New York: Cambridge University Press), 1986, pp. 1–2, 15, 219–227.

11 Thomas Mann, "Germany and the Germans," in *Thomas Mann's Addresses Delivered at the Library of Congress, 1942–1949* (Washington, DC: Wildside Press, 1963), p. 62.

12 The Einstein–Freud Correspondence, p. 12.

13 Emanuel Rice, *Freud and Moses: The Long Journey Home* (Albany, NY: SUNY Press), 1990, p. 25.

14 Jones, *Sigmund Freud*, vol. 3, p. 235.

15   Peter Gay, *Freud, A Life for Our Time* (New York: W.W. Norton, 1988), p. 640.

16   W.H. Auden, *In Memory of Sigmund Freud,* Poets.org, https://www.poets.org/poetsorg/poem/memory-sigmund-freud.

CHAPTER 9

1   Eduard Bernstein, *Evolutionary Socialism* (New York: Schocken Books, 1961), p. 166.

2   Thomas Piketty, *Capital in the Twenty-First Century,* translated by Arthur Goldhammer (Cambridge, MA: Harvard University Press, 2014), p. 1.

3   Thomas More, *Utopia,* translated by Robert M. Adams (New York: W.W. Norton, 1975), p. 90.

4   William Shakespeare, *King Lear* in *The Riverside Shakespeare* (Boston: Houghton Mifflin, 1974), 4.1.67–70, p. 1282.

5   David Schweingruber and Ronald T. Wohlstein, "The Madding Crowd Goes to School," *Teaching Sociology,* vol. 33, no. 2 (April 2005), pp. 138–140.

6   Elias Canetti, *Crowds and Power* (New York: Viking Press, 1962), pp. 29–34.

7   Christian Borch, "Body to Body: On the Political Anatomy of Crowds," *Sociological Theory,* vol. 27, no. 3 (September 2009), p. 290.

8   "Pussy Riot," Wikipedia, last modified February 16, 2018, https://en.wikipedia.org/wiki/Pussy_Riot.

9   Jason DeParle, "The Sea Swallows People," *New York Review of Books,* February 23, 2017, p. 31.

10   Catherine Edwards, "The Italian doctor giving hope to thousands of migrants," The Local Italy, August 10, 2016, https://www.thelocal.it/20160810/the-doctor-who-has-assisted-every-migrant-arriving-at-lampedusa.

11   Larysa Kozovaya, "Director of Film about Nemstov: 'Boris was uncomfortable with Russia sending its men to the war and concealing it,'" Unian, July 25, 2016, https://www.unian.info/world/1436057-director-of-film-about-nemtsov-boris-was-uncomfortable-with-russia-sending-its-men-to-the-war-and-concealing-it.html.

12   "Jewish Population of Europe in 1933: Population Data by Country," *Holocaust Encyclopedia,* United States Holocaust Memorial Museum, https://www.ushmm.org/wlc/en/article.php?ModuleId=10005161.

13   "The fight against jihadism is the great challenge of our generation," Gouvernement.fr, May 10, 2016, http://www.gouvernement.fr/en/the-fight-against-jihadism-is-the-great-challenge-of-our-generation.

14   "Un Chien Andalou," Wikipedia, last modified January 26, 2018, https://en.wikipedia.org/wiki/Un_Chien_Andalou.

15   Samuel Beckett, *Waiting for Godot* (New York: Grove Press, 1954), p. 51.

16   "Harold Pinter: the most original, stylish and enigmatic writer in post-war British theatre," *The Telegraph,* December 25, 2008, https://www.telegraph.co.uk/news/obituaries/3949227/Harold-Pinter-the-most-original-stylish-and-enigmatic-writer-in-the-post-war-revival-of-British-theatre.html.

17   Peter Weiss, *The persecution and assassination of Marat as performed by the inmates of the asylum of Charenton under the direction of the marquis de Sade* (London: Calder and Boyars Limited, 1964), p. 107

18   Gabriel García Márquez, "The Solitude of Latin America," Nobel Peace Prize Address, December 8, 1982, http://www.nobelprize.org/nobel_prizes/literature/laureates/1982/marquez-lecture.html.

19   Ultra-red, "Mission Statement," http://www.ultrared.org/mission.html.

20   Italo Calvino, *Invisible Cities,* translated by William Weaver (New York: Harcourt Brace Jovanovich, 1974), p. 165.

21 Francis Fukuyama, "The End of History?" *The National Interest,* Summer (1989), p. 1, https://www.embl.de/aboutus/science_society/discussion/discussion_2006/ref1-22june06.pdf.

22 Benjamin Disraeli, *Sybil, or The Two Nations,* Project Gutenberg, https://www.gutenberg.org/files/3760/3760-h/3760-h.htm#link2H_4_0013,Book 2,Chapter5.

23 James Kanter and Elisabetta Povoledo, "E.U. Leaders Sign Rome Declaration and Proclaim a 'Common Future' (Minus Britain)," *New York Times,* March 25, 2017, https://www.nytimes.com/2017/03/25/world/europe/rome-declaration-european-union.html.

EPILOGUE

1 Albert Camus, *Resistance, Rebellion and Death,* translated by Justin O'Brien (New York: Modern Library, 1963), p. 114.

2 Aleksandr I. Solzhenitsyn, *The Gulag Archipelago* (New York: Harper and Row, 1974), p. x.

BIBLIOGRAPHICAL NOTES

CHAPTER 1

My discussion of Mann's *Mario and the Magician* uses Thomas Mann's *Death in Venice and Seven Other Stories* (New York: Vintage), 1954. The issues considered in *Mario and the Magician* permeate some of Mann's other major works, especially *The Magic Mountain* (1924) and *Dr. Faustus* (1947), two large reflective philosophical novels, widely recognized as two of the most important novels of the twentieth century.

Two excellent critical studies of Mann in English are Harry Hatfield, *Thomas Mann* (New York: New Directions, 1962) and Hermann Kurzke, *Thomas Mann: Life as a Work of Art*, trans. Leslie Wilson (Princeton, NJ: Princeton University Press, 2002). T.J. Reed's *Thomas Mann: The Uses of Tradition*, rev. ed. (Oxford: Clarendon Press, 1996), is very good at placing Mann's work in its historical context and discussing Mann's political views. Nigel Hamilton's *The Brothers Mann* (New Haven, CT: Yale University Press, 1979) is excellent on Mann's close ties to his family and his political development.

The Cambridge Introduction to Thomas Mann by Todd Kontje (Cambridge: Cambridge University Press, 2011) is a good place to start if you want a general overview. Reading the Kontje introduction alongside the series of essays by major scholars of Mann edited by Ritchie Robertson, *The Cambridge Companion to Thomas Mann* (Cambridge: Cambridge University Press, 2002) will give one a good picture of Mann's long and fertile career as a leading writer and intellectual. Richard Parker, *Here, the People Rule: A Constitutional Populist Manifesto* (Cambridge, MA: Harvard University Press, 1994) uses Mann's story as a way of discussing some of the problems of democracy.

The story has been adapted several times as an opera. The best-known version is in English, first performed in 2005. The composer is Francis Thorne and the librettist is J.D. McClatchy. A recording was released by Albany records in 2006. As well, there is a 1994 German-language film of *Mario and the Magician* directed by Klaus Maria Brandauer.

CHAPTER 2

For my discussion of *A Room of One's Own* I used the New York and London edition published in 1981 by Harcourt Brace Jovanovich. My discussion of *The Waves* used the edition, edited with an introduction and notes by Kate Flint, published in London by Penguin Books in 1992.

Other novels by Woolf of note that deal with some of the issues she explores in *The Waves* include *Mrs. Dalloway* (1925), *To the Lighthouse* (1927), and *Orlando* (1928).

Woolf wrote the influential essay *Three Guineas* in 1938. Woolf's diaries, letters, and journals are important material for her aesthetics and epistemology as well as revealing a great deal about the context of her times.

Of the many biographies, those by Quentin Bell, *Virginia Woolf: A Biography*, 2 vols. (London: Hogarth, 1972), Julia Briggs, *Virginia Woolf, An Inner Life* (London: Penguin, 2004), and Lyndall Gordon, *Virginia Woolf: A Writer's Life* (Oxford: Oxford University Press, 1984) are especially fine introductions.

A good book-length discussion and reading of Woolf's essay is *A Room of One's Own: Women Writers and the Politics of Creativity*, by Ellen Bayuk Rosenman (New York: Twayne Publishers, 1995). Woolf's feminism is well analyzed and understood in both Naomi Black, *Virginia Woolf as Feminist* (Ithaca, NY: Cornell University Press, 1994) and *Virginia Woolf, A Feminist Slant*, ed. Jane Marcus (Lincoln, NB: University of Nebraska Press, 1983).

The cultural and social context of Woolf's London is well presented in Christine Froula's *Virginia Woolf and the Bloomsbury Avant-Garde: War, Civilization and Modernity* (New York: Columbia University Press, 2005). *Language, Time and Identity in Woolf's The Waves* by Michael Weinman (Lanham, MD: Lexington Books, 2012) is a worthwhile study of the novel. Emma Sutton's *Virginia Woolf and Classical Music: Politics, Aesthetics, Form* (Edinburgh: Edinburgh University Press, 2015) includes an interesting discussion of *The Waves*, associating it with Wagner's *The Ring*.

CHAPTER 3

I quote extensively from Ortega's most famous work, the 1932 English edition of *The Revolt of the Masses* (New York: W.W. Norton and Company) in this chapter. I also use Ortega's *Mission of the University*, translated by Howard Lee Nostrand (Princeton, NJ: Princeton University Press, 1944). Other works by Ortega dealing with issues in this chapter include *The Dehumanization of Art, and Notes on the Novel*, translated by Helene Weyl (Princeton, NJ: Princeton University Press, 1948), *History as a System, and Other Essays Toward a Philosophy of History*, translated by Helene Weyl (New York: W.W. Norton and Company, 1961), and *Meditations on Quixote*, translated by Evelyn Rugg and Diego Marin (New York: W.W. Norton and Company, 1963).

The first important and comprehensive study of Ortega's thought in English is that of José Ferrater Mora, *José Ortega y Gasset: An Outline of His Philosophy* (New Haven, CT: Yale University Press, 2nd rev. ed., 1963). It stands up well and remains indispensable as an excellent introduction and assessment. Victor Ouimette's *José Ortega y Gasset* (Boston: Twayne Publishers, 1982) is another good overview, as is Andrew Dobson's *An Introduction to the Politics and Philosophy of José Ortega y Gasset* (Cambridge: Cambridge University Press, 1989).

Ortega as a Europeanist is well considered in Harold C. Raley's *José Ortega y Gasset: Philosopher of European Unity* (Tuscaloosa, AL: University of Alabama Press, 1971). In Robert McLintock's *Man and His Circumstances: Ortega as Educator* (New York: Teachers College Press, 1972), the author takes Ortega's concept of "social pedagogy" as the central motif. It needs to be read critically, though it has some valuable insights. John T. Graham's *Theory of History in Ortega y Gasset* (Columbia, MO: University of Missouri Press, 1997) is thoughtful and comprehensive, and Patrick Dust, ed., *Ortega y Gasset and the Question of Modernity* (Minneapolis, MN: Prisma Institute, 1989) has a number of good essays, including ones on technology and humanism, and on *The Revolt of the Masses*.

The most complete bibliography is still Anton Donoso and Harold C. Raley's, *José Ortega y Gasset: A Bibliography of Secondary Sources* (Bowling Green, OH: Philosophy Documentation Center, 1986).

CHAPTER 4

All quotations from *The Threepenny Opera* come from Bertolt Brecht, *The Threepenny Opera*, in English by Desmond Vesey, English lyrics translated by Eric Bentley, with a foreword by Lotte Lenya (New York: Grove Press, 1964). All quotations from *Mahagonny* come from Bertolt Brecht, *The Rise and Fall of the City of Mahagonny*, trans. W.H. Auden and Chester Kallman (Boston: David R. Godine, 1976).

John Willett's works on Brecht have had immense influence in the English-speaking world. He remains the best introduction to the playwright. Willett translated and edited *Brecht on Theatre* (London: Methuen, 1964, 1974), a collection of Brecht's critical writings. In addition, Willett wrote *The Theatre of Bertolt Brecht* (London: Methuen, 1977) and *Brecht in Context: Comparative Approaches* (London: Methuen, 1984).

Other fine studies include Martin Esslin's *Brecht: A Choice of Evils* (London: Methuen, 1984), Ronald Hayman's *Brecht: A Biography* (London: Weidenfeld and Nicolson, 1983), and John Fuegi's *Brecht and Company: Sex, Politics and the Making of the Modern Drama* (New York: Grove, 1994).

Walter Benjamin's *Understanding Brecht* (London: New Verso, 1983) has been influential in doing what the title states. *The Cambridge Companion to Brecht*, edited by Peter Thomson and Glandyr Sacks (Cambridge: Cambridge University Press, 1994), is a useful introduction and overview.

The context of the times can be found in Eric D. Weitz's *Weimar Germany: Promise and Tragedy* (Princeton, NJ: Princeton University Press, 2013) and Peter Gay's *Weimar Culture: The Outsider as Insider* (New York: Harper and Row, 1968).

Ronald Sanders's *The Days Grow Short: The Life and Music of Kurt Weill* (Los Angeles, CA: Silman-James Press, 1980) is a very good biography, as is Ronald Taylor's *Kurt Weill: Composer in a Divided World* (London: Simon and Schuster, 1991). Ethan Mordden's *Love Song: The Lives of Kurt Weill and Lotte Lenya* (New York: St. Martin's Press, 2012) is very useful. Kim H. Kowalke's, *Kurt Weill in Europe, 1900–1935: A Study of His Music and Writings* (Ann Arbor, MI: UMI Research Press, 1979) focuses on Weill's early years.

CHAPTER 5

Of all the topics in this book, that of Black culture in Paris and Europe around 1930 is the least researched. A good start is to look at *La Revue du Monde Noir* (Paris: Jean-Michel Place, 1992), published in its original version, in both French and English. Some of Paulette Nardal's later writings for the publication *La Femme dans la Cité* are collected in *Beyond Negritude: Essays from 'Woman in the City,'* translated by T. Denean Sharpley-Whiting (Albany, NY: SUNY Press, 2009).

Shireen K. Lewis, *Race, Culture, and Identity: Francophone West African and Caribbean Literature and Theory from Negritude to Creolite* (London: Lexington Books, 2006) has one of the best discussions of the Nardal sisters and their environment. See also the brief article by Shireen K. Lewis, "Gendering Négritude: Paulette Nardal's Contribution to the Birth of Modern Francophone Literature" (*Romance Languages Annual*, vol. XI, 1999).

T. Denean Sharply-Whiting's "Femme negritude, Jan Nardal, La Dépêche africaine, and the Francophone New Negro," *Souls*, Fall (2000), pp. 10–11, on the website www.columbia.edu/cu/ccbh/souls/vol2no4/vol2num4arti.pdf, is useful, as is Sharpley-Whiting's *Negritude Women* (Minneapolis, MN: University of Minnesota Press, 2002).

The atmosphere in Paris during the Joséphine Baker years is well presented in three works: Ean Wood, *The Joséphine Baker Story* (London: Sanctuary, 2000); Benetta Jules-Rosette, *Joséphine Baker in Art and Life: The Icon and the Image* (Urbana, IL: University of Illinois Press, 2007); and Lynn Haney, *Naked at the Feast* (London: Robson, 2002).

J.L. Hymans's *Léopold Sédar Senghor: An Intellectual Biography* (Edinburgh: Edinburgh University Press, 1971) is excellent. Janet G. Vaillant's *Black, French, and African: A Life of Léopold Sédar Senghor* (Cambridge: Harvard University Press, 1990) adds to the insights of Hymans.

The colonial exposition of 1931 is best documented in Jennifer Anne Boittin's *Colonial Metropolis: The Urban Grounds of Anti-Imperialism and Feminism in Inter-War Paris* (Lincoln, NB: University of Nebraska Press, 2010) and Patricia A. Morton's *Hybrid Modernities: Architecture and Representation at the 1931 Colonial Exposition, Paris* (Cambridge, MA: MIT Press, 2000). Nicholas B. Dirks, ed. *Colonialism and Culture* (Ann Arbor, MI: University of Michigan Press, 1992) includes essays dealing insightfully with the understanding of colonial sociology and culture.

CHAPTER 6

There is an abundance of material on the visual arts of the period. Hal Foster et al., *Art since 1900: Modernism, Antimodernism, Postmodernism*, vol. 1 (London: Thames and Hudson, 2011) provides a very good survey. Robert Hughes's *The Shock of the New* (New York: Alfred A. Knopf, 1991) is interesting, provocative, and insightful. George Heard Hamilton's *Painting and Sculpture in Europe, 1880–1940* (London: Penguin Books, 1967) is comprehensive.

For Surrealism, Patrick Waldberg's *Surrealism* (London: Thames and Hudson, 1997) will give one an understanding of the dimensions of the movement. Maurice Nadeau's *History of Surrealism* (Cambridge: Harvard University Press, 1989) is also very good. Dalí was often purposely enigmatic, but Victoria Charles's *Dalí* (London: Sirocco, 2004) provides a good overview of his life and work. William S. Rubin's, *Dada, Surrealism, and Their Heritage* (New York: Museum of Modern Art, 1977) is fine on context and influence.

A good introduction to *Magritte* is Suzy Gablik's *Magritte: World of Art* (New York: Thames and Hudson, 1985). Dawn Ades, Neil Cox, and David Hopkins, *Marcel Duchamp* (London: Thames and Hudson, 1999) provides a fine analysis. John Richardson's *A Life of Picasso: The Triumphant Years, 1917–1932* (New York: Knopf, 2010) is very good on Picasso's life and times. Hilary Spurling's *Matisse the Master: A Life of Henri Matisse: The Conquest of Colour, 1909–1954* (New York: Alfred A. Knopf, 2005) is excellent. Braque, sometimes undeservedly, does not get the attention given to Picasso. Karen Wilkin's biography *Georges Braque* (New York: Abbeville, 1991) is helpful in addressing this issue.

John Willett's *The New Sobriety, 1917–1933: Art and Politics in the Weimar Period* (London: Thames and Hudson, 1978) is wide-ranging and definitive. Stephanie Barron, *German Expressionism: Art and Society* (New York: Rizzoli, 1997) is very good on the movement. Two good studies of Grosz are Hans Hess, *George Grosz* (London: Studio Vista, 1974) and Beth Irwin Lewis, *George Grosz: Art and Politics in the Weimar Republic* (Princeton: Princeton University Press, 1991).

CHAPTER 7

My discussion of Huxley's novel uses quotations from the edition published by Grafton Books, London in 1977. Huxley's *Brave New World Revisited* (1958) is an important reflection on the novel and its reception. Other novels by Huxley of interest include *Crome Yellow* (1921), *Point Counter Point* (1928), and *The Doors of Perception* (1954).

The most comprehensive recent biography is that of Nicolas Murray, *Aldous Huxley* (New York: St. Martin's Press, 2002). Milton Birnbaum's *Aldous Huxley's Quest for Values* (Knoxville, TN: University of Tennessee Press, 1971) is a very good discussion of Huxley's personal intellectual voyage, focusing on both what Birnbaum terms Huxley's spiritual self and his societal self. George Woodcock, one of the finest analytical writers of his generation, wrote *Dawn and the Darkest Hour: A Study of Aldous Huxley* (New York: Viking, 1972), still worth reading because Woodcock's intellectual breadth was as wide as that of Huxley.

Jerome Meckier's *Aldous Huxley, from Poet to Mystic* (Zurich: Lit, 2011) focuses on Huxley's beginnings as a poet and the influence his poetry had on the development of his mysticism in later life. Meckier edited *Critical Essays on Aldous Huxley* (New York: G.K. Hall and Co., 1996), a very good set of articles about the author and his work. Another useful group of essays is *Huxley's Brave New World: Essays*, edited by David Garrett Izzo and Kim Kirkpatrick (London: McFarland and Co., 2008).

Two interesting studies of *Brave New World* are Peter Frichow's *The End of Utopia* (Lewisburg, PA: Bucknell University Press, 1974) and David Leon Higdon's *Wandering into Brave New World* (Amsterdam: Rodopi, 2013).

CHAPTER 8

My discussion of Freud's work, *Civilization and Its Discontents,* uses the edition translated by James Strachey (New York: W.W. Norton and Company, 1961). The standard biography of Freud is still Ernest Jones's *Sigmund Freud: Life and Work*, 3 vols. (London: Hogarth Press, 1953–1957). Jones was both a friend and a colleague, and his work has many insights into Freud's meaning. Peter Gay's *Freud: A Life for Our Time* (New York: W.W. Norton, 1988) is very good on both Freud and the context of the times. It also contains an excellent bibliographical essay. A good short biography is O. Mannoni's *Freud* (New York: Vintage Books, 1974). The most recent comprehensive biography is the very good work by Élisabeth Rudinesco, *Freud: In His Time and Ours* (Cambridge: Harvard University Press, 2016).

Paul Roazen's *Freud: Political and Social Thought* (London: Hogarth Press, 1969) discusses many of the ideas in this chapter. Another work on Freud's social thought, Philip Rieff's *Freud: The Mind of the Moralist* (Chicago: University of Chicago Press, 1979) is illuminating. J.C. Flugel's *Man, Morals and Society: A Psychoanalytical Study* (London: Duckworth, 1955) is still worth reading.

The most influential works assessing the quality of Freud's work are Adolf Grünbaum, *The Foundations of Psychoanalysis: A Philosophical Critique* (Berkeley, CA: University of California Press, 1984), and Paul Kline, *Fact and Fancy in Freudian Theory* (London: Methuen, 1972). The feminist issue is discussed in Nancy Chodorow's *Feminism and Psychoanalytic Theory* (New Haven, CT: Yale University Press, 1979) and Juliet Mitchell's *Psychoanalysis and Feminism: Freud, Reich, Lang and Women* (New York: Pantheon, 1974).

In the English-speaking world the attacks on Freud have been led for several decades by Frederick C. Crews, who has made a career out of criticizing him, recently calling him someone who made his reputation "by boasting, cajoling, question begging, denigrating rivals, and misrepresenting therapeutic results" (Frederick Crews, "Freud: What's Left?," *New York Review of Books*, February 23, 2017, p. 6). Crews's edited book, *Unauthorized Freud: Doubters Confront a Legend* (New York: Viking 1998), puts together a number of essays by critics of Freud, including Frank Cioffi and Frank J. Sulloway. Crews recently published *Freud: The Making of an Illusion* in August 2017 (New York: Metropolitan Books), in which he stated, he "trace(s) the many steps that took [Freud] from modest conventional prospects to a cult of personal authority that overrode every scientific and ethical constraint." See the review by George Prochnik in *The New York Times Book Review* of August 14, 2017, for an assessment.

CHAPTER 9

The finest survey of Europe in contemporary times is Tony Judt's masterwork, *Postwar: A History of Europe since 1945* (New York: Penguin, 2006). Also useful are Philipp Ther's *Europe since 1989: A History* (Princeton, NJ: Princeton University Press, 2016) and Mary Elise Sarotte's *1989: The Struggle to Create Post–Cold War Europe* (Princeton, NJ: Princeton University Press, 2009). Martin Dedman, ed., *The Origins & Development of the European Union 1945–2008: A History of European Integration* (London: Routledge, 2nd ed., 2009), provides history and analysis of this important topic.

Immigration matters are insightfully discussed in Jennifer Welsh's *The Return of History: Conflict, Migration and Geopolitics in the Twenty-First Century* (Toronto: Anansi, 2016). Alexander Betts and Paul Collier's *Refuge: Transforming a Broken Refugee System* (Oxford: Oxford University Press, 2017) analyzes the current problem and offers a perspective on changing the way the world deals with its refugee crisis. Paul Gifford and Tessa Hauswedell, eds., *Europe and Its Others: Essays on Interperception and Identity* (Oxford: Oxford, Peter Lang, 2010), includes pieces that discuss the identity issue surrounding the Other from both the point of view of the Other and that of Europeans.

No single history of the Catholic Church in the modern world is comprehensive and sufficiently analytical. The following works on major popes and their reigns are worthwhile: John Cornwell, *Hitler's Pope: The Secret History of Pius XII* (New York: Viking, 1999); Thomas Cahill, *Pope John XXIII: A Life* (New York: Viking, 2002); Tad Szulc, *Pope John Paul II: The Biography* (New York: Scribner, 1995)

Two entries into the culture of postmodernism are Steven Connor, *Postmodernist Culture* (Oxford: Blackwell, 1989) and Thomas Docherty, ed., *Postmodernism: A Reader* (New York: Columbia University Press, 1993). Postmodern thought has influenced scholarship on crowds and mass man in Elias Canetti's *Crowds and Power* (New York: Viking Press, 1962), a breakthrough work, and Christian Borch's *The Politics of Crowds: An Alternative History of Sociology* (Cambridge: Cambridge University Press, 2012) is a very thoughtful analysis.

Thomas Piketty's *Capital in the Twenty-First Century*, trans. Arthur Goldhammer (Cambridge, MA: Harvard University Press, 2014) is essential to an understanding of how capitalism works in modern Europe and the West. Also useful are Joseph E. Stiglitz's *The Price of Inequality: How Today's Divided Society Endangers Our Future* (New York: W.W. Norton, 2012), and Chrystia Freeland's *Plutocrats: The Rise of the New Global Super-Rich and the Fall of Everyone Else* (New York: Penguin, 2012).

David Trotter's *Cinema and Modernism* (Oxford: Blackwell, 2007) provides a very good discussion of film. Mildred Friedman's edited collection, *Gehry Talks: Architecture and Process* (New York: Universe Publishing, 2002) is worth looking at for understanding architecture in the early twenty-first century. The essays in Lois Parkinson Zamora and Wendy B. Faris, eds., *Magical Realism: Theory, History, Community* (Durham, NC: Duke University Press, 1995) are wide-ranging and comprehensive.

Jonathan Israel, *A Revolution of the Mind: Radical Enlightenment and the Intellectual Origins of Modern Democracy* (Princeton: Princeton University Press, 2010) provides background for the issue of the viability of liberalism and democracy. Also of interest is Robert Kagan's article "Is Democracy in Decline?: The Weight of Geopolitics," *Journal of Democracy*, vol. 26, no. 1 (2015).

Four works, among the many now being published, are worth citing regarding the present state of Europe. They are: Ruth Wodak, *The Politics of Fear: What Right-Wing Populist Discourses Mean* (Thousand Oaks, CA: Sage Publications, 2015), Edward Lucas, *The New Cold War: Putin's Russia and the Threat to the West*, 3rd ed. (New York: Palgrave Macmillan, 2014), Desmond Dinan, Neill Nugent, and William Patterson, eds., *The European Union in Crisis* (London: Palgrave, 2017), and Timothy Garton Ash, "Is Europe Disintegrating?," *New York Review of Books*, January 19, 2017.

ADDITIONAL READING

Benjamin, Walter. "The Work of Art in the Age of Mechanical Reproduction." In Hannah Arendt, ed., *Walter Benjamin: Illuminations*. New York: Schocken Books, 1969.

Berman, Marshall. *All That Is Solid Melts into Air: The Experience of Modernity*. New York: Simon and Schuster, 1982.

Bracher, Karl Dietrich. *The German Dictatorship: The Origins, Structure and Effects of National Socialism*. New York: Praeger, 1970.

Bradbury, Malcolm, and James McFarlane, eds. *Modernism, 1890–1930*. Harmondworth: Penguin, 1976.

Brenan, Gerald. *The Spanish Labyrinth: An Account of the Social and Political Background of the Civil War*. Cambridge: Cambridge University Press, 1960.

Butler, Christopher. *Modernism: A Very Short Introduction*. Oxford: Oxford University Press, 2010.

Darius, Sara. *The Senses in Modernism: Technology, Perception, and Aesthetics*. Ithaca, NY: Cornell University Press, 2002.

Figes, Orlando. *Natasha's Dance: A Cultural History of Russia*. New York: Henry Holt, 2002.

Gay, Peter. *Modernism: The Lure of Heresy*. New York: W.W. Norton, 2008.

Glynn, S., and J. Oxborrow. *Interwar Britain: A Social and Economic History*. London: Allen and Unwin, 1976.

Graves, Robert, and Alan Hodge. *The Long Weekend: A Social History of Great Britain, 1918–1939*. London: Hutchinson, 1963.

Greene, N. *From Versailles to Vichy: The Third Republic, 1919–1940*. New York: Crowell, 1970.

Hughes, H. Stuart. *Consciousness and Society: The Reorientation of European Social Thought, 1890–1930*. New York: Octagon Books, 1976.

James, Harold. *The German Slump: Politics and Economics, 1924–1936*. Oxford: Clarendon Press, 1986.

Laqueur, W., and G.L. Mosse, eds. *The Left-Wing Intellectuals Between the Wars, 1919–1939*. New York: Harper, 1966.

Levinson, Michael, ed. *The Cambridge Companion to Modernism*, 2nd ed. Cambridge: Cambridge University Press, 2011.

Luebbert, Gregory M. *Liberalism, Fascism, or Social Democracy: Social Classes and the Political Origins of Regimes in Interwar Europe*. New York: Oxford University Press, 1991.

Lunn, Eugene. *Marxism and Modernism*. London: Verso, 1985.

Lyttleton, Adrian, ed. *Liberal and Fascist Italy, 1900–1945*. Oxford: Oxford University Press, 2002.

Lyttleton, Adrian. *The Seizure of Power: Fascism in Italy, 1919–1929*. London: Routledge, 2004.

Maier, Charles S. *Recasting Bourgeois Europe: Stabilization in France, Germany and Italy in the Decade after World War I*. Princeton, NJ: Princeton University Press, 1975.

Marks, Sally. *The Illusion of Peace: International Relations in Europe, 1918–1933*. New York: Palgrave Macmillan, 2003.

Naylor, Gillian. *The Bauhaus*. London: Studio Vista 1968.

Parkinson, David. *History of Film*. London: Thames and Hudson, 1995.

Rainey, Lawrence. *Institutions of Modernism: Literary Elites and Public Culture*. New Haven, CT: Yale University Press, 1998.

Rees, Goronwy. *The Great Slump: Capitalism in Crisis, 1929–1933*. New York: Harper and Row, 1970.

Rieger, Bernhard. *Technology and the Culture of Modernity in Britain and Germany, 1890–1945*. Cambridge: Cambridge University Press, 2005.

Salzman, Eric. *Twentieth Century Music: An Introduction*. Upper Saddle River, NJ: Prentice Hall, 2002.

Schwartz, Vanessa, and Leo Charney, eds. *Cinema and the Invention of Modern Life*. Berkeley, CA: University of California Press, 1995.

Taylor, Charles. *The Sources of the Self: The Making of Modern Identity*. Cambridge: Cambridge University Press, 1989.

Weitz, Eric D. *Weimar Germany*. Princeton, NJ: Princeton University Press, 2007.

INDEX

Abravanel, Maurice, 68
abstract expressionism, 191
Academia Catavencu, 183
Achebe, Chinua, *No Longer at Ease*, 102
Achille, Louis Thomas, 95, 102; on the Salon Clamart, 89, 90; on style of clothing, 97
Adorno, Theodor, 84
alienation, in experience of being uprooted, 101–2
Alternative for Germany (AfD), 168, 210–11
Anderson, Benedict, 62, 167
Anderson, Maxwell, 85
Anderson, Sherwood, 60
androgyny, 33, 40, 41
anti-Semitism, 186–87; in postwar Europe, 2, 152
anxiety, uneasiness of postwar society, 148, 153, 213
Apollinaire, Guillaume, 97
architecture, post-1945 culture, 197–98
Arendt, Hannah, and nature of evil, 32
Arnold, Matthew, 130
Aron, Raymond, 60
A Room of One's Own (Woolf), 34, 41, 45–46
Arp, Jean, 73
Arrau, Claudio, 68
art: architecture, 197–98; artists as culture heroes, 120–21; artists as social/political commentators, 123–27; as autonomous, 119; *bandes dessinées*, 197; Black/

African art, 97; collage technique, 118–19; Cubism, 107, 108, 118–19; cult of the original, 113; Dada, 110–11; diminution of visual arts, 191; Expressionism, 81, 107; expressionist art of Berlin, 73; the Fauves/Fauvism, 107, 122; Futurism, 107; German Expressionism, 123–27; Impressionists, 191; intellectual reversal of cultures, 108; language, and images, 110; mimesis, 107–8, 118–19; multiple realities of representation, 108; Nabis, 107; and photography, 108; post-1945 culture, 191; Post-Impressionists, 191; postwar climate, 7; postwar experimentation and invention, 2; sculpture, and public installations, 197; street art, 197; Surrealism, 81, 114, 115–18; technique of juxtaposition, 81, 110; triptych form, 123, 126–27. *See also artists by name*
Aszdzienik, 183
Atwood, Margaret: *The Handmaid's Tale*, 203; *Oryx and Crake*, 203
Auden, W.H., 3, 81, 123; *The Age of Anxiety*, 144; *In Memory of Sigmund Freud*, 162; *Musée des Beaux Arts*, 45
Austria: accountability for past behaviour, 187; and Fascism, 13; Nazi *Anschluss*, 161
authoritarianism: and mass man, 54; and nationalist ideologies, 177, 184; and presence of violence, 21, 51, 147, 201
autonomy movements, 217

241